THE CONTROLLING MINDS

THE CONTROLLING MINDS OF ASIA

BY
THE SIRDAR IKBAL ALI SHAH
Author of "Fuad: King of Egypt"

ILLUSTRATED

HERBERT JENKINS LIMITED
3 YORK STREET ST. JAMES'S
LONDON S.W.1

A
HERBERT
JENKINS'
BOOK

First printing 1937

Printed in Great Britain by Wyman & Sons Ltd., London, Reading and Fakenham

The book contains the account of the following personages of Asia and Islam:

Mustapha Kamal	- - -	- Turkey
Gandhi	- - - -	- India
Aga Khan	- - -	- International Islam
Nadir Shah	- - -	- Afghanistan
Feisal	- - - -	- Iraq
Ibn Saud	- - -	- Arabia
Fuad	- - - -	- Egyptian Islam
Reza Shah	- - -	- Iran
Sun Yat Sen	- - -	- China

DEDICATION

THIS BOOK IS DEDICATED TO THE MEN, WHOSE LIFE-SKETCHES ARE INCLUDED IN THIS VOLUME: BECAUSE THEIR EFFORTS SHALL LEAVE INDELIBLE MARKS UPON THE HISTORY FAR BEYOND OUR OWN LITTLE DAY

LIST OF ILLUSTRATIONS

His Excellency Ghazi Mustapha Kamal Pasha *facing page*	12
Mr. Gandhi — — — — — — — ,, ,,	50
His Highness the Aga Khan — — — — ,, ,,	88
His Late Majesty Mohamed Nadir Shah Ghazi ,, ,,	128
His Late Majesty King Feisal of Iraq — — ,, ,,	170
H.M. Sultan Ibn Saud — — — — — ,, ,,	224
His Late Majesty King Fuad of Egypt — — ,, ,,	258
H.M. Reza Shah Pahlavi — — — — ,, ,,	276
Dr. Sun Yat Sen — — — — — — ,, ,,	296

THE CONTROLLING MINDS OF ASIA

THE CONTROLLING MINDS OF ASIA

MUSTAPHA KAMAL

NOTHING riles more than an oft-repeated half-truth. Nothing is more difficult to deny, and nothing harder to kill. It persists because of the obvious truth on both sides of the hyphen.

Mustapha Kamal Pasha is a man of many *aliases*. Officially, he now appears to the world as His Excellency Kamal Ataturk, but he is also known as the " Grey Wolf " and the " Dictator."

His is the temperament which can afford to smile at the *nom de guerre* of " Wolf," but which expands into righteous indignation at the mere mention of the word " Dictator." Here, when his wrath has cooled, his reaction is one of *noblesse oblige*. That Kamal does dictate cannot be denied, but he is at pains to place emphasis on the constitutional difference of the position of one who secures unreserved acceptance of " requests," and one who merely orders.

Kamal Ataturk is a dictator, but he differs fundamentally from his more famous prototypes. He sees in himself the constitutional head of a constitutional machine, laboriously evolved and cemented upon the ashes of an effete Sultanate.

In a world of dictatorships, and threatened dictatorships, comparisons are inevitable. Benito Mussolini, Stalin and Kamal are outstanding personalities. One other, Reza Shah, has made of himself a monarch. In this, perhaps, he is wise, for while none the less a dictator, he has achieved absolution, for there is the world over a tacit understanding that the hereditary head is sacrosanct in respect of invidious criticism Such, however, had yet to apply to those Masters o Men who have yet to found a House.

Kamal has no inhibition. An earnest disciple o the Young Turks, he was anti-Caliphate from the beginning. For long he had to shroud his rea intentions, but when the moment was ripe, he stoo disclosed. He invited obloquy, and he was not dis appointed, but the quavering occupant of the Yildi Kiosk had to go—and he went, at dead of night and as a fugitive, with a few handfuls of persona jewels hurriedly scrambled together in sheets c ordinary newspaper, to seek refuge upon British warship—the inevitable asylum of exile monarchs.

The man of action—the saviour of a dissolute an shortly to be rejuvenated Turkey—he had the countr at his feet. Power was his for the taking, but he wa big enough, and courageous enough, to build cor stitutionally. He had seen enough of the evils c undue centralization with all administrative channe directed to the Yildiz Kiosk and everything subservier to the will of the Sultan.

HIS EXCELLENCY GHAZI MUSTAPHA KAMAL PASHA
President of the Turkish Republic

It was an immense moment in the life of modern Turkey, and the decision then to be made was fraught with consequences which would have inevitable reactions throughout the Asiatic world. Kamal had to decide between the West and the East. In reality, it was a decision between the Western concept of nationality, and the Eastern, or Turkish, ideal of a unified Islam. It was at once a question of religion *versus* country.

The Sultan Abdul Hamid had sought to glorify his Empire by the reanimation of Islam. His failure was abysmal, and Turkey was wrecked upon the shoals of his ideals. When the world flew to arms, the unifying power of Islam failed to resuscitate a regime which was rotten at the core. Under the domination of the Yildiz Kiosk, every effort was directed toward an ideal which meant that an Empire of enormous extent must wallow in antique disorder. Everything modern was stigmatized as a perversion; every forward advance was frowned upon as dangerous. Every waking moment of the Sultan was spent in examining his defences against the infiltration of Western ideas.

Everyone knows how Kamal decided. Later generations alone will be able to determine the full measure of his achievements, for with a stroke of the pen he decreed something which was momentous. He abolished, not only the Sultanate, but the Caliphate, and the world of Islam has yet to recover from the shock.

What manner a man is he who has this truly amazing post-war record? Easily the best-dressed figure in modern Turkey, Kamal Ataturk is a man of surprising extremes. He combines an extraordinary taciturnity with an ability to let flow a deluge of words which literally drowns the hearer in fact and eloquence, as witness the memorable occasion when, in October, 1927, he addressed the assembled deputies at Angora from the fifteenth to the twentieth, and delivered himself of a spate of nearly half a million words. Ordinarily, his daily output of words rarely exceeds the century—less, indeed, than his daily consumption of cigarettes, of which he is an inveterate smoker.

This is the man who has brought to the ancient East so much of the materialism of the West. In so doing he had to dispose of an absolute monarchy, inspire a people who had been contemptuously left by victorious Allies as beyond further effort and notice, fight a war with Greek armies swollen by the incidence of a great world conflict, outwit such past masters in diplomacy as Lloyd George and the venerable Clemenceau, and mould into one interests so conflicting that no one but a Colossus would have essayed the task.

For one who is a rebel at heart, and whose earlier years were marked by numerous escapades in which the quality of restraint was not unduly obvious, Kamal's sense of proportion and perspective on attaining the Presidency has amazed foreign observers. The son of a minor customs official in the town of Salonika, who died and left his wife and son in straitened circumstances, it is remarkable that even at an early age there should have appeared the military exquisite with the rebellious heart. Kamal rebelled at school—at each of three institutions to which he owes his education. He was entered in a clerical school in which all teaching was based upon the Koran. Even then Kamal was a budding free-thinker, and he revolted. His father was inclined to agree with him, and Kamal was enrolled on the student roll of a school conducted on more progressive lines. Within six months he had a difference of opinion with the principal. Kamal received a whipping. Convinced that he had been unfairly treated, he walked home, vowing that he would never again submit to such treatment. He never did.

Before a further outlet could be found for Kamal's scholastic endeavours, his father died, and the bounty of an uncle had to be requisitioned. Two years in the fields and the cowsheds only served further to assure the self-dependence of one who was eventually to dominate Turkey, and it was a sturdy-minded youngster who, with the financial assistance of an aunt, sat for the entrance examination to the Military College at Salonika. He passed, and worked so assiduously that he was shortly transferred to the Academy of Military Art in Constantinople. Here he was one of those selected for training for the General Staff, and he devoted his time to his studies and to the teachings instilled by a free-thinking secret society. Three days after he was gazetted, and while he was preparing to leave the Academy, he and the other members of the society were raided while they were in secret conclave. Kamal accompanied the police to the local prison, and was confined to a cell which was to be his home for several weeks. It seemed that the end of his career had come before it had fairly opened. The secret society had taken unto itself the name of "Vatan," signifying Fatherland, and the word was one which was as anathema to the Sultan. The least that Kamal could expect would be a court-martial and dismissal from the service, and perhaps he was doomed to several years in a fortress. Kamal was given plenty of time in which to cogitate on his fate. The Sultan never hurried in such matters.

From where he sulked in his cell, the youthful Kamal could observe the walls of the Yildiz Kiosk, where the Sultan, perpetually haunted by the fear of assassination, also brooded on his unenviable lot. In the hundreds of compartments of the royal palace, the Sultan was a virtual prisoner, and a singularly unhappy one. Never twice in succession did he sleep in the same bedroom, in order to foil the knife of a possible intruder. Never did he eat until the food, which had been specially prepared, had been sampled in his presence, and even then he would personally indicate which particular portion of a dish must be eaten by those of his entourage.

The youthful delinquent had to contend with a man who was frightened nigh unto death, and his thoughts were not rendered any the more palatable when he learned that the Inspector-General of the Army took a very serious view of the case, and intended to take a close personal interest in the conduct of the judicial examination.

Yet the intrigue and chicanery against which even

then he was beginning to rile, was to prove his salvation. One influential Minister supported the Inspector-General in his view of the affair. That was sufficient for another influential and rival Minister to take the opposite course, and to decry the whole incident as nothing more than youthful effervescence and coltish indiscretion. For many weeks the ministerial battle was fought over the young man's body, until even the Sultan became tired of the subject. He settled the matter out of court, as it were, by transferring Kamal from Constantinople and attaching him to a cavalry regiment in Damascus.

It is one of the ironies of fate that a soldier who was to play such an important part in his country's battles, and conjure up armies, and achieve victories when all else declared the military situation irrevocably lost, should so nearly have been branded as a felon before being returned to the obscurity of an uncle's farm. In this he had something akin to the famous Kitchener, whom he so closely resembles, for it is on record that Kitchener, when he sought to enter the Egyptian cavalry after his exploration work in Palestine, was all but rejected because of his indifferent horsemanship.

Kitchener, too, was an economic soldier. He won his battles without piling up his country's bills. Kamal has won his without the necessity of incurring bills, for the sole and simple reason that there was none who would advance him credit. His armies had no equipment, so he sought the ploughshares, and produced armaments. They had no transport, so he commandeered the village donkeys and oxen.

His later ability to exploit a situation and to extricate himself from a seemingly impassable morass, was reflected in other of his early escapades. When he was banished to Damascus he precociously decided that the place did not agree with him, and he made overtures to a highly-placed officer in Salonika to secure a transfer. The request embarrassed the general, for he was fully aware that Kamal was *non persona grata* at court, but he was still further disturbed when Kamal appeared on his doorstep with the *naive* tidings that he had deserted his post in Damascus. Kamal was ordered back to duty in no uncertain voice, but before he could leave news came from Constantinople. Briefly, it was to the effect that the higher command had been acquainted with Kamal's defection, and had issued a warrant for his arrest. That would have been too much for the ordinary soldier, and a problem defying solution for the average civilian, but Kamal remained unperturbed. There was then a certain unpleasantness between the Porte and Whitehall respecting possession of one of the Red Sea ports. Kamal solved the seemingly impossible by proceeding with all haste to the spot, giving out that he had been given command of the Turkish forces there, and so completely mystified a not very well informed staff in Constantinople that the matter of the warrant was conveniently forgotten, and he was actually thanked for his services to the State. Obviously, such a man was not of the ordinary rut. He was destined either for great things or an appalling disillusionment. As it was, good fortune remained on his side. He achieved his temporary ambition, and was transferred to Salonika, then the political Mecca of the more advanced of the Young Turks.

Turkey, a land of mystery, of incessant intrigue and of appalling and pathetic inefficiency, had yet much to teach Kamal. Beneath his waywardness and his wild extremism, he was a thinker. He became enveloped in the work of the Committee of Union and Progress, the principal and most virile of the many secret organizations of the Young Turks, but it was not long before he also became a critic.

Kamal certainly took an active part in the revolt of officers in 1908, and he was with the forces which marched on Constantinople and forced reforms from a timorous Sultan, but even then he was not entirely at his ease. Prior to that he had had an highly significant conversation with his mother, to whose gently expressed misgivings he had replied uncompromisingly : " Yes," he said, " I am a rebel against the Padishah. The man whom you invest with the power of the saints is really impotent. We intend to deprive him of power and liberate the country from him."

The Sultan maintained an army of spies, and Kamal was regarded in Constantinople as a good soldier but a dangerous young man. His military career underwent many more vicissitudes. Once, as a major, he was actually deprived of his command, but the intrigue which had saved him when newly gazetted again came to his aid, and he was reinstated. When the Great War broke out, he was still under a political cloud, but he insisted upon seeing service. He was gazetted lieutenant-colonel, and became a divisional commander under that redoubtable and clever soldier, General Liman von Saunders, who had been loaned to the Porte by Germany before the War. General Liman von Saunders had proceeded to Constantinople ostensibly upon a military mission, but the diplomatic papers which were exchanged at the time between the various embassies made it evident that none of the Powers were blind to Germany's real motive.

Gallipoli is a lasting memorial to the resolution of a Kamal when beset by odds. Significant of the man himself are a number of incidents when he came into direct conflict with the British. Almost foolhardy was he in some of his daring—this man who was always impelled by the one thought of restoring the faded glories of his country. It must have been that destiny had selected him for a great mission—otherwise he would never have survived the results of his earlier indiscretions or the deliberate effrontery which he displayed at Gallipoli when, on two occasions at least, his personal disregard of danger turned the scales against the invader, and left for them but the husk of a glorious failure. That he should be wounded in one of these encounters, he accepted with that philosophical phlegm which was so characteristic. In another encounter his watch was smashed to pieces by a British bullet.

Gallipoli made the name of Mustapha Kamal, and he became known to the multitude. He was hailed as the "Victor of Ariburnu and Anafarta." Yet this man was still an idealist. He was still a thinker. Although the British had been forced to evacuate the ground which he had held with such un-Turklike tenacity (it was characteristic of one of the world's most gentlemanly fighters that fierce resistance of the day should be the prelude to a retirement to a new defensive position by night), Kamal was not blinded by the fog of war. He returned to Constantinople in no jubilant frame of mind. Indeed, he was convinced that those whom he had just vanquished would win the war. He had the temerity to say so, and it again was remembered that Kamal was dangerous. Incontinently he was transferred to the Caucasus, well away from all spheres of mischief.

Kut fell, Baghdad fell, and the Turks were being pushed from Palestine. The great fortress of Erzerum had long ago fallen to the Russians. In its extremity, the Turkish high command bethought itself of Kamal rusticating in the Caucasus. He was made a general, and ordered to retake Baghdad. This, he said, was beyond the capabilities of the Turkish armies, and he refused the command. Headstrong, impulsive, but with the uncanny and irritating ability of being always right, he was a thorn in the side of the Minister of War, and those who advised him.

That fine Oriental conception of the fitness of things saw a use for one who could ask an unending series of inconvenient questions. The Porte, with malicious ingenuousness, sent him to interview Ludendorff and the Kaiser. So forceful and so tactless was he with the great field-marshal on the subject of his next objective, that Ludendorff was constrained to ask Turkey's youthful general whether he preferred a cigarette or a cigar. There are more delicate ways of evading a dangerous issue, and less direct methods of intimating to a young man that his queries savour of the indiscreet and impertinent. With the Kaiser he was even less successful. He complained with unrestrained bitterness of the buffetings which Turkey had received, and asked for a categorical assurance that effective help would be forthcoming. So hurt was the Kaiser in his dignity that he carefully refrained from shaking hands with Kamal when he left. As Kamal was the only one to be denied the honour, it can be taken that the All Highest was more than ordinarily incensed.

Kamal returned from his visit to Germany more firmly convinced than ever that Turkey was but a tool in the hands of men who had already lost. He sought an interview with the Sultan, and had the courage to suggest peace pourparlers. Such a suggestion was incredible, for the German military mission in Constantinople was insistent that the forthcoming offensive by Ludendorff would curl up the Allied armies. Yet almost did Kamal convince Vahededdin. In the end he prevaricated, and that hesitancy was to cost him his throne. As firmly as he was convinced that Germany would lose the War, so was he certain that modern Turkey could expect nothing of the new Padishah. From that moment, Kamal was an implacable enemy of the Sultan.

Jerusalem, and most of Palestine, went the way of Baghdad, and again Constantinople turned to Kamal. He was sent to Syria to stem the tide, but when he reviewed the troops assigned to him, he knew the position to be hopeless. He arrived on the northern Palestine front but a few weeks before the final debacle and the military achievements of Lord Allenby. He was ill with fever when the final blow was delivered to Turkish arms on this sector, but he rose from his sick bed and brought the stricken Turks to heel not far from Aleppo. There his indomitable courage infused the hungry, dispirited rabble with new hope. He formed a line beyond which the victorious Allied armies deemed it inadvisable to advance. He had at least demarcated a frontier.

This marked the end of the first phase of Mustapha Kamal's meteoric career. He had been a wilful playboy, he had been a rebel scowling at the waywardness of fate, and, when one considers the remarkably poor resources at his command, he had been a remarkably successful general. Now the playboy was to disappear. The rebel was to come uppermost, and the *flair* for military strategy subordinated to the end.

Kamal returned to Constantinople, its silvery palaces still shimmering in the golden sunshine, and its minarets still peering upwards in mute appeal to heaven; but a city of sadness, of fear, and of want, nevertheless. He, too, was unemployed, and that most helpless of all male creatures—an unemployed general. With the collapse of Turkey's might, he had asked for the post of Commander-in-Chief. Like Don Quixote tilting at windmills, he would fight for an honourable peace. His request was ignored. The

Porte had little time to think of generals; it was concerned too much with its own safety, and the very last thing it wanted to do was to unleash a headstrong soldier who might give offence to enemies who had already given great portions of the old Ottoman Empire to the Arabs, was to promise another great tract to the Jews, and had a greedy eye on the small portion that remained to the Sultan —Asia Minor and an insignificant section of Europe.

Sultan Vahededdin had one pulsating desire at this time, and that to fawn at the feet of the victors. He even went so far as to order the arrest of a number of his Ministers and senior officers in order that these gentlemen might be handed over to the Allies as human sacrifices. He was very moved and very angry when these functionaries made good their escape.

While the Sultan was plotting his schemes whereby he might retain some semblance of his authority, this hard-headed general without a job rented a house in a Constantinople suburb, and sat down furiously to think.

He came to several inexorable conclusions.

Wriggle and genuflect as it might, the Porte could not save an Empire which was already smashed to fragments. The Empire was finished, and with it the ancient conception of a universal Islam. The old order had had a long trial, and had failed, and Abdul Hamid's conception of Pan-Islam had been insufficient to bind together peoples of a single faith, but of varying national prejudices and racial characteristics.

Very well, Pan-Islam should go. With it should go the Power that had dragged down a mighty Empire into a morass so frightful that the Turkish people sprawled supine and helpless. With the disappearance of the Sultanate and the Caliphate there should rise a new Turkey—a Nationalist Turkey—which should be cemented together by ties of blood rather than of faith.

Kamal's was cold logic, entirely bereft of sentimentalism for the great past, for historical tradition, or for the great pundits, either temporal or spiritual. And it was evolved in an unpretentious rented villa.

Kamal dared tell no one of his deductions. He had to deal with a large and powerful element which was fanatically disposed to regard the institution of the Caliphate as sacrosanct.

He sat down coldly and deliberately to weigh the pros and cons of an almost impossible situation, and it was characteristic of him that he should decide that time was entirely in his favour. Given time, and the Porte would inevitably bring about its own eclipse.

A general had made his decision. He swung the Porte into some deep recess of his brain, to be dealt with later. He concentrated on other factors. There were the Powers to be considered.

While the world statesmen were engulfed in a peaceful tumult even more tempestuous than that of war, Kamal remained in his villa and became a philosopher. America was already showing the way. She was anxious to get out of Europe, and the commitments which only a high-minded president could envisage. Kamal developed that line of reasoning. He saw the great Allied peoples hungry for peace— peace almost at any price, once the fangs of Germany had been drawn. He saw in Great Britain and her colonies, and in France, a disposition toward the irritable with statesmen who should quibble and bargain over remnants, for the great nations, in the course of four years of war, had been coached and dragooned into thinking and concentrating on first principles. Millions and billions had been spent on the war. Millions and billions must be made out of the peace. There must be a race for trade, with the devil taking the hindmost. How well he read the situation!

Thus far logic took him. It is always perilous to stake much on the logical, because human frailties are so diverse. In the case of Albion they could so easily be perverse, but even here Kamal read the signs correctly.

Come what may, would Whitehall desire to see Turkey absolutely mangled? He thought not. The key to the situation was Constantinople. It had been a bone of contention before. It should remain as one if a Turkish general without an army could make it so. Kamal reasoned that Great Britain would watch with perfect equanimity the break up of the outer Turkish Empire, but would hesitate to apply the guillotine if this should at once sever and apportion Constantinople.

Kamal came out into the limelight. In order to dispossess the Sultan he declared that he must be saved. It was a battle-cry that received immediate and enthusiastic attention. All could see, when Kamal pointed it out, that the Sultan was no better than a prisoner. In Constantinople the Allied troops were there to render concrete the "requests" of the Allied High Commissioners, and there was no Turkish Government save in the will and the dictates of the conquerors. Public opinion rallied to Kamal.

What would he suggest?

To men tired of inactivity, any proposal which promised movement would be welcomed.

There could be no unfettered expression of opinion in Constantinople, he said. Therefore, Parliament should take immediate steps to remove itself from the orbit of foreign influence and meet in Anatolia.

Kamal decided that he should go to Anatolia with powers. Was he not out to save the Sultan? The Sultan gave him his blessing.

Unaccountably, unrest broke out in Anatolia. The Allies desired that a trustworthy Turkish officer should proceed there to restore order. Kamal was selected. With papers sealed, signed and countersigned, Kamal set out, once more a force. Once again fate had thrown this human diabolo high into the ascendancy.

While this was being engineered, there occurred one of those rifts in the Allied lute which Kamal, with true Oriental perspicacity, had relied upon as inevitable. Italy had seized Fiume, to the consternation of the rest of the Allies. Venizelos, ever alive to the main chance, declared that he had evidence that Italy was also determined to seize Smyrna. At the same time he disseminated reports, which even yet lack substantiation, to the effect that the Christian peoples of Smyrna were being massacred. He appealed to the kindly and fastidious soul of President Wilson. Would it not be well, he suggested, if kindly-disposed Greek forces repaired to Smyrna to prevent this wanton slaughter of Christians? Almost falteringly, President Wilson agreed that it would.

On the very morning that Mustapha Kamal set out from Constantinople on his mission to Anatolia, Greek troops began to disembark at Smyrna. The Turkish resident stood appalled. There was an explosion of racial animosities, and hundreds of Turkish citizens lost their lives. Thousands were transported to Greece as prisoners and as hostages. As a ludicrous tail to the War to End War, there was that day initiated yet another ferocious conflict which was to drag on for three further years, and to draw Greece deep down into the mire of the most shameful humiliation.

In that hour Kamal was provided with his most potent weapon. He had no need to sound the tocsin. Venizelos had sounded that, and the Turkish peoples, ennervated and impoverished by a continuous cycle of wars, yet heard and rallied.

The cry went forth: "The Greeks, . . . The Greeks. . . . Anyone but the Greeks. . . . The ancient enemy. . . . This despised rabble. . . . To become lords and masters of the Turks!"

Kamal, normally the silent, let forth a stream of indignant and burning invective. The stream became swollen, and surged as a mighty river. It became an irresistible flood of national wrath, and to Kamal fell the Herculean task of directing it. Would he succeed?

He looked around him. The Turkish armies, broken in war, had been torn asunder by the Allies. There were small bands of ill-armed men scattered over the country-side, but at long-intervening distances. Kamal set himself the task of formulating a fighting machine to meet this new invader. Never, perhaps, had a general shortly to embark on a three-years' war with a modern army ever contemplated less illuminating material.

The Porte, in its habitual panic, heard of Kamal's overtures to the disbanded army, and he was recalled to Constantinople. He ignored the summons, except to reply: "When we have independence, I will return from Anatolia."

Kamal's resolve to fight the Greeks became a mass movement—a national impulse. It was the self-expression of a people, and the accepted rulers of the nation had no part in it; in fact, they deprecated it. Kamal, however, conjured an army from the rag-tail and bob-tail of the villages, and he induced the youngest of Turkey's generals to take command. He seized the telegraph lines, and he told his scattered units that delegates should be sent to Sivas, there to take part in a National Congress. With the request went the dictum: The Central Government is no longer capable of performing its functions. . . . Independence can only be secured by the will and energy of the nation.

Thus was the Porte informed of its ineptitude and

of its impending doom. It is not to be supposed that the Sultan and his ministers sat lightly under the scarcely-veiled inuendo. They took steps to curb the activities of this dangerous fanatic. While cursing the impulse which had caused them to send this firebrand general to Anatolia in order to remove him from dangerous influences nearer at hand, they gave emphatic orders to all to break off all negotiations with Kamal, and to regard him as a criminal and a rebel.

Nevertheless, the National Congress was held at Sivas, and a harassed Turkey was presented with two governments. Embarrassed Allied High Commissioners and slightly supercilious Allied statesmen in Paris and where else they staged their peace pourparlers, regarded the scene with pessimism and as much detachment as they could muster.

Before long the Porte was importuning. "Dear Mustapha," said the Grand Vizier in one of those rare moments when he was allowed the use of the telegraph, "please go on leave. Please go anywhere, but cease your activities."

Endearments failed as orders had done, so the fiat went forth. Kamal was stripped of his rank, and the world was informed that all who had intercourse with him were guilty of high treason.

Kamal's answer was to initiate a fierce guerilla warfare against the Greeks in Smyrna. And he was still saving the Sultan. Nothing had yet passed his lips respecting his real purpose in life.

It was, perhaps, only natural that Kamal should be elected President of the preliminary National

Congress which was held at Erzerum, though there were those present who were tactless enough to ask why he should. At this conference it is noteworthy that a loyal address was submitted to the Sultan, and allegiance to the person of the Sultan and Caliph was emphasized.

Vahededdin, however, had enough natural subtlety to appraise these tributes to his throne and being at their true value. If no one else in Turkey yet suspected Mustapha Kamal's design, he saw in them a direct threat to the monarchy. He determined that this wayward ex-general and his supporters should be exterminated. He wanted to dispatch a considerable army to Anatolia to round up the malcontents, but the Allied High Commissioners strenuously objected. This would be contrary to the terms of the Armistice. It would mean rearming!

The Sultan, not to be outdone, issued orders for Kamal's arrest, " wherever he might be found," and as a stiffening to these, he arranged with the Kurdish tribesmen for a revolt. The Kurds were to descend upon Sivas and to take all the members of the Assembly prisoner. The Sivas Assembly was held, as has been indicated, and Kamal, brushing aside a not inconsiderable opposition, was voted chairman. Here again a loyal address to the throne was voted. One can imagine Kamal, as chairman and president, accepting the motion with his tongue in his cheek.

The discussions at Sivas were brought to an abrupt termination by unpleasant news. The warlike Kurds were almost at the gates, and the Nationalist troops hesitated to attack. Kamal mounted a battalion on mules, and disposed of the Kurds who fled with such precipitancy that their chief left behind his correspondence.

The Sultan's plot was thus laid bare, but the time for the *dénouement* was not yet. Kamal suppressed that part of the correspondence which inculpated the ruler, and merely apostrophised the Constantinople Ministry. The people were still loyal to the Padishah and had no inkling of the schemings of this man they so blindly followed.

Vahededdin became "the Exalted Ruler and Glorious Caliph," *pro tem.*, and he was urgently requested by telegram to dismiss his "traitorous" Cabinet. The Grand Vizier, to whom the fruits of office were sweet, was not to be caught so easily, however. By the simple expedient of withholding all telegrams addressed to the palace, he rendered Kamal's carefully-laid scheme as nought.

Kamal countered, and informed the Grand Vizier that unless his telegrams were delivered all communication with the capital would be cut. He gave the minister twenty-four hours in which to consider the position. At the expiration of that period, the Grand Vizier still being unwilling to commit suicide, the telegraph lines were severed. Thus, without yet being fully aware of the fact, those who had gathered around Kamal were committed to revolution. Now, whether they would have it or not, their beloved Padishah represented Constantinople, and the vast Turkey that lay beyond was without his sphere of influence. In the *passe* thus skilfully designed, someone had to assume the leadership of the Turkey beyond the environs of the capital, and who except Kamal?

Vahededdin was forced to parley. The Allied High Commissioners were beginning to point out that as Sultan his domains appeared to have shrunk. In order to retain his throne, he agreed to dismiss his Cabinet, and for the moment Kamal had to declare himself satisfied. In point of fact, he could do little else. His was a tortuous path, and when one is leading a nation by the nose, one has to proceed warily.

Constitutionally, of course, the Sultan had won the game. He had been asked to dismiss his Cabinet, and had done so, installing a compromise Ministry in its place. Therefore, there was no room for the Committees set up by the Sivas Congress—Committees which were, in effect, Mustapha Kamal—and the position of the Nationalists became difficult. From all sides there arose a demand that they should cease their activities, but Kamal, on the plea that the " nation " was waiting to see whether the new Cabinet " deserved the confidence which had been reposed in it," and other pretexts, succeeded in keeping these bodies in being.

This man, so curiously devoid of Oriental circumlocution, caught at the imagination of the Turkish peasant. Here was someone who seemed to know what he wanted, and, what was perhaps more important, what they wanted. Accustomed, over the centuries, to pious platitudes and to phraseology designedly ambiguous and beyond their comprehension, they turned to the cryptic " Yes " and " No " of Mustapha Kamal as a tired worker turns his brow to the refreshing breeze. The success of British civil servants in India and elsewhere is largely attributable to their ready facility in giving prompt and fair decisions to which they adhere, and this trait of Kamal's came to the peasantry as something unique.

This man had promised them independence. He had declared that the hated and despised Greek should go. He had gone further, and said that no matter what the conquering Allies decided, Turkey itself should retain her fabric, and her being. It was a terrific boast for one individual to make, but there was none other so to strike at fundamentals, and Kamal had the ear of the people.

Let Arabia go, he said. Let them take Syria, but beyond the line where I halted the Allied armies, they shall not pass. That which is truly Turkey, shall remain Turkey.

In the interim, Mr. Lloyd George, who so woefully misjudged the Oriental in most of his contacts with them, spoke in the Guildhall and said what was to happen to Turkey in respect of the Peace Treaty. When he sat down but little remained of Turkey or of the old Ottoman Empire—at least, in prospect.

Among the people Kamal had become almost a legendary figure. He declared that he would save them from the wrath of this "wild-haired oppressor from the Welsh hills" who knew so little of the Oriental and his ways, and who judged Turkey by the Yildiz Kiosk. The people whispered together at Kamal's coming, and said, one to the other, that this man was Beloved of Allah, than which there is no higher praise. They turned instinctively and trustingly toward him, accepting of his guidance and obeying his behests simply and without question.

The politicians, however, were not so *naive*. They distrusted one who was inclined to be autocratic. They, who thrived on circumlocution, were apt to regard as gauche the simple and forthright affirmations of this out-of-work general who got things done. This man had secured the dismissal of a Cabinet, and new elections were in prospect. The elections were held, and the Nationalists returned to an enormous majority.

In Anatolia, however, the Nationalists were one thing. In Constantinople, within the shadow of the Palace, they were another.

Kamal deemed it expedient not to trust his person to the atmosphere of the capital, but he sent his newly-elected Nationalists to the Chamber with instructions to elect him leader. The deputies proved pusillanimous. On the one hand they feared the Sultan. On the other they were jealous of the growing power of Kamal. They elected another.

This might well have spelled the end of Kamal, but he was one who could digest a reverse, and turn it to his own advantage. He ignored Constantinople, and remembered his promise to rid Turkey of the Greeks. He stole, and otherwise captured munitions from Allied war dumps, and harried the Greeks. Furious that a general turned brigand should have violated the sanctity of their war stores, the Allies turned the guns of their fleets on Constantinople, but as they forbore to fire this *coup de théâtre* became little more than a farcical *coup de chapeau*.

Great Britain proceeded a *posse ad esse*, and sought to dragoon this irrepressible opportunist *à main armée*. She landed troops in the capital, and seized the public buildings, including the telegraph offices. Many arrests followed, and the Nationalist Deputies who had denied their leader in the newly elected Chamber lost no time in taking to their heels, and with hatred of the Sultan in their hearts who, they declared, had sold his country to the foreigner, made all haste to regain the confidence of the Giant of Angora.

Kamal was not slow to seize the opportunity thus presented to him of further embarrassing the Porte and the Allies.

"*Aut inveniam viam aut faciam*," he declared in an inspired moment, but in the meantime Constantinople, in the hands of the enemy, can no longer be regarded as the true capital. That is to be found elsewhere—at Angora.

Enraged by this checkmate, Vahededdin called upon his mightiest thunder. As Caliph, he excommunicated Kamal, and all those who associated with him.

Move and counter-move across the chessboard of Fate.

Still maintaining his contention that Constantinople had passed into the limbo of the lost, Kamal declared the recent elections invalid, and issued writs for a new one. He added that the new Deputies would assemble in Angora.

He set up his revolutionary government in an old and disused schoolhouse in this ancient and sleepy Oriental town. A small kerosene oil lamp provided the illumination for the affairs of State which were inscribed on a medley of paper that came easily to hand, pack-saddles doing duty for the usual furbishings of a deep-seated bureaucracy.

With the previous backsliding of his Deputies well in mind, Kamal took pains to see, when his elections had been held, that he was elected both President of the Assembly, and President of the Ministry. Armed with both legislative and executive authority he was not a dictator, but only a hair's breadth divided him from the dictatorial and the constitutional, if revolution can be styled constitutional.

A year and a half had passed since the armistice, and still peace terms had to be imposed upon Turkey. Mr. Lloyd George, in order to give effect to his Guildhall utterances, produced the Treaty of Sevres which, if anything, proved to be even more exacting than his speech had promised.

Vahededdin sent an army against Angora, and the terms of the armistice were thus submitted to a further breach. The Sultan's forces, not viewing their task with enthusiasm, were defeated, and the Allies had allowed a further concession without producing the desired effect. Mr. Lloyd George became doubly incensed, and concentrated all available naval forces at the Golden Horn. To maintain this amazing chess-like farce, Kamal concentrated his ragged, bare-footed warriors before the Greeks in Smyrna, and got severely trounced.

In a moment his mantle fell from him. Mustapha Kamal, the Beloved of Allah, was hailed as a traitor by those who had previously regarded him as only a little less than divine.

The Nationalists remembered that they were revolutionaries first, and Kamalists afterwards, and they spoke darkly of Madame Guillotine to whom Kamal should be the first to bow his head in deference.

Instead of being caught up in the general wave of pessimism, Kamal ignored the demands for his head. Many Nationalists had become Bolshevik-conscious, and began to address each other as "Comrade." Secret preparations were made for a Communist rising against Kamal, and the Padishah. Kamal countered the intrigues of the Communist leaders, and forced them to seek asylum in the ranks of the Greeks. The irregular bands which they had mustered he incorporated in his own forces.

Back in Constantinople, the Allies had forced the Sultan to sign the Treaty of Sevres, and they gave him six months in which to carry out its provisions. They might just as well have asked for the moon.

Aujourd'hui roi, demain rien, thought Vahededdin. The public treasury was empty, and the privy purse inordinately thin. Beyond adding his signature to the Treaty of Sevres, the Sultan gave the document little consideration.

The general state of muddle was now wonderful to behold, and the Allies sought to inject into this some semblance of order. Although not a single provision of the Treaty of Sevres had been brought into effect, they called a conference. To be on the safe side, they insisted that Angora, as well as Constantinople, should be represented.

Pleased beyond measure that he should at last have wrung reluctant recognition from the Powers, Kamal went further. A conference, by all means, he agreed, but why include Constantinople? There was no longer any government there, and Turkey's sole authority was vested in the National Assembly at Angora.

At the same time Kamal made overtures to the Padishah. All the ruler was required to do was to recognize the National Assembly at Angora, and all would be well. If he refused, then he would run the risk of losing his throne. For the first time Kamal hinted at the major schemes which had fired his revolutionary purpose.

With an adroitness not usually associated with Western diplomacy, the Allies extricated themselves from a difficulty by cancelling their joint invitation, and issuing two distinct and separate ones, one to Constantinople, and the other to Angora. Thus was honour satisfied, and the play went on. At the conference, which was entirely abortive, the Angora representative was the only one to speak. He from Constantinople remained silent. The conference was ostensibly to bring about a cessation of the hostilities between Greek and Turk in Smyrna, but racial animosities were too bitter for compromise. On each side it was a case of all or none.

The conference failed, and both Greek and Turk retired to prepare for the fight which was to be fought to the bitter end with a ferociousness and a contempt for human life which was astounding. The Greeks were at the throats of their ancient enemies. Led by their King Constantine, they would once again see the ancient Constantine a Christian citadel. Once again the holy church of Sophia should house the Cross, and the crescent should be expelled. Against this crusading spirit there was Turkish steadfastness based on an animal desire to live. If the Greeks won, it was extermination. Therefore they must win and drive these Europeans into the sea.

The rest of the world sat back to watch the bloody conflict which ensued, and so interested became the Powers in the varying fortunes of the contestants that the Padishah was practically forgotten.

While engaged in this life and death struggle with his country's ancient enemy, Kamal had to contend with other malcontents who should have been his friends. A powerful Opposition developed, principally composed of "leaders" who had seen the straws in the wind and gathered that big events were portending. They argued that more luscious fruit would be to their portion if Mustapha Kamal could be side-tracked. They stamped the country. This Kamal, they said, prattles of independence, yet his principal aim is to dispossess the Sultan that he may reign in his stead. Fortunately for Kamal, his armies suffered further reverses, and retired to the very doors of the Assembly. This brought the horrors and the realities of war to the hearthstones of the politicians, and rapidly they changed their tune.

Kamal, they pleaded, should lead the army in person. No other Turkish general possessed the

facility for ensuring victory. They approached
Kamal, hand to forehead, and he agreed to lead his
men to victory, even though all seemed lost. He
made one stipulation, however. He had no intention of becoming embroiled in a personal encounter
with the Greeks from which he might not be
able to extricate himself at any given moment,
and allow the politicians a free hand while his
attention was directed toward winning a fight.
He agreed to become commander-in-chief provided
all the rights and powers of the Assembly should
be vested with him. The Deputies retired precipitately under the blow. This, they said, was
too much. But not for long. The Greek armies
continued to advance — they were actually to
come within sight of Angora — and the Deputies
capitulated.

Kamal beat back the Greeks, but only when both
sides were exhausted. Gone was the grandiose
scheme of running these invaders into the sea. They
had to be allowed to crawl there unmolested while
the Turkish armies remained in situ licking their
own wounds. That the crawl did eventually become
a run is true, but the barb was applied not so much
by Turkish arms as by that baneful thing, Greek
politics. King Constantine fell out with Venizelos,
and incidentally with himself, and Greece as a force
was ended.

Someone did eventually remember Vahededdin
sulking in the Yildiz Kiosk where, with Oriental
fatalism, he awaited the end. It became necessary
for France to conclude an agreement with Turkey.

She ignored the Sultan, and came to terms with Kamal.

In his final brush with the Greeks Kamal desired passage through the neutral zone. This he was denied, but he marched through all the same. His path took him in the direction of the much debated Straits, and the Allies strengthened their garrisons there. Kamal had directly challenged the Powers, and he determined to carry the war with Greece right across the Dardanelles. Mr. Lloyd George took fright, and issued the battle-cry, "War on the Kamalists." It seemed that another European conflagration was at hand. Fortunately for the world, the response to Mr. Lloyd George's appeal was lukewarm. France, at least, had had enough of Turkey, and said so by diplomatically withdrawing her troops from the danger zone. The close-cropped Kamal stood menacing the long-locked Welshman; and public opinion in England was with this clean-fighting Turk who had accomplished so much with so little. There was in England a great admiration for what he had done, and it was not forgotten that, except on the legitimate battlefield, his revolution had been accompanied by almost a complete absence of bloodshed. Kamal had proved himself no terrorist. Essentially he was a moderate, and anyone who is moderate in the face of extreme provocation—and Kamal had had to withstand much, even from his friends—was certain of a friendly Press in England.

Two forces were halted, almost at the bayonet-point, while the talkers settled the fate of thousands

—perhaps hundreds of thousands. On one side there was a soldier whose chief desire was peace (an attribute of most great soldiers), and on the other, very fortunately, was another. General Harington, commanding the British forces, took every prudent course to prevent an explosion.

Among the statesmen it was not so much whether there was to be another war, but whether yet another piece of paper, this time the Treaty of Sevres, should be consigned to the waste-paper basket. The waste-paper basket won, and Mr. Lloyd George slid down from his giddy eminence, never more to scale the heights.

An armistice was signed, and modern Turkey was free, with the exception of the clauses which bound the Straits in the bonds of disarmament.

For some months Kamal toyed with the fiction of a monarchy. All powers were vested in the people, and the Sultan, although Sultan, did not reign. The next steps were logical. The Sultan should be Caliph without being Sultan . . . there should be no Caliph.

The Revolution was complete.

Kamal still had other battles to fight—notably those at Lausanne, but the principal was in the boudoir. He became enamoured of a high-spirited lady—a Mohammedan lady in the best sense of the word—virile, modern, essentially well-educated, and in every sense a suitable partner for one whose principal characteristic was dourness. For months the pair fenced, Kamal waging an inner battle with what he conceived to be his duty to the State. He had Kitchener's strong views on the subject of marriage. Kamal even went on a long journey to escape from temptation, but the lady won. He returned with amazing speed, and his proposal was typical of the man. Rushing from the motor which had conveyed him, he stumbled into Latife's presence, and blurted: "We shall be married." He was.

To Latife, Kamal owes much. She has been able to soften the effects of his difficult nature. Even now he is a man who cannot be bothered by the knowledge whether a man is a friend or an enemy. He can be charming, of course, but he can also offend, often unwittingly. With Kamal, men naturally align themselves into one or other of two camps —friends or enemies—and Kamal remains completely unmoved.

He has a nervous irritability before petty obstructions, and he loses patience with the insignificant. He has overcome so much; he has created a mighty edifice out of nothing; he is impatient of trifles. One day he will be taciturn; the next he will be loquacious, and then because he has something of import to impart. One moment he will be affable, and the next moment abrupt. This does not make for friendship among those who do not understand the real worth of the character underneath.

A doctor would perhaps tell why Kamal is prone to these nervous reactions. Under the terrific strain of war, intrigue, and a restless and all-consuming desire, he remained Sphinx-like. In a Westerner, even in a Northerner, this would have been sufficiently remarkable. In an Oriental it was little less than astounding. Yet it was a pose, and it was held at the sacrifice of mighty pools of endurance. Half of Kamal's success is attributable to the fact that one could never read his thoughts from his expression. His face never mirrored his mind. Always was he enigmatic. This took toll of his nervous resources. A mighty war was waged with the impulse to find relief to an intolerable strain in the invective and fulminations of lesser men. Toward the end of his fight for independence—when he had yet to make his last desperate throws against a recalcitrant Assembly, and against a powerful enemy in the field, he turned to alcohol for the solace and stimulant which no human could accord him. He drank deeply. He found that it gave his overworked nervous system a temporary repose, and assisted him in determining momentous decisions. Alcohol is a hard master. In Kamal's case it is no longer that. He no longer seeks its doubtful joys, and regrets the day when he did. His recourse to stimulant was dictated by a distrust of his fellow men—a distrust which was certainly founded on a foundation lamentably solid. Latife has held the balance, and has prevented that mistrust from becoming acute. That even keel, that sure balance, have stood Turkey in good stead. Amidst the shoals of post-war diplomacy, Turkey has been guided by a sure hand, so sure in fact that when Turkey asked that the Dardanelles should be refortified, the Powers, almost excessively urbane, rushed with remarkable celerity to the Geneva lakesides to grant the request.

Turkey, instead of the despised among nations, has risen to high esteem. The face of the country has been radically changed, and the old order has passed. The fez is no more, and the veil is going.

Omnia mutantur, nos et mutamur in illis.

GANDHI

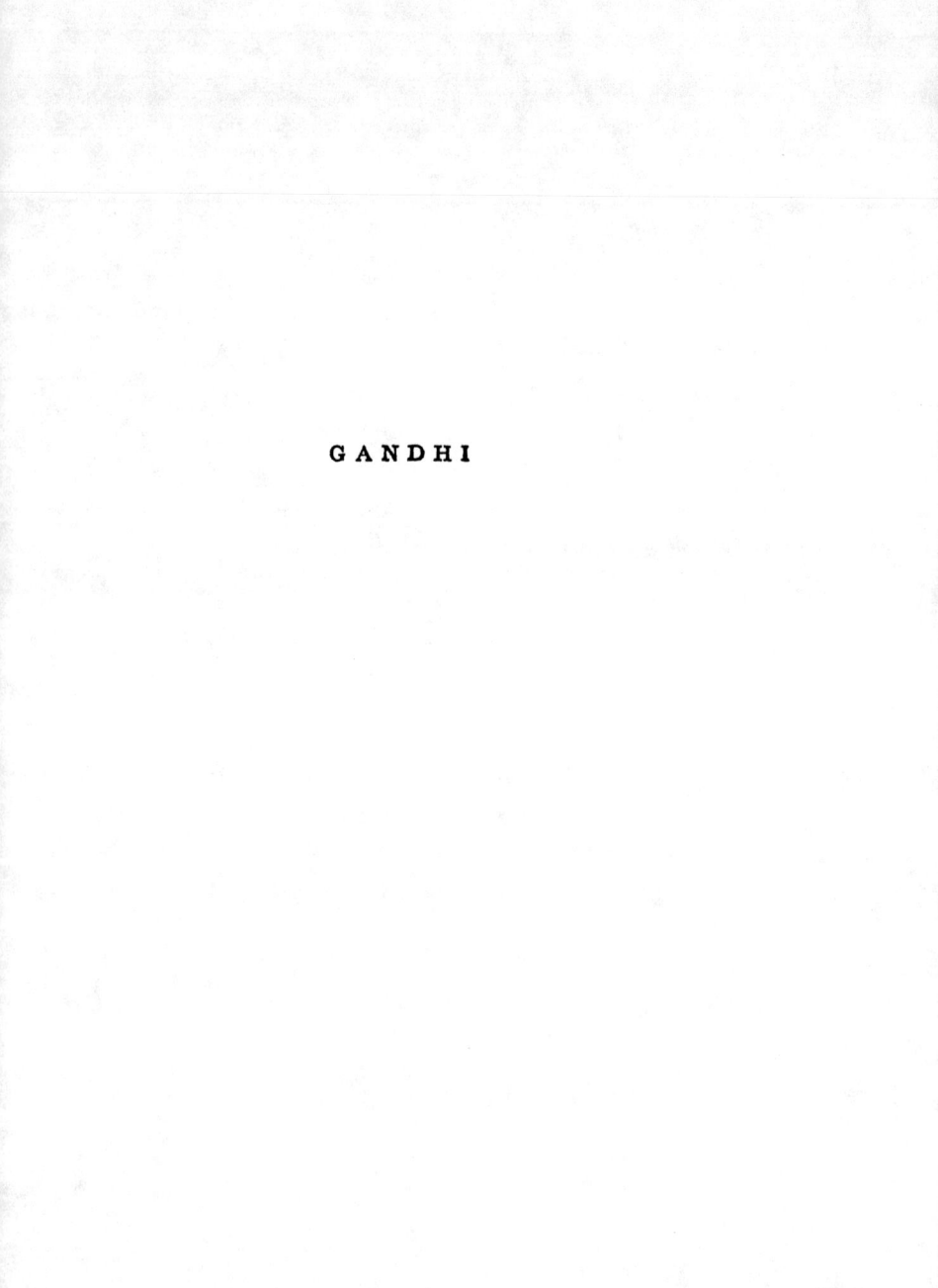

GANDHI

LIKE Tolstoi, Mohandas Karamchand Gandhi preached "Thou Shalt Not Kill"—and there was death.

Like Tolstoi, he advocated peace and goodwill to all men. Everywhere, men were eager to eat of the fruit of his philosophy, but further than this they were reluctant to go. A mundane streak in their character called them back to realities—that terrible world of facts and figures which, in these days, has even invaded the East. Being Orientals, and with an innate courtesy, they did not term him mad, as others did Tolstoi. They were far more devastating —they Deified him. He became the Saint—the Mahatma.

Christ was spurned in His day, yet He attracted a great following. Gandhi, although orthodox, paraphrased Christ with a like result; but whereas Christ's teachings have withstood the analysis of time, there is little in those which are Gandhi's, other than those admittedly of the Great Teacher's, which will bear the test of logic, or even of expediency.

Gandhi made a fundamental error when he sought the ear of the multitude. If he was to succeed he had to gather to his banner the young idea—the hordes of students which make the intelligentsia of modern India. He failed, in the main, because he was psychologically wrong. To those who have laboriously reached the higher teachings, only words on a high and unctuous plane will grip. The more difficult they are of comprehension, the better. Gandhi approached his audiences, and he told them of the things they had heard as children at their mothers' knees. He taught the principles of peace and love. He reverted to the religious reformers of a thousand years ago, and when he required a means to meet an end, he delved even further, and resurrected from antiquity much that was Indian history when Christ was a modern.

Gandhi's audiences had been drilled in a hard school. He really did not attempt to capture the masses until after the Great War, and the East, as much as the West, suffered from the Great Depression. His listeners were at grips with life—a life which was proving hard and merciless, and they could see, after they had been with him a little way, that but few of his lofty ideals, and but few of the fundamental truths which he espoused, were applicable to life as it has been evolved to-day. Quite frankly—Gandhi made no secret of it—this Mahatma wanted his countrymen to revert with him to the time when time in the modern sense was not ; when man tilled for the necessities of life, and spun the yarn which would give them covering. Modernity was as anathema to him. The giddy whirl of modern civilization he regarded as satanic. His watchword was " Simplicity." The facetious interpreted this as " Simple."

Mr. Gandhi

Express Photos

Gandhi took the Indian student too seriously. He failed to realize that some Universities of India were not so much centres of learning as political institutions in which the principal faculty was not knowledge of life, but how to rid Hindustan of the hated tutelage of Britain. There could be no peace and goodwill to all men in such an atmosphere as this. The younger element demanded blood and fire. In this, Gandhi sadly disappointed them, hence his decline.

To me, I admit, Gandhi has always been very ordinary, and I have been completely uninfluenced by his spell. When in his presence I have had the uneasy conscience of the unbeliever; I have felt as must do the sceptic at the seance. The waves of ecstacy which were transmitted to others, and which caught up so many in a delirious abandon, left me cold and critical. Perhaps this is unfair on the Mahatma, because I have felt the same in the presence of others, notably in that of Mr. Lloyd George. I have listened to the latter's audacious oratory, and have heard the wildly enthusiastic plaudits of the multitude, yet all the time, with the atmosphere charged and electrical around me, I have visualized the sentences of the Welsh wizard in print. In cold black-and-white, short of their delightful cadences, bereft of their telling inflections, they become so ordinary, so much so that one is constrained to wonder whether the reporter has not placed his "Laughter" and "Cheers" in their parentheses from a sense of duty rather than as an indication of merit.

Mr. Winston Churchill affects me in a way exactly

the opposite. As an orator he is not on the same plane as Mr. Lloyd George, but his utterances, when rendered into print, sparkle and flash with the joy of life.

In much the same way I would describe Gandhi's utterances as brilliants rather than gems. They shine, but they do not scintillate.

So much for Gandhi's reception in India. What of it in England?

It was Prince Lichnowsky, pre-war German Ambassador in London, and a keen student of humanity, who said : " The Briton loathes a bore, a schemer and a prig."

To the European mind, Gandhi was frequently boring. Long before he left the political stage he had ceased to interest the newspapers, and therefore the public, principally because he was so monstrously monotonous. He was a schemer, but not of the genus which makes head-lines, and he adopted a pose which, in the eyes of superficial observers, stamped him as a prig. It can be taken that London, usually so receptive and courteous to political adversaries, was not amused. Scarcely could it restrain the yawn which is the acme of bad breeding in the presence of a guest. Only in the East End did the real Gandhi become evident. There his name is revered. He did much to assist the poor, and he was made boisterously and roughly welcome. He was far more at home in the simple quarters of the poorer part of the Empire's great metropolis than he was in the Palace of St. James's or in the sumptuous surroundings of the West End.

Gandhi never understood the " average " Englishman, if such a person exists, and Gandhi was never understood by the vast majority of Englishmen. Their mentalities were as poles apart. He was never *persona grata* with the official element, as other Indian politicians of the Left Wing have been, principally because he was so embarrassingly ready to forgive officialdom its sins. Officialdom did not want to be forgiven. It might be prepared to admit that it makes mistakes on occasions, but sin—never.

To British minds, Gandhi was the Erratic Philosopher—the High Priest of Disarray—and that offended the essentially tidy and ordered mind of the Englishman. This much was understood. Seldom was expression given to these sentiments, because Englishmen have long memories. They remembered that he had done much for the downtrodden among his countrymen, and in the days of the Boer and Zulu Wars had done good work in charge of Indian ambulance corps. In the minds of the vast majority of Englishmen, Gandhi occupied the place apportioned to so many of their own kin. I have in mind some wealthy Britishers in this connection who insist upon airing their somewhat unorthodox views at all times and in all places. Some of them even have newspapers in which they flog their own particular " isms " to the bare bones. The Englishman would resent any untoward attack upon these individuals because he realizes that they are sincere, and the Englishman will put up with much for sincerity. In the same manner, public opinion in

England resented the lampooning of Gandhi which was conducted in some journals, and cartoons depicting him as a toothless, bald-headed, shrivelled creature clad in a loin-cloth were considered to be in extremely bad taste. The Mohammedan and the Englishman have many things in common, and one of them is a strong dislike of satirizing the unbalanced. Gandhi was never unbalanced, but in the view of many Westerns he came perilously near to be included in this category—near enough for ridicule to be characterized as bad form.

A patriot, a philosopher, and a publicist of no mean note, the world only heard of Gandhi when he decided to give up his practice at the Bar to become a stormy petrel in South Africa. Prior to that he had seen something of the world, and he was unfortunate in that he had several serious falls with a colour prejudice that has now been broken down to a very material extent.

He was born on October 2nd, 1869, and he received an education which was the best that his time could offer. Like so many thousands of young Indians of his era, and subsequently, he had a yearning for the gown and white linen collar of the Counsel. With thousands of other young men, forensic ability was there. It had not to be cultivated, for the Hindu especially is born with a gift of argument which, in comparison, renders the voluble Irishman as one of God's dumb creatures. Throughout the Eastern centuries, a halo of magnificence has attached to the office of cadi and pleader. It is still there, even though many thousands of young men have been on the rack of disillusionment and the legal profession is the most crowded of all.

Young Mohandas Karamchand Gandhi first came to London in the days when the hansom cab bowled merrily through the streets, and, after Rajkot and Bharnagar, he found both the people and the climate excessively cold. Then, far more than now, the Englishman was insular. His home was a veritable castle, and even clerks, in the fastnesses of their own habitat, never so much as dreamed of knowing their next-door neighbour until the ladies of the households had exchanged cards. A timid young man from India, completely out of his environment, and perhaps more than a little apprehensive as to the manner of his reception, could hardly hope to be comfortable in such surroundings. In a land where the people make a fetish of minding their own business and of cultivating a polite ignorance of the presence of all who had not gone through the formality of an introduction, loneliness and an infuriating inferiority complex was inevitable. Even in these days, London can be the most inhospitable place in the world to the stranger within its gates, but it was so much more so then.

Gandhi consumed his dinners in the Middle Temple and studied in lonely state. Inevitably he was called to the Bar. With his natural abilities, and a life which was necessarily devoid of entertainment, his law books provided him with a single outlet.

He returned to his native India to make his mark as a barrister, but he found the way exceedingly hard. First in Bombay, and then in Kathiawar, he tempted Dame Fortune, but her smiles were wan, and without warmth. One has to be an outstanding personality quickly to achieve success at the Bar, and luck is an element which has to be there in preponderant quantities. Mere ability counts for little.

There is little material solace to be found in shilling briefs, especially when fourpence has to be returned to the individual who introduced the client, and Gandhi gave up the struggle. There was then, as there is now, a large Indian population in South Africa, and Gandhi decided to emigrate.

He was successful, and within a comparatively short period was earning three thousand pounds per year.

It was while in South Africa that Gandhi was turned out of a Christian church, being curtly informed that one of his colour could not be allowed to sit in the same religious building as a white man, but it was not this which convinced him that the lot of the Indian in South Africa was intolerable so much as the conditions, of which he had first-hand experience in his legal practice.

He found that his fellow Indians were subject to many startling inequalities and countless indignities. They were denied their fundamental rights as British subjects. Land tenure was difficult, where it was not absolutely impossible, and Indians suffered from a thousand-and-one disabilities. Gandhi commenced to agitate, but the results of his agitation were not inspiring. They were heartbreaking.

In his acute disappointment he turned for a weapon which would make these arrogant whites see reason, and Passive Resistance was born. Eastern culture and Indian history are rich in examples of the efficiency of the purely passive. One can trace it back to the Greeks, so that Gandhi was not so very original, even though he is held as the author and the instigator of the movement.

Even Alexander the Great had to submit to the forces of passive resistance, and it was the passive which stemmed his advance into India, and caused him to halt in the region of the Beas River (the Hyphasis). Before he reached the Beas, Alexander had been severely mauled in battle by Porus before the latter finally submitted, and his men became dispirited. They were told that they would be opposed by eighty thousand horse and two hundred thousand foot, eight thousand armed chariots, and six thousand fighting elephants when Alexander sought to pass the Ganges, and they merely sat down and refused to go farther. Alexander, grieved and enraged, shut himself up in his tent and threw himself to the ground. To retreat, he declared, would be to acknowledge himself vanquished. To his men he said that he owed them nothing for what they had hitherto done, yet his men remained respectful but obdurate. They crowded round his tent in suppliant manner, lamenting, but still resolved not to march farther, and before this passiveness, Alexander had to bend.

It was this ancient weapon of passive resistance which was to be welded on to the body politic in

India at a much later date, and to appear under the guise of Non-Co-operation.

A successful lawyer in South Africa, and one earning a competence which would be the envy of many of his confreres from the Middle Temple, Gandhi suddenly rose to a task of tremendous responsibility, and one which was to be successful and completely passive only if the leader showed the way to the passive. He gave up his highly lucrative practice and assumed a leadership which hitherto had been so lamentably lacking.

Here the Mahatma displayed one of his finest traits. Never have his critics, never have the sceptics, been able, even remotely, to suggest that he had a personal axe to grind in any of the movements which he fostered. He gave his all and eschewed the fleshpots. He was not even keen on personal aggrandisement; certainly not on personal preferment.

In so many great movements, whether successful or not, the true touch of the ascetic has been lacking. In many later-day cults the founders and principals have blended the commercial with the spiritual, and the unbelievers have had the mental satisfaction of gauging the huge sums which have accrued through the generosity of disciples. Not so with the Gandhi cult. Gandhi asked no more than a covering for his head, a sufficiency of simple material to provide bodily warmth, and for sustenance his principal diet was goat's milk.

The ascetic is always difficult to attack, but I do not believe that Gandhi renounced so much in order to disarm the critics. He did so because it was part of his creed of the passive. He believed that the material and the truly passive could not, and would not, mix.

This young man worked and became the most interesting and dominating figure in Asiatic affairs in South Africa. He knew the seriousness of Indians' ailments there far better perhaps than the Secretariat in India, and he strove with all his might to provide a solution for the puzzling and perplexing problems which arose. Sufficient is it to say that to a very large measure he succeeded, though not until he had been forced to leave South Africa and to continue the battle elsewhere.

During the Great War, Gandhi, who had won considerable renown in South Africa for his handling of the Indian Ambulance Corps, turned actively to the assistance of the British, believing that the measure of India's advance toward self-government would be largely determined by her response to the Empire's call for succour in the hour of her great need. He, and other leading Indians, were encouraged in this belief, notably by Mr. Lloyd George, who, in August, 1917, declared that India's war activities had been such that the existing system of British rule in India was to be regarded as but the prelude to the conferring of responsible government. This speech was one of the least of the disservices which Mr. Lloyd George conferred upon the East.

Believing then that by the fulfilment of her obligations as a member of the British Commonwealth of Nations, India was strengthening her demand to be freed of the shackles imposed by the Minto-Morley

Reforms and to the full enjoyment of her liberties as a member of the British Commonwealth, Gandhi raised an Indian ambulance corps and conducted a recruiting campaign in the Kaira district. He worked wholeheartedly. Here, for the nonce, he emerged as a materialist.

India impatiently awaited the end of the War, for she had got into the habit of placing a literal interpretation upon the promises of Great Britain's representatives. If a member of the Indian Civil Service said that a thing should be so, then it was so. There was no quibbling.

The Armistice was signed, and confidently India awaited developments. She expected to see the promised return for the great sacrifices in money and man-power which she had made in the general cause of Empire; but the war which had just ended had been the worst in all the world's history. Millions of lives had been lost, and more property and more senses of value had been destroyed than in any other great conflict. It was perhaps natural that there should follow a period of decadence, confusion, chaos and unrest. Unrest, indeed, filled the air, not only in troubled Europe, but throughout the entire world. The old balance had been disturbed. All was still oscillating, and into this turmoil there crept an irritable irresponsibility, an impatience with time; the old was despised; the new cult of snatch and take was permeating all.

The Government of Great Britain, faced with the tremendous task of bringing a great nation back to normality—a task no whit less onerous than that of dealing with erstwhile Allies and enemies within the framework of peace—was distracted almost beyond endurance. So little time could it devote to India, which was told to sit still and to possess its soul in patience, that there arose a widespread belief that India's war sacrifices had been in vain, and that the country would revert to the status which was hers at the outbreak of the War in 1914.

It has to be admitted that there was much to foster this suspicion. True, the British Government assured India that everything was being done to expedite another measure of reforms, but events elsewhere within the Empire were such as to cause considerable distrust. In South Africa, where Gandhi had made a pact with General Smuts in 1914, the question of the status had, in the meantime, become exceedingly acute. Alarmed by the promises of Whitehall in respect of India becoming a full, self-governing member of the British Commonwealth, South Africa, and particularly the Krugersdorp Municipal Council, took time by the forelock and acted. A committee of inquiry was set up, and the outcome was the passing of a Bill which cut right through the letter and the spirit of the Gandhi-Smuts agreement, and, while protecting the existing rights of Indians to trade in certain defined areas, prohibited the acquisition of land by Asiatics.

This was not all. In East Africa, the white population passed resolutions suggesting that the presence of Indians there was not in the best interests of the African population. In Uganda, anti-Indian restrictions were imposed.

Gandhi saw in this the death-knell of all his hopes. He was a bitterly disappointed man.

I was in Lahore, in the Punjab, in the early part of 1919, and I can hear now the mutterings and the murmurings. The good faith of the British Government was impugned. In every word and in every action of officialdom, India saw a vast change to what had been during the days of the War. There were tremendously enthusiastic meetings at the Bradlaugh Hall, and processions and demonstrations. The air became electrical. One sensed the coming explosion. The authorities sought powers under the Rowlatt Act of ill-omen, and the Punjabis saw in these restrictive measures the affirmative answer to the question : " Has Great Britain renegaded ? "

Stories, unfortunately true, came seeping into a Lahore palpitating with ill-suppressed excitement. The Sikhs had looted Amritsar. The banks had been forced, and the European managers murdered. Their bodies were thrown on to pyres which had been fed with kerosene. Kasur had gone, and there had been trouble in Ferozapore. An ominous silence fell over the vast walled city of the Punjab capital. Not far from the walls there was, and still is, the Zam Zama gun around which Kipling's Kim was wont to play. Tradition said that he who held the gun held the Punjab. Should there be a sortie from the city, and should the gun be taken ? British troops in Mian Mir were five miles distant, and the local box-wallah sahibs, now precariously mounted as the Punjab Light Horse, could be discounted.

While the hotheads of Lahore talked, the military

moved, and the "city" remained quiet. Subsequently, when the troops had been hurriedly dispatched elsewhere, it was defying authority, and a large contingent was to march upon Government House, to be stopped by a thin line of red-turbaned policemen when it had proceeded half-way, but the opportunity for real action, if any was ever contemplated except by the very few, which is extremely improbable, was irrevocably lost.

There came the appalling news from Amritsar. General Dyer, convinced that the Punjab was in revolt, decided that rebels must be taught a lesson. There followed the ghastly tragedy of Jallianwallah Bagh. In a large walled garden—a park almost—demonstrators were ordered to disperse. They would, or could, not—there is no need to go into the ethics of the case—and hundreds were mown down.

The news of this event stunned India, as it was to stun England and the rest of the world when details of the affair were eventually allowed to become known. It stunned Gandhi.

He was then fifty years of age, and he thereupon decided that no longer could one put one's faith in Englishmen. He unfurled the black flag of Swaraj, and he enunciated the principles of Non-Co-operation.

Non-Co-operation, he declared, must contain not a single element of violence. Love for all men must be the key-note of the movement. Non-Co-operation must be the noble act of self-sacrifice by the sons and daughters of India on behalf of the Motherland.

There was a marked tendency at the time to absorb the teachings of Bolshevik Russia because these promised early results, but Gandhi would have nothing of the new. He pinned his faith on the old, and that which was peculiarly fitted to the mentality of India. To those who protested and would have more direct action, he maintained that the Russians had gone forward too fast, and that they would have to retreat almost as rapidly in order to extricate themselves from their own impetuous destructiveness. He visualized many of the compromises which Communism would have to evolve in its backward movement, particularly the Communist leaders, cap in hand, pleading with the capitalists whom they had doomed to destruction for the financial sinews with which to carry on the war against the Imperialists.

There was an immediate and terrific response to the appeal for non-co-operation, but the mass discipline which such a cult demanded was not there. How could it be ? It was a dream philosophy, and Gandhi sought to apply it to minds which, in the Punjab at least, frequently terminated a hockey match with a pitched battle, not for the ball, but among the players. Gandhi was dealing with inflammable material, and it is not surprising that his efforts were attended by such disorder and so many clashes with authority.

Through all the turmoil, Gandhi retained the poise of an early Christian martyr. When his train was met by the police at a small wayside station, and he was escorted from the trouble zones, he maintained his remarkable *sang froid*. He was Gandhi the imperturbable, Gandhi the Sphinx-like, Gandhi the dreamer—Gandhi, a man with a fixed goal, from his advance upon which nothing could shake him, nothing could deter him, not even the collapse of his Non-Co-operation campaign.

The broad terms of the Montagu-Chelmsford Reforms were made known, and they fell woefully short of the promises so glibly made by Mr. Lloyd George when the utmost war efforts had to be conjured from India. They were received first with a cry of incredulity, then a howl of anguish, and finally a long-sustained scream of hate. This hate was vivid and real. Not only were the Montagu-Chelmsford Reforms a pious recantation of the pledge of a British Prime Minister, but they inevitably set back the clock for a further decade. Constitutional machinery works but slowly and cumbrously, and it would be a further ten weary years before India would see the wheel go full cycle. It is not surprising that the first reaction was to reject the constitutional advances so sparingly offered, and thoroughly to non-co-operate. Equally inevitable was it that with the course of time those who were sternest in their denunciation of the reforms should become weary of watching those who did co-operate batten on its advantages, and should, with repugnance still uppermost, drop Mr. Gandhi to the extent of entering the Councils and the Assembly.

Before this could happen, however, the hateful fires were to be fed by events singularly unfortunate, and with which the name of Gandhi has to be associated.

The principal of these, and one which was attended by untold loss, misery and loss of life had its fulcrum in the effervescence of Mr. Lloyd George. He was going to legislate Turkey out of existence, and there arose the Caliphate movement, designed by Muslims to assist their co-religionists in Turkey who stood in such danger at the hands of the Christian Powers. Mr. Lloyd George's continued reference to the fates of Turkey sustained excitement in India, and Gandhi took the unprecedented step of identifying himself with a movement essentially and expressly religious. The brothers Shaukat and Mohamed Ali had previously been conducting an intense agitation on behalf of Turkey, and Gandhi allied himself with them, lending his system of Non-Co-operation to the cause of the Prophet. He called for the resignation of titles, for a boycott of the courts of justice, for the withdrawal of children from schools, and for a refusal to co-operate with the Government in any form of public activity.

This blending of forces convinced many Muslims of the sanctity of their agitation, and they, too, delved into the past for inspiration. They resolved upon the ancient expedient of migration—in other words, they determined to shake from their shoes the dust of a land ruled by those who were seemingly enemies of their Faith. Thus was the fateful Muhajrin exodus conceived, which caught up thousands in unbalanced religious zeal and culminated in distress and impoverishment for untold numbers.

Thousands of families, more particularly in the north of India, sold their holdings for miserably inadequate sums to those who were only too eager to profit from their religious zeal, and with a sublime faith they set out for the northern frontier to pass through Afghanistan to the promised land. They were pitifully equipped for such an enterprise. At first Afghanistan gave them a welcome, but when they continued to flood across the border, they speedily provided acute problems for a country which never has a surplus of anything, except perhaps robust appetites, and orders were given to close the frontier.

We had the grim and grisly picture of thousands dying by the wayside for want of food, without hope and without plans. They had sold their homes; they had expended their all; they were outcaste. Fortunately, a "satanic" Government came to the rescue. It did all that was possible to restore these misguided persons to their homes, but it was inevitable that in such a mass movement the casualties would be tremendous.

This was one of the movements which Gandhi inspired. When the grim harvest was reaped he sought refuge behind his Sphinx-like smile. I never heard him utter one word of remorse, apology, or regret.

I recall other incidents—that in Bombay when King Edward VIII landed there to commence his Eastern tour as Prince of Wales. A tumultuous reception was accorded the Prince, notwithstanding Gandhi's exhortations for non-co-operation, and the high feelings which this inflamed led to serious riots and to action by the police and military. The official list of casualties fell far short of the reality, as they always do in such cases, because relatives drag their dead and wounded away and hide them, for fear of further inquiries by the authorities.

Again in Madras, His Royal Highness was accorded an enthusiastic reception. The processional route was thronged by a dense mass, dozens deep, and for the main part the Non-Co-operators concentrated in a square to the rear of Government House. After His Royal Highness had passed into Government House the rowdy elements suddenly bethought themselves of the fact that the majority of police and military were on the processional route. I entered the square unthinkingly, and my car was held up by a dense mob of wildly-gesticulating humans. I was wearing the badge of "satanic" servitude—a morning coat—and the scene was ugly. The roaring manifestations rose to a high crescendo. In the centre of the square was a pillar around which flowers and palms had been pyramided. One enthusiast, probably a warm disciple of Charles Chaplin, caught a palm by the stem, just above the heavy earthenware pot, and swung it. When he had completed the requisite number of gyrations, and had achieved a sufficient impetus, he released its hold, and it tore its way through the crowd, felling half a dozen.

That was the signal for mass action. In a few seconds not a flower, or a palm remained around the pillar, and the driver of my car lay sprawled across his seat with an ugly gash across his forehead.

I looked ahead and saw six red-turbanned policemen, and they were running—away. I did not blame them. They were six against many thousands.

Heartened by the rout of the traditional enemy, these Non-Co-operators assailed a tram which had been halted by a solid wall of humanity. A number went to one side of the vehicle and, despite the protests of the affrighted passengers, heaved it over. They repeated the game with another tram.

I looked elsewhere—I was unable to concentrate anywhere for long because of the hail of stones and filth—and I saw a party engaged in firing a cinema. The Parsee owner objected, and he stalked forth with a revolver. Six shots rang out, with what result I do not know, for I was suddenly required to deal with a madman who evinced a strange but earnest desire to batter my head with a *lathi*.

I had climbed over the seats of my car, had edged my unconscious driver away, and had taken his place at the wheel. I had succeeded in covering, perhaps, three yards in double that number of minutes, when suddenly the throngs around me began to melt. From a road leading into the square came the sound of firing. It was the Leinsters advancing to quell the rioting. Bullets fell around me with unpleasant frequency, but fortunately the firing was restrained. The troops were not out to kill so much as to intimidate and restore order. Nevertheless, there were casualties, and as I made my escape from the square I counted more bodies around me than subsequently figured in the official lists. Undoubtedly the majority of these were removed before it was possible for those responsible to count the cost of non-co-operation.

In the subsequent years Gandhi dropped and

retrieved Non-Co-operation much as one may do a hot brick, but as a disciple of peace and brotherly love he acted strangely and inconsistently when waves of terrorism swept over Bengal, the North-West Frontier Province, and the United Provinces. In order to cope with organized mass murder, it was necessary for the Government to promulgate a series of Ordinances, but Gandhi allowed the Ordinances, and not the murders, "to cast a gloom over his thoughts."

His prison experiences multiplied, and it was from prison that he decided to take part in the Indian Round Table Conferences in St. James's Palace, in London. He was an honoured guest in both places, but with a remarkable perversity he said far less at the Conferences than he ever did in prison. Gandhi was faced with the necessity of once again reverting to realism, or remaining an enigma. He chose his rôle as Mahatma, which was politic, if not very helpful, for the Round Table Conference had degenerated so much into a battle with those who were reluctant to grant India her freedom, as a battle between the guests on the apportionment of the promised feast. It was all so exceedingly embarrassing, for the time of the Conference was taken up, not with sessional debates, but with backstairs bickerings and East-end murmurings, while the Indian delegates made a forlorn attempt to compose their differences and present a united front at the Conference table.

This internecine warfare was fought on the principle of communal representation. As the mouthpiece of the Congress party, Gandhi was constrained to declare that there could be no special reservation of seats in the Councils, or special electorates for any minorities other than Muslims and Sikhs. The consequence was that Gandhi had an unpleasantly large dose of his own medicine when he returned to Bombay, for the depressed classes had taken umbrage at his waywardness, and went to extreme lengths to counter the extensive programme of welcome which had been arranged by the local Congress. Bands of the depressed, armed with the formidable *lathi*, went through the streets tearing down the decorations set up by zealous Congressmen, and some thousands took up a strategic position opposite the Ballard Pier where Gandhi was to disembark. When the steamer arrived, there was an assault *en masse* on the Congress workers, and many of the reception committee retired to hospital with broken heads. It is exceedingly probable that Gandhi would have found it impossible to land if the much-maligned police had not appeared. They collected nearly two thousand *lathis* from the infuriated depressed, not to mention sundry broken bottles and knives. Thereafter the depressed had to confine their welcome to waving black flags and chanting hostile battle cries.

Gandhi gave the multitude a smiling acknowledgment as he descended the gangway. When he sought to board his car there was a raging mob of Congressmen on one side shouting a welcome, and a furious concourse of the depressed on the other shrieking condemnation.

Notwithstanding this, Gandhi refused to believe that the depressed classes were angry with him. { He had a remarkable facility for ignoring the obvious. " I deny that they are angry with me," he said. " They are bone of my bone and flesh of my flesh. I would love to die so that they may live with perfect dignity and self-respect."

With so much disunity among Indians, and the onus having been thrown upon the Government of making a communal award, it was necessary to create a diversion to mask the rather pathetic failure at St. James's. Consequently, within a few days of Gandhi's return, Congress resolved to revive defiance of the law, to boycott British goods, and to restart picketing. Gandhi, on his part, sent a long ultimatum to the Viceroy, Lord Willingdon, in which he offered to suspend action if the Viceroy granted him an interview and also gave him facilities to tour the provinces, "so that he could personally study conditions."

Within a few hours, the only possible action had been taken. Gandhi was arrested once more and conveyed by car to the very comfortable quarters which were more or less continually maintained for his convenience in the Yeravda Gaol, near Poona. Gandhi had been interned here before, and he had quite an affection for the attendants kindly provided by a beneficent Raj.

It was also necessary to arrest Mrs. Gandhi, and Gandhi's son, Ramdas, but they were not accorded the extraordinary courtesies extended to the Mahatma. They had to be content with short terms of imprisonment.

It was while in Yeravda that Gandhi staged his series of famous fasts. His first in September, 1932, was designed to force the Government to make fundamental changes in its communal award. Gandhi was told that he could secure his release if he would agree to certain restrictions on his movements, but he refused the offer. He declared that he was not willing to buy his liberty on such terms, and therefore had to remain in prison. This fast came to an end when certain adjustments to the communal award were made.

Gandhi could have regained his liberty at any time by calling off civil disobedience, but in point of fact he remained in Yeravda for sixteen months. On May 1st, 1933, Gandhi announced his intention to undertake an " unconditional and irrevocable fast for twenty-one days," on behalf of the work of eradicating the evils of untouchability. By this time he had completely abandoned the *non possumus* attitude he had taken up at the Round Table Conference, and was now the champion of the depressed classes.

Explaining the origin of his decision to fast, Gandhi said that a tempest had been raging within him for some days. The voice became insistent, and said, " Why don't you do it ? " He resisted, but in vain.

He added that a study of the evil of untouchability since the days of the Round Table Conference had convinced him that it was far greater than he had thought it to be. Money, external organization and political power would help the untouchables, but this must be accompanied by self-purification, which could only come about by fasting and prayer.

"I have no desire to die," he went on. "I want to live for the cause, though I hope I am prepared to die for it. But I need for myself, and my fellow-workers, greater purity. Shocking cases of impurity have come to my notice. I want more workers of unassailable purity."

Gandhi gave out that he would commence to fast eight days later. As his previous fast had been for eight days, and as after the expiration of that period, doctors had announced his condition as "serious," the opinion was expressed that he would not survive a fast of twenty-one days.

Gandhi himself, however, remained quite optimistic, declaring that older men than he had survived such an ordeal. He took the precaution of sending a telegram to the Government in which he made clear that his fast was projected for reasons wholly unconnected with the Government, and solely connected with the Untouchable movement, and "in obedience to a peremptory call from within received about midnight."

He added: "I have to take twenty-one days' unconditional and irrevocable fast with water, soda and salt."

"The fast," he continued, "might be commenced at once, but for my being a prisoner, and my anxiety to enable the local authority to receive the necessary instructions for arrangements during the fast, and to avoid all possible embarrassment to the Government."

Actually, of course, he placed the Government in a serious dilemma. The fast was admittedly non-political, and it had three courses open to it. Gandhi could be allowed to complete his fast in prison on the assumption that he would there find the necessary rest and peace which would be denied him by those who would throng around him were he released. He could be permitted to remain in the gaol in the hope that a further peremptory voice from within would persuade him to give up the fast, and that then, if no voice came, he could be released if his condition became critical.

The Government, however, had to consider the administrative risks and inconveniences involved should Gandhi die on their hands, either in gaol, or in transit after his condition became critical. Had he died in such circumstances it was practically certain that a purely social and religious issue would be confused with a sordid political controversy.

It was decided to release the Mahatma forthwith, it being understood that this was an act of grace which did not imply that Gandhi agreed to the immediate cessation of civil disobedience, and that as a man of honour he would not take advantage of the act of grace.

Mr. Gandhi was removed to the house belonging to Lady Thackeray near Poona, and there he commenced his fast. When he had completed it, an audience of two hundred persons, including Hindus, Muslims, Parsees, Europeans, and members of the depressed classes, gathered in the hall of the house.

As twelve o'clock struck, announcing the expiry of the prescribed twenty-one days, Gandhi's bed was wheeled in. He lay motionless among the pillows, and it was seen how wasted he had become in three weeks. His eyes were sunken, and the hand and lower arm which projected over the sheet were tremulous and thin. Nevertheless, Gandhi had sufficient strength and will power to smile upon those had who come to greet him.

It is recorded :

" All the Hindus present sang a hymn. Dr. Ansari read a passage from the Koran dealing with fasting. A small group of Christians followed with two verses of the hymn ' When I Survey the Wondrous Cross,' and a Parsee sang a Parsee song. A poem which Rabindranath Tagore had composed specially for the occasion was recited by Gandhi's secretary, and Gandhi's own favourite hymn brought the devotional part of the ceremony to a close."

Gandhi, before drinking a glass of orange juice presented by an untouchable boy, said in his weak voice :

" I do not know exactly what God expects from me now, but whatever it may be I know He will give me strength for it."

Gandhi knew then that he had lost his grip upon Congress. Months before, indeed on the day he had landed at Bombay after his disastrous visit to the Round Table Conference, his life-long friend, Mr. V. J. Patel, former President of the Legislative Assembly, had told him as much.

In October, 1934, when it was becoming increasingly evident that as a leader of the masses he was a spent force, Gandhi began to hint that he desired to retire from the Congress, giving as a reason " the absence of solid support for his amendments to the constitution of Congress."

Later in the same month, when the All-India Congress Committee met in Bombay, Gandhi addressed the gathering. He was an old man, but a shadow of the man he had been. His fasts had wrecked his health, and his voice was thin and quavery. He said that he wanted to retire from the Congress organization if it was possible for him to secure the blessings of the Committee.

He went on to say that he felt that the Congress was being suppressed by his presence, and was not giving natural expression to its views. At the same time he deplored the artificiality and corruption in the movement, and the overpowering desire to wrangle. He added that if Congressmen would not cleanse themselves of such things he had no option but to retire.

He went on to emphasize that he desired to retire in order to give the Congress the opportunity to train itself. He desired to retire in order that he could also grow himself. He was leaving in order that he might develop the power of non-violence.

Gandhi remained the High Priest of the Passive until the end.

He concluded his very pathetic oration—for in this he saw the grave of all his hopes, of all his schemes—with a final exhortation on the powers of his cult.

"India," said this emaciated wisp of a man, "will never get liberty without non-violent means, and without non-violence expressed in terms of civil disobedience. Independence is impossible without civil resistance. I know of no historic instance of purely constitutional means having clothed any nation with liberty."

Gandhi still entertained an affecting simplicity ; a plaintive belief in the efficacy of prayer and of meditation ; and a hope, deep down, that he might yet regain the hold upon the public imagination which he had lost.

With the vision of the ashram to which he was retiring before him, Gandhi indicated that he might return, and say :

"Now I can lead you to the goal, and we can march in perfect safety."

Congress was taking its leave of a general, and a Mahatma. It was bidding farewell to one who had the most disturbing qualities of the ascetic, the cynic, the paterfamilias, and the rebellious child.

He was one who could declaim with perfect sincerity, " Hearken little children, and come unto me," yet contemplate with a baffling and irrational equanimity the appalling results which attended his incursion into Muslim politics, and the Muhajrin debacle.

He could blind himself to the painfully obvious, and yet retain faith in an ideal.

Gandhi forgot that human beings are born egotists, and that they do not love one another unselfishly. Rather do they hate one another.

He made another fundamental error when he appealed to the sentimental. It was useless for him to say that it was wrong to be violent, that it was unethical to use force, that it was immoral ever to be otherwise than completely passive. That was, as abundantly proved, the way to incite violence.

He preached love, and the brotherhood of man, and he was idealist enough to believe that when he had delivered himself of his sermons, the very souls of his hearers would be changed.

When Gandhi indicated that he might return to the Congress and say: " Now I can lead you to the goal, and we can march in perfect safety," he was the last poet of his own agony. He was the doctor at his own deathbed. For him the ashram, prayer, meditation—and obscurity.

Even at this stage it is difficult to get to grips with the mentality of this idealist with the shaven skull, thick lips, and protruding ears. His pronouncements were frequently so diverse and torn from the line of logical sequence. Some, at least, of these will live.

" Europe to-day is only nominally Christian," he said in 1930. " In reality it is worshipping Mammon."

"India's aim," he said on another occasion, " should be to repudiate Western civilization," and with that he condemned all things British—magistrates, teachers, alienation from Hindu culture, and modern medical science. " India," he reiterated, " must go back to the sources of her ancient culture." Yet he claimed, in August, 1920, " I am not a visionary. I claim to be a practical idealist."

" Hindus, Parsees, Christians or Jews," he declaimed, " if we wish to live as one nation, the interest of any one of us must be the interest of all. The only deciding consideration can be the justice of a particular cause."

Much of his philosophy was based upon a poor conception of India's potentialities, and a conception at variance with realities.

" Bravery on the battlefield is impossible for India," he said once, " but bravery of the soul remains open to us. Non-co-operation means nothing less than training in self-sacrifice. I expect to conquer you by my suffering."

" If," he said, " Indians have become the pariahs of the Empire it is retributive justice meted out to us by a just God. Should the Hindus not wash their blood-stained hands before we ask the English to wash theirs? . . . Untouchability has degraded us. . . . India is guilty . . . England has done nothing blacker. . . . We are no better than brutes until we have purged ourselves of the sins we have committed against our weaker brethren."

And yet again, and here perhaps we have the explanation of much of Gandhi's confused thought, " I am trying to introduce religion into politics."

It was Tagore who said of Gandhi : " His soul is perpetually anxious to give, and he expects nothing in return—not even thanks. . . . If I were to be strangled, I shall be crying for help, but if Gandhi were strangled I am sure he would not cry. He would laugh at his strangler. If he has to die, he will die smiling."

This is the same man who, when he first went to England, took lessons in elocution and in dancing, to fit himself for the polite world. Half-way through his dancing lessons he came upon Ruskin's " Unto

This Last," and the dancing lessons ceased. Afterwards he read Tolstoy's "The Kingdom of Heaven is Within You," and it fitted into his philosophy.

His views on art are worth quoting. Speaking of Oscar Wilde he said : " He saw the highest art only in outward forms, and therefore succeeded in beautifying immorality. All true art must help the soul in realizing its inner self. In my case I find I can do entirely without external forms in my soul's realization. I can claim, therefore, that there is truly sufficient art in my life, though you might not see what you call works of art about me. My room may have blank walls, and I may gaze out upon the starry heavens overhead that stretches in the unending expanse of beauty. What conscious art of man can give me the scene that opens out for me when I look up to the sky above with all its shining stars? This, however, does not mean that I refuse to accept the value of human production of art, but only that I personally feel how inadequate these are when compared with the external symbols of beauty in nature."

Gandhi sought to clothe all his subjects, " Hindus, Parsees, Christians or Jews," in one distinctive covering. He believed that by so doing he would bring about a mass sense of equality.

Writing from Ahmadabad gaol in 1923, he said :

" Personally, after deep thought, I have come to the conclusion that if there is anything to serve as an effective and simple symbol . . . it is the adoption of charka and pure khaddar dress prepared from hand-spun yarn by the rank and file of the communities. Only universal acceptance of this cult can supply us with a common idea, and afford a common basis of action."

Thus there came into being the well-known Gandhi cap.

From the same gaol, and almost at the same time, he wrote : " Hindu-Muslim unity must be our creed to last for all time, and under all circumstances."

Yet Gandhi was against removal of the system of caste.

" I am certainly against any attempt at destroying caste," he wrote. " The caste system is not born on unequality; there is no question of inferiority.

" Caste is the projection in the world of the principles of reincarnation, and nature will, without any possibility of mistake, adjust the balance by degrading a Brahmin if he misbehaves himself."

This was akin to telling the hungry and destitute not to despair, for in the next world they would inhabit the Kingdom of Heaven. It indicated a sublime faith, but it was too completely devoid of this world to find full flavour.

Gandhi would have all in a common mould, but he would retain the caste system, and he expected to achieve Hindu-Muslim unity when he expounded the following on the vexed question of cow-killing :

" The central fact about Hinduism is cow protection. Cow protection, to me, is one of the most wonderful phenomena in human evolution. The cow, to me, means the entire sub-human world. Man, through the cow, is enjoined to realize his identity with all that lives. Why the cow was selected for apotheosis is obvious to me. The cow is the best companion. She is the giver of milk in plenty. Not only does she give milk, but she also makes agriculture possible. This gentle animal is a poem of pity. Protection of the cow means protection of the whole dumb creatures of God. Ahimsa (non-killing: non-violence) is the gift of Hinduism to the world, and Hinduism will live as long as there are Hindus to protect the cow."

But Gandhi could still stigmatize the Hindus. He said:

"I loathe and detest child marriage. I shudder to see a child widow. I have never known a grosser superstition than that the Indian climate causes sexual precocity. What does bring an untimely puberty is the mental and moral atmosphere surrounding family life."

How different was Gandhi to Kamal. Gandhi's was a movement away from Europe and her civilization. Kamal's is still toward Europe, and hers.

Gandhi, frail and ascetic, harrowed and racked by religious superstition, at the height of his power held sway over millions. He was reverenced and worshipped as a demi-god.

One scene remains in my mind, as an evidence of this little man's emotional appeal. It was in 1924, and Gandhi had just been released after two years in prison.

During his incarceration his followers had been out-manœuvred by the new party in Congress, the Swarajists, and the Swarajists were well organized and disciplined. The Swarajists attended the meeting of the Congress working committee in full force, and they protested with vigour against Gandhi's virtual dictatorship of the Congress. Finally the Swarajists brought into force the principal Swaraj weapon—they left the meeting in a body.

Gandhi regarded this as a defeat. He had sponsored a motion, and it had been passed. He withdrew it.

Though out-manœuvred in the formal proceedings, this arch-psychologist had another weapon to his armoury. He sat quietly, and talked. He spoke of his defeat, of the pitiful state of India, and tears flowed down his cheeks. The tears flowed faster, and this was the signal for a strange phenomenon, and one which would certainly be impossible of reproduction in prosaic Europe. The entire gathering began to weep in sympathy, and the eyes of all were unashamedly tear-stained. One by one, all swore undying allegiance to the man who had attacked them at their weakest point—that of emotionalism. He had more than regained his lost ground.

With this power, and this grasp of psychology, he disturbed the very heart of India. For long it was no consideration to the masses that his ideals were impossible. They cared not a whit that this Heaven-sent leader was out of touch with reality.

For many years, the more frequently Gandhi failed to produce that which he had promised, and the more often he pleaded guilty to abysmal failure, the higher he rose in the esteem of the people.

He termed the British Government "Satanic," and millions believed him.

They still believe in the Satanic, but they have forgotten that Gandhi coined the phrase.

THE AGA KHAN

THE Aga Khan is no longer a mystery to the Western world, although a great deal of misunderstanding still exists in respect to his unique position in the world of Islam. To that purely mythical being, the " average " man, he is a person rich beyond the dreams of avarice, who is singularly fortunate on the Turf. In the view of the same unlikely being he has a weakness for Europe, and all that Europe can offer, and the ties that bind him to the East and to the great religious foundation of which he is the undisputed head appear to be remarkably elastic. This same person seeks an analogy, and for the want of something better places him on the same plane as the Archbishop of Canterbury, or the Pope. Having thus erroneously " placed " him to his own satisfaction, he is then apt to become somewhat critical and to ask, " If this man is a great religious leader, why is he not among those whom he leads ? "

A very pertinent question this, because though it is one built upon false premises, it is one that is very frequently put.

The very unique position occupied by His Highness the Aga Khan has no counterpart in the West. There is nothing that is comparable. He is a spiritual Lord without temporal being. He is a man without a country, a world figure without a home. Millions bow in humility before his name. He is the living descendant of the Prophet, but the very Faith of which he is the living embodiment deifies the wanderer upon the earth. It is an axiom of the Believers that, allegorically at least, the spirit of martyrdom should be there.

The Aga Khan, when he succeeded, at a very early age, to the patrimony of his father, received no vast domains. This Prince stepped into no cumbrous heritage, and the orbit of the activities which were to be his were ill-defined. The sceptre which was his was that of the House of Man, and the House of the Prophet. He had not to live the drama of life circumscribed by frontiers and borders. His was not to be a stewardship presented in so many acts. His domain was limitless, and if world events should have had their pivot in Europe rather than in the East, that was at the dictate of a Higher Being, and was not fortuitous. In all the great events of the war and post-war period which had their centre in the East, it will be found that the Aga Khan was there, ready to throw his weight upon the scale of reason and order. He possesses the facility of being in the right place at the right time, and his rovings have proved a great asset. When great problems reared their fungus-like growths, the Aga Khan was able to lend a much-wanted sense of perspective. Pyramidical detail associated with proximity was not there either to intimidate or to deter him. He brought a fresh mind to the scene, untrammelled by the petty.

HIS HIGHNESS THE AGA KHAN

Elwin Neame

This is not an apologia—for the Aga Khan requires none—but an explanation. Effectively to administer the great trust which is his, it is incumbent upon His Highness that he should retain the broadest of outlooks, and be above any suspicion of favouritism which might accrue were he to bind himself down to fixed terrain. He has necessarily to be a world figure. In so doing he is maintaining the tradition of his line.

In the main the European fails to realize this, principally, of course, because he does not know. He gazes at one of the photographs with which the illustrated periodicals are plentifully bestrewn, and murmurs, " Oh, the Aga Khan." He has won another golf-match, or has topped the winning list of racehorse owners. Not one in a hundred thousand who instantly recognize these reproductions of the Aga Khan's likeness has any conception of the power and romance behind this agile, sturdy figure. Really to understand one has to span the centuries, for the story of the Aga Khan is steeped in the deep mysteries of the ancient East. His story did not begin with his birth, but more than thirteen hundred years ago, for he is directly descended from Ali, the son-in-law and cousin of the Prophet. Thus we find the secret of the veneration which is accorded His Highness by millions of his Faith the world over. In it also lies the secret of the source of the immense funds which he administers on behalf of the Faithful.

The Aga Khan has had the courage to march alone through the troubles of our afflicted world, and his very detachment has caused multitudes to march behind him in times of great and international discord. A passionate lover of the arts, and the possessor of one of the keenest eyes in the world for a horse, he is essentially human, and he has made his life one long, continuous effort to attain the ideal of peace. Always ready to wage war, and to call upon his followers to aid the right, nevertheless his creed has always been peace in the ultimate. His power and immensity spring from the aura which surrounds his name, and his remarkable individuality, rather than from his surroundings.

He believes that all must work, and that nothing can be achieved without hard work. Always has he preached the gospel of physical fitness in order that work might be enjoyed. He refuses to confuse work with labour, or industry with penance. In his mind there is a sanctity attaching to work, and he is impatient of the idler. Those who tarry by the wayside, he says, have the souls of thieves.

The amount of work which the Aga Khan daily accomplishes is prodigious. He caught my somewhat apprehensive eye on one occasion when a secretary presented him with a truly formidable pile of correspondence, and he smiled.

"We must," he said, answering my unspoken question, "give the best that is within us. We must all work hard, as nothing can be achieved without hard work. If one is hasty, one rushes to the accomplishment of nothing. And if a man works only with worldly success or gain in his mind, or of honours that are likely to accrue, he ceases to be the true craftsman. Work should have its own rewards."

"Many of the young people," he added, "do not place sufficient value upon the qualities of patience and perseverance. They seek to reach their goal too quickly. The striving in these days is for originality, and—there is so little scope for the original, for more often than not we find that it has been done before."

This philosophy perhaps explains the remarkably even temperament of the Aga Khan. He is not a dreamer, although he refuses to rush. When he acts, he has the force and the strength of mathematical calculation behind him. Many would-be get-rich-quick schemers who have approached him with their designs have discovered this to their chagrin.

He is a great admirer of nature. He admires its beauties so much, and he finds them so perfect, that if God were to call him and suggest a change, he would answer: "All is perfect." This, however, does not prevent him in obtaining the best that nature can provide. His selectivity at the stud gives a case in point. Perhaps his views can be best summed up if it is said that he has no use for the erotic.

It may or may not have been noticed that the Aga Khan never seeks the limelight. When it is thrust upon him, he accepts the inevitable with a resigned shrug of his broad shoulders. Similarly, this descendant of the Prophet abhors show and display.

This much is evident in the Aga Khan's home in Bombay. It is an immense structure, but no one would term it a palace. Rather is it a great administrative centre—a place for quiet and unobtrusive work.

Here the atmosphere is essentially Persian, and of the old school, with just a tinge of the India that was in the days of the Great Moghuls. There is colour, there is air and sunlight, and there are magnificent gardens in which the birds are encouraged to gather. No gaily caparisoned servants bar one's entrance as one makes for the gates; there is a complete absence of ceremonial, and the personality of the poseur is entirely lacking. Simplicity and old-world Eastern courtesy is the keynote. It is here that the mighty finances of the Ismailian order are directed and controlled.

It is impossible to see His Highness, or any of the Aga Khans who preceded him, in proper perspective. without recalling something of the past. It is not enough to say that a man is linked with history. Without at least indicating some of the major links, much of the romance attaching to the individual is lost, and unappreciated, yet for the sake of brevity it is possible to jump the centuries, and to leave the ancients for something a little more modern while still maintaining the thread of the story of the Aga Khans. In so doing one leaves behind much that is rich in romance—great battles on the banks of the mighty Euphrates and Tigris, assassinations, and millions fighting for the sanctity of their Faith.

Until the beginning of the last century the scene was almost entirely set in an Old Testament environment—in Iraq, Persia, Syria, Palestine, Egypt, and the Valley of the Jordan. Then, in 1817, we find that the descendant of Ali and the head of the Ismailians had taken up his head-quarters at Yezd, in

Persia. He had very considerable renown for piety, for he lived in a licentious age. His name was Shah Khalilulah, and he was rather too outspoken in criticism of the ways of the Persian Court for him to be popular with those other than of his own Faith. He died suddenly, with a knife in his back, placed there by one who sought favour and advancement of the Shah of Persia. So summarily to dispose of the head of a great sect promised trouble, and the Shah of Persia was more than a little apprehensive of the consequences which might ensue.

In order to demonstrate his repugnance of the act of the assassin, he had the miscreant thrown into an icy-cold pool, and then beaten with rods until he died. The son of the dead Khalilulah was invited to Court, and marked favour was shown him. This was Muhammad Hussain. Eventually he married a daughter of the Shah of Persia, and was appointed Governor of Mohelati. To mark his preferment he was vested with the hereditary title of the Aga Khan.

The Shah of Persia died, and the first Aga Khan found himself in a position of considerable difficulty. The Shah had left many sons, and all became protagonists for the throne. Before many days had passed a many-sided civil war was in progress, and the Aga Khan was called upon to lend his support. He had no option but to assist the son who had been nominated as successor by the Shah. He was appointed Commander-in-Chief, and as such undertook a number of highly successful campaigns. There was, however, a fly in the ointment of success, for the kingly aspirant lacked a royal treasure chest, and the Aga Khan was required to finance his wars from his own resources. When he had routed the other pretenders, and had brought the campaign to a successful conclusion, the Aga Khan tendered his bill to the new monarch. It had assumed somewhat alarming proportions—wars cannot be conducted for nothing—and the Shah was without funds. The tax-gatherers had yet to be appointed. The Shah sought a novel way out of his embarrassment. He directed the Aga Khan to assume the overlordship of two provinces, and to recoup himself from the taxes he was empowered to collect. The arrangement proved to be an admirable one, but it excited the cupidity of the newly appointed Prime Minister who, as the principal officer of the State, saw no reason why another should fare better than he. This functionary utilized the powers which were his, and decreed that the Aga Khan had no right to the taxes which he was collecting with such diligence. As Commander-in-Chief, the Aga Khan considered that his position was sufficiently strong to maintain that he had.

More internecine warfare broke out, with varying fortunes to either side, and the conflict was eventually brought to a close with an honourable settlement. The Aga Khan agreed to lay down his arms, and the Prime Minister agreed to allow the head of the Ismailians his just possessions. It takes two to keep a bargain, honourable or otherwise, and no sooner had the Aga Khan disbanded his forces than he found himself a prisoner in a dungeon in Teheran.

It was at this stage that the Shah, mindful of his

own person, recalled the fact that the Aga Khan was also the leader of a powerful people, and in order to obviate the unpleasant, he ordered his immediate release. The Prime Minister, however, was not to be foiled so easily. The Aga Khan should be freed, but it was not difficult to arrange a remarkable scarcity of food wherever he wandered. It became necessary for the Aga Khan once more to beat his forces to battle, but this time not so much to defeat the armies of the Prime Minister as to cut a way through to safety and freedom. The Aga Khan, after much travail, succeeded in reaching the comparative security of Afghanistan, and there to make his first contacts with the British—contacts which have been maintained from that day to this.

The Aga Khan met the British officers then in Kabul, and he was induced by them to leave the Afghan capital, and to take up his residence in Sind, where there were very large colonies of Ismailians. Here the warrior refugee came under the notice of Sir Charles Napier, the famous British general, and Sir Charles persuaded the Aga Khan to abandon for the time being the plans he was then maturing for a return to Persia, and for yet a further fight for his own. Sind was then being added to the sphere of influence of the East India Company, and the Aga Khan, at his own expense, raised and maintained a body of irregular cavalry, and, debouching on the right bank of the Indus, secured for Sir Charles British communications with Karachi. So meritorious were the services rendered by the Aga Khan that a grateful British Government conferred upon him the hereditary title of "Highness," and provided him with a pension commensurate with his estate.

It was this first Aga Khan who relaid the foundations of his illustrious line in Bombay, where thousands of Ismailians poured offerings into his coffers.

This bearer of the title had much in common with the present. With his Persian associations he had a wonderful eye for a horse. Horses were his passion, and he had agents scour the East for representative specimens with which to form the basis of the racing establishment for which he became famous.

Some of the earliest memories of Sir Aga Sultan Muhammed Shah, the present Aga Khan, are of happy hours spent in the stables maintained by his grandfather. He can recall, too, how his grandfather, when too old to take a more active interest in the racecourse, would ride to the scene on a pony led by a groom. To the last, the first Aga Khan considered the horse to be the only worthy means of transportation.

The purpose of the present Aga Khan has been unobtrusively to work for the bridging of that gap which divides the Suni and Shiah, and to rouse all Muslims, irrespective of creedal differences, to an appreciation of their responsibilities in a world which has progressed far since the Prophet first gave his teachings to mankind. It has been a laborious task, but he has succeeded to a degree which at one time seemed impossible, and the drift is still toward unity and enlightenment. At an early age he was called upon to give the lead against fanaticism following the murder of a number of men of the Shiah Faith who had been converted to Suni-ism. Feeling naturally ran high, and Bombay and the Deccan was in a turmoil, but this young leader acted. In his eyes, those who perpetrated these deeds in the name of religion were nothing more than murderers and assassins, and before a vast concourse of his followers in the Jamat Khana in Bombay, he said so, in unbridled language. He excommunicated the murderers, and directed that they should be denied burial in Shiah graves. He emphasized then, as he has done on countless occasions since, that between followers of the Prophet there should obtain the closest bonds of amity and friendship, and he intimated that any of his followers who went beyond this precept could count upon his stern displeasure. The dread decree of excommunication made it evident to both Suni and Shiah that this was a young leader who would not countenance extremism, and the lesson he preached then has never been forgotten.

The Aga Khan was the forerunner of the modernist spirit in Islam. He fought for the emancipation of women, and for the more modern education of men long before other "progressive" movements in Islam had reared their heads, and whereas his tutelage pointed to the sane and balanced road of advancement, his forward thrust has been attended by none of those upheavals which have been a concomitant of similar expressions of modernity elsewhere. Long before Turkey was to be precipitated into that series of swift, breath-taking incidents which was to result in the jettisoning of the Caliph—incidents which were more cultural and economic than political or religious—and long before the Arab peoples came to their awakening, and Amanullah was to set all Afghanistan at his heels, the Aga Khan was telling Muslims that they must embrace a new philosophy, and seek the rich heritage which comes from the tree of true knowledge. He was a pioneer, and it goes without saying that he was a courageous one, for he had to break through barriers of prejudice and custom. Above all, he had to overcome an amazing lethargy, and to instil into a people who saw virtue in unprofitable religious meditation a desire for achievement and for advancement. It was no light task which the Aga Khan undertook, and it was one which would have defeated a man with less pertinacity. Muslim education was then centred almost entirely upon and around the Koran. Trade was regarded with repugnance, and the Muslims of India especially were in a torpor. There the Muslims constitute a minority community, and His Highness looked ahead to the days when the British Raj would fulfil its pledge and admit India to a full partnership in the British Commonwealth of Nations. He saw that those of his faith were woefully unprepared for the contingency, and he commenced the great work of rousing them.

Then, the Muslim conception of life began with the recitation of prayers and ended with the great pilgrimage. Mainly through the efforts of the farsighted leader, Aligarh College was raised to the status of a university. The Aga Khan was forthright in his insistence upon higher educational values, and his views on this difficult subject were enunciated with vigour when he presided over the Muslim Educational Conference in Delhi at the time of the Coronation Durbar of the late King Edward VII. Such a statement of policy would now cause no great furore. Then, in the state of Muslim unpreparedness, it created a tremendous sensation, for here was the leader, the lineal descendant of the Prophet, telling Muslims that they were intolerably wrong in many of their interpretations.

" We are undertaking a formidable task," he said, " when we attempt to correct and remodel the ideals of our people, but for the task before us we Indian Muslims have many advantages. We have the advantage of living under a Government which administers justice evenly between rich and poor and between persons of different breed and class ; in the second place, we enjoy complete freedom to devise plans for the amelioration of our people. We have no reason to suppose that our deliberations will be abruptly closed if we propose schemes of education other than those approved by the Government . . . we know that under the protection of British rule we shall be allowed to work out to the end any plans for social or economic salvation which we may devise. . . . These are privileges which our co-religionists in Turkey and Persia, who are not British subjects, do not possess. . . . How have the Indian Muslims taken advantage of the opportunities which Providence has placed in their way ?

" We must all acknowledge with shame and regret that so far we have failed. . . . There are a certain number of old-fashioned schools which continue to give, parrot-like, the teachings of the Koran, but even in these places no attempt is made to improve the morals of the boys, or to bring before them the eternal truths of the Faith. . . . The most moral and the most genuine of Muslims often tell you that as long as they expend their energies in prayer and in pilgrimage, they are certain that, though they do not do the best, yet they do no harm.

" It is to this class that I appeal. I desire most earnestly to impress upon them my conviction that if they continue in their present attitude of aloofness, it means the certain extinction of Islam, at least as a world-wide religion."

The Aga Khan not only attacked the men directly for their sloth, but he had the courage to attack them in a more vulnerable spot. The force and vigour which he applied to the problems of education he also brought into play for the improvement of the lot of Muslim women.

"A cause of our present apathy," he said with intense conviction, " is the terrible position of Muslim women, due to the Zenana and Purdah systems. There is absolutely nothing in the Koran or in Islam, or the example of the first two Muslim centuries, to justify this terrible and cancerous growth that has for nearly a thousand years eaten into the vitals of Islamic society. . . . The heathen Arabs in the days of ignorance, especially the wealthy young aristocrats of Mecca, led an extremely dissolute life, and the scandals of Mecca before the conquest were vile and degrading.

"The Prophet, not only by the strictness of his laws put an end to this open and shameless glorification of vice, but by a few wise restrictions made the former constant and unceremonious companionship of men and strange women impossible. . . . From these necessary and wholesome rules has developed the present system of purdah, which means the permanent imprisonment and enslavement of half the nation. . . . This terrible cancer must either be cut out, or the body of Muslim society will be poisoned to death by the permanent waste of all the women of the nation. Purdah, as it is now known, did not exist till long after the Prophet's death, and is no part of Islam."

His Highness suffers no illusions as to the sex, but he has always insisted that no fair or reasonably-minded person who has read the Koran can doubt for one moment that freedom of will and individual responsibility is there insisted upon.

Laughingly, the Aga Khan will declare that women will sometimes do the exact opposite of what is expected of them. On one occasion he observed to me, apropos of this delicate subject: "You can never tell what a woman will do, but that is in unessentials. There is no reason why purdah should continue to obtain; there is no reason why there should be a continuance of that fatal fatalism in Muslim thought which discourages effort, and which has been one of the principal causes of the non-progressive spirit of modern interpretation of Islam."

Other great Oriental leaders have subsequently discovered the force behind the Aga Khan's insistent teachings. In Turkey and Egypt the veil is going, because of the realization that purdah restricts the intellectual development of women.

"I say," said the Aga Khan, "that this cause has brought the modern Muslim society down to its present low level of intellect and character. How low we have fallen one can easily find out by comparing Muslim general intelligence with even the most backward of Slav-European States." His Highness said that a quarter of a century ago. That appreciation of Muslim society, then so lamentably true, would not be applicable to-day, and the Aga Khan has been greatly responsible for the upward movement.

So low was the then state of Muslim thought that the Aga Khan was even constrained to declare that anything like popular self-government would be unsuited to the conditions of India. At that time this criticism was also true, but His Highness has considerably modified his views since then, and he took a keen personal part in the last series of Round Table Conferences on the constitution of India which were held in London in St. James's Palace.

A lesser man, or one who had not come to a correct appraisal of values, could not have achieved so much, for the Aga Khan, when he set out to rouse the Muslims of India, was treading on dangerous ground. His appeal was issued not only to the Shiahs, but to the entire Muslim community, and the Aga Khan was dealing with very inflammable material.

He was out to rouse, but when the movement was initiated it had to be kept in check. He succeeded where others failed. Here, in order to emphasize this great achievement, it is necessary to make one of those odious comparisons. All will remember the spectacular European tour of ex-King Amanullah, and of his consort, Queen Souryia. King Amanullah took stock of Europe much as did the Aga Khan in his early travels, and he returned to Kabul imbued with the same fiery zeal which had entered into His Highness.

When Amanullah looked upon the Muslims of Afghanistan through eyes opened by European travel, he found them in much the same state that the Muslims of India were in when the Aga Khan made his great decision to infuse life and movement into his countrymen. He said that there must be schools, and that there must be advancement, and he was impatient to see the results.

Above all, he desired to be king of an entirely Westernized people. He made a fatal and theatrical error when he attempted to anticipate the reactions to his progressiveness.

The Aga Khan, when he first unfurled the banner of advancement, told his hearers that popular self-government was an ideal that was many generations away. Amanullah gave his orders for new ideas and for the general unveiling of women, and expected his people immediately to respond and to assimilate the new teaching in a night. The revered tribal leaders must be fashionable, and ape those of the West. He bade them forsake their picturesque national garments and attire themselves in unbecoming morning coats and top hats bought wholesale from the merchants of Europe.

The unfortunate men, forbidden to walk the streets of the capital unless so strangely accoutred, and not daring to promenade without because of the ridicule which would be heaped on their heads by the hillmen, were wont miserably to change their garb under the shadow of the walls of Kabul.

No more poignant hurt can be administered to an Afghan than through his dignity. He may be poor; he may even be hungry; but his dignity is always a precious possession from which he will not lightly be parted. He lost the goodwill of the chiefs as he had already lost that of the mullahs. Because Amanullah was precipitate, and because he had failed to weigh all considerations, he lost his throne. The mullahs whispered that their ruler had been accursed by the infidel, and that these strange orders were the manifestations of the Evil One.

When, in order to finance his schemes, some of Amanullah's much-favoured officers collected advance land taxes, the people were more than ready to believe the mullahs, and this attempt at progress brought, not advancement but a cruel civil war, and an even more unpalatable " peace," when for nine months a water-carrier's son held the Arg Palace of Kabul, and terrorized the country.

His Highness the Aga Khan, although outspoken in his addresses, had to tread warily, and although he encountered considerable opposition from the older generation, he won over the younger men little by little. His Highness, of course, was able to speak with unique authority. When he criticized so severely modern interpretations of the Koran, he spoke not only as a descendant of the Prophet, but as one who had given deep and serious study to his subject.

Under the tutelage of his father he received a thorough grounding in Muslim and Persian history, but it was his mother, the Lady Ali Shah, who realized that a mere knowledge of Oriental literature would be insufficient to equip her son for the great work to which he would eventually be called. At her instigation he was placed in the hands of an English tutor, and thus, hand in hand, as it were, with his religious training, which proceeded daily until he reached his majority, he was introduced to a wider sphere of learning which widened his outlook. When, therefore, he declared that the traditional forms of piety in the Muslim world were not in accordance with the example set by the Prophet, the young men, at least, gave him heed. With that His Highness was content. Twenty-five years have passed since then, and these young men are now not so young, and the young men that have followed have naturally adopted the new philosophy.

One incidence of the economic advance of Muslims has been a substantial increase in the funds which pour into the Shiah treasury, and a proportionate increase in the responsibilities of the Aga Khan. It is only occasionally that the veil is lifted on this aspect of the Aga Khan's labours, and it is usually in times of great calamity that these funds are dispersed.

The subscribers to the great co-operative society of which His Highness is the principal, literally number millions, and they are to be found not only in India, but in Zanzibar, along the coast of Eastern

Arabia, in the Persian Gulf, and, indeed, throughout the entire East. Each individual makes periodical contributions according to his estate to the Aga Khan and to Muslim finances in general. The money flows into Bombay in one never-ending stream—cheques, much befingered bills upon ruche merchants of little-known bazaars, gold coins of many realms, mohars, rupees, nickels, and even the modest copper pies the size of a farthing, and worth in reality but a third as much.

In each district there is a properly appointed official known as a Mukhi, and it is he who receives the contributions from the Faithful and transmits them to the central treasury in Bombay. Here the accounts are maintained by the Mukhi-in-chief, and this official is directly responsible to the Aga Khan. Only His Highness and the chief Mukhi know the extent of finances, but the treasury must now hold many millions of pounds, the majority of it in coin and bullion. In this centre in Bombay there is probably more wealth than there is in the Bank of England at any one time, yet it goes practically unguarded. Guards are, in fact, unnecessary. No Eastern would dream of touching a halfpenny of this enormous wealth.

There are, of course, considerable outgoings at all times. Amongst many rules which the Aga Khan has laid down there is one that is golden, and that is that no member of the Faith should go hungry. Not only does the district Mukhi receive contributions, but he also distributes money to those in need. There is no question of a loan about any of these transactions—usury of any kind being as anathema to the Muslim soul. These are free gifts for which there is no future accounting.

Also, through the Mukhis disbursements are made for educational, religious and other purposes, and it is through the Chief Mukhi and through him and the district Mukhis that His Highness maintains touch with his people. A very strong check is kept on these officials, for every Ismailian knows that he has direct access to the Aga Khan. Should any member of the Faith declare that he wishes to see the Aga Khan in person, the Mukhi cannot refuse to put the application forward. When such an application is made, and the Aga Khan considers that the circumstances warrant a personal interview, the Mukhi has to accompany the applicant. Thus is His Highness assured of hearing both sides of a story.

The Aga Khan has a specific object in keeping so much ready money available. The experiences of his youth taught him the value of money, and he resolved then that the finances should be placed upon the soundest of sound footings. In the past, Muslims have suffered from lack of ready capital whenever great sums have been required to keep abreast of modern developments, and in other ways also.

The Aga Khan was only twenty when he was called upon to exercise his latent administrative ability, and to call heavily on the funds stored in Bombay, and he resolved then, that as far as he was able, he would always see that there was a sufficient reserve to meet any contingency. The deadly scourge of cholera laid its blighting hand on great tracts of India, and the scourge was followed by a great famine. The wells and the rivers dried up, the crops wilted, the cattle died for want of pasture and water, and a purely agricultural community was bereft of all means of livelihood. Hungry in thousands of cases, and completely penniless in hundreds of thousands more, these unfortunates had scant hopes of ever restoring their lost fortunes, even if they could tide themselves over to the next, and very improbable, harvest, for in many instances the people had even been forced to eat their seed grain.

Only the Aga Khan is aware of the magnitude of the sums then distributed to assist these starving thousands in their travail. He had immense camps erected, where all who were hungry were supplied from food kitchens; dispensaries and hospitals were set up, and corps of helpers enlisted to collect the afflicted in the stricken areas, and to place them in isolation camps. Later, in innumerable instances, money was provided for the purchase of seed grain, agricultural implements and cattle.

Since that day the immense barrage schemes which have been introduced into India have turned millions of acres of fallow desert into smiling cornlands, and the bogy of famine is no more, but the Aga Khan has had reason for satisfaction in his early resolve to build up funds in harrowing circumstances much more modern. Soon after the Great War calls were made upon the treasury for vast amounts, and the reason lay in the delays in signing the peace treaty with Turkey and in the fulminations of Mr. Lloyd George against the Crescent.

THE AGA KHAN

The wildest rumours flashed through Hindustan, and the British Premier was accredited with the intention of humbling Islam to the dust. The Aga Khan toured the country and did his utmost to dissipate the worst effects of Mr. Lloyd George's speeches in respect to the Caliphate, but rumours of the character then flying the country travel faster than humans, even in these days of greatly accelerated speed.

Throughout the centuries migration from the land of the oppressors has obsessed the Oriental mind. The Jews did it long ago when the Red Sea was cloven to facilitate their progress, and as a pacific counter to oppression, or fancied oppression, the ultimate resort to migration has remained as an idea fixed ever since.

Reference has already been made to the part which Mr. Gandhi played in this mass movement of the Faithful toward the asylum of Afghanistan and beyond, and to the fact that many thousands of ill-informed Muslims thronged the roads leading northwards with the sole idea of removing their persons from the shadow of the Union Jack. Literally hundreds of thousands of humans, of all ages, found themselves upon an alien roadside, and with no haven of refuge. Many hundreds of miles behind them were homesteads which had been sold to eager buyers for the proverbial song.

Suffering and privation on a gigantic scale loomed grimly. Indeed, it was already there, and to this day the number of deaths has never been satisfactorily computed. The Aga Khan, who had retained a firm grip of his adherents throughout the early stages of the Non-Co-operation Movement, and, indeed, eventually killed the movement as an effective force by inducing his followers to accept and work the reforms, called the Muslim leaders together, and made personal tours among those who would follow the emigrants, and to a very material extent succeeded in localizing the drift away from India.

He made urgent representations to a sympathetic Indian Government, which resulted in many returned emigrants being resettled on the land they had so foolishly sold, and his purse was opened, and remained open, until it had been drained of tremendous sums.

None of the money earmarked for the cause is expended by His Highness on personal matters. He has a very large fortune of his own, which has been considerably augmented in his lifetime. Few who see him on the racecourse, or in the Legations and Embassies of Europe, realize that he is an astute business man, and one who insists upon being sure of the potentialities of a project before loosening the strings of his privy purse. There has grown up in some circles a belief—based on the great sums at the disposal of His Highness, and on his ready disbursements—that it is only necessary to approach and interest the Aga Khan for a scheme to be assured of financial backing.

Those in the ranks of the disappointed are legion, for this belief is widely held, and not a day passes without His Highness being invited to invest in something. For his own protection he had to erect a barrier between himself and the importunists, and for many years the Aga Khan has had at his disposal a small corps of experts who rigidly scrutinize every project which is presented for his attention and the *bona fides* of those who proffer them. Notwithstanding the singularly large proportion of promoters who have failed to satisfy the Aga Khan's experts as to their own personal qualifications, His Highness retains a high appreciation of the probity of the West and of its commercial standards.

In thirty years' effort, the Aga Khan had so galvanized the Muslims of India that he was able, in its entirety, to withdraw his strictures on the ability of India to absorb the principles of popular self-government, and he came out very strongly in the purely political aspect of the community's aspirations during the dangerous days of 1930 and after.

When the British Government decided to dispatch to India a statutory commission to inquire into the working of the reforms, Sir John Simon and his confreres were met by Non-Co-operation *in excelsis*. His first view of the Appolo Bundar was of a sea of black flags which bore the unwelcome and uncomplimentary slogan of the moment. This was terse and to the point, and it was: " Simon, go back ! "

This situation was fraught with considerable danger, and objectionable and unsavoury incidents became an everyday occurrence. Mr. Gandhi cried, " Boycott," and his followers obeyed him, and there were sanguinary clashes between those who would receive the Commission at its face value, and those who would relegate it to Whitehall minus the evidence it had come to collect. The prison populations grew and grew until the prisons could hold no more, and the accommodation of the hospital casualty wards was strained to the utmost.

The Aga Khan had maintained a firm grip of the Muslims in the equally dangerous days of 1919. Fearful lest his compatriots should become embroiled in the general turmoil, he once again made a spectacular incursion into the politics of the day, enjoining Muslims and all of sane and moderate opinion, to eschew the evils of Non-Co-operation, and to adopt precisely the same tactics as had proved so successful for the Muslim community in 1919. The Aga Khan threw his weight on the side of moderation, and largely through his efforts the Simon Commission was enabled to present a report to Parliament. Without the intervention of His Highness, the Statutory Commission would have returned empty-handed, and its inquiry would have been rendered negative and abortive by a solid wall of Non-Co-operation.

The 1919 reforms created a furore. The publication of the Simon Commission's Report caused another. It indicated a constitutional advance which fell short of what was demanded by the Swarajists, which was, of course, unadulterated Home Rule.

Mr. Ramsay MacDonald called a Round Table Conference in London. The Swarajists met the suggestion with peals of ribald and derisive laughter, and Mr. Gandhi again uttered the fateful word "Boycott." There would have been a complete boycott if the Aga Khan had not decreed otherwise. He saw that it had adequate representation on the Muslim, and the Swarajists, still in India, could only watch the proceedings from afar with jealous and apprehensive eyes.

The fear was expressed that the Muslim minority would secure political ends which would be detrimental to the Hindu majority. Outside of Islam, the Aga Khan was easily one of the most unpopular figures in India at this juncture, and when the delegation returned from the Round Table Conference its reception could not have been more frigid or hostile.

The banners of Non-Co-operation were raised even higher, and the most strenuous efforts were made to woo Muslims from their allegiance. They were invited to take part in "hartals" (the closing of shops), and there was much intimidation where persuasion failed in its object. There was a little crumbling at the edges, but in the main the Muslims of India maintained a united *bloc* which, when combined with the astuteness of Lord Halifax (then Lord Irwin), who fought Gandhi with his own weapons, resulted after a long period of turmoil, with the jails again full to overflowing, in the much-criticized Irwin-Gandhi pact.

This pact enabled Mr. Gandhi to save his face and to take part in the second Round Table Conference in person, with results already well known.

This conference broke down on the communal issue, yet almost were the dissentients brought together in accord. The Aga Khan laboured day and night for the settlement of communal discord, and it seemed that he would be successful. The desire of the Muslim community, he impressed upon all, was that Hindu, Muslim, Sikh and Christian should live together in perfect amity. There were certain elements which proved recalcitrant, and Mr. Gandhi was manacled by the exhortations of the Congress for whose being he was so largely responsible, and the delegates had to return.

India is still battling with the complex machinery which makes for federation. By the majority it is assumed that the principal enunciated in the report of the Simon Commission was a new and startling development, but actually it had been in the mind of the Aga Khan for many years, and he had worked wholeheartedly for its consummation.

As long ago as 1919, His Highness came to the conclusion that no reform scheme for India could be complete or satisfactory if it left out of account the Indian States, which cover one-third of the Indian Empire. He then declared that it was necessary to deal with the problem presented by the States before discussing the constitution of the central authority. "The States," he continued, "cannot be mere spectators of the constitutional changes now impending. To reduce the princes gradually to the mere position of great nobles, and to let the power and the individuality attaching to their States to pass out of their control would be a crime against history, art, and even nationality. On the other hand, the present standard of relations between the protecting Power and the protected States cannot go on after British India reaches the first stages towards self-government. . . . In Federalism we find a system that will meet the need both of British India and of the States. . . . No scheme of reconstruction can be complete without taking into consideration the seventy million people in these Indian States. . . . The history of the past, no less than the justice and the symmetry to be sought to-day, leads to the conclusion that we need a Federation which can be entered by the greatest provinces and the smallest Indian raj alike without loss of internal freedom, and yet with the assurance that in all Federal matters they will pull together for a united Empire."

If the Aga Khan had advanced political views a quarter of a century ago—views which have now been largely incorporated in statute—he had also very original pronouncements to make on the vexed subject of caste. He has always held that there is a strong affinity between low standards of public health and moral and material degradation. He has proved the truth of this contention among his own followers, more particularly in Zanzibar, and in other centres which at one time were notoriously unhealthy. There, with the Muslim community racked with disease, he provided facilities for recreation and sport. The young men, devoid of vitality, and misanthropic, required much rousing, but he dragooned them on to the hockey fields and into similar sporting endeavours until the dormant competitive spirit did the rest. In two decades there has been a marked improvement in the public health in these areas, and the Muslim community can no longer be described as " backward."

Similarly in India, the Aga Khan has given expression to views which have not commended themselves to the more orthodox of Hindus. In maintaining that in a country which had to contend with such diverse scourges as plague, cholera, smallpox, leprosy, malaria and a hundred other ills, it was the under-nourished who succumbed. Here he impinged on the extremely delicate question of caste, but he was undeterred from fighting the battle for the depressed, maintaining that it was vitally wrong that one-sixth of India's millions should be artificially segregated and kept apart from the main stream of national life.

Long familiarity with all-pervading poverty, he declared, led to the application of the term "submerged," not on the basis of poverty, but of membership of the "untouchable" communities. He insisted that if the task of national improvement and consolidation was to be taken in hand, there would have to be a wider meaning to the description of "depressed" than that of the mere position of a number of inferior sections in relation to the Hindu caste system. "To-day," he said, "the generalization that an outcaste cannot escape from the invidious bar of birth requires qualification. Whatever the disabilities of the depressed classes may have been when India was a purely Hindu society, for centuries past the power of strictly legal prevention of obtaining a better social position has been enforceable in restricted areas only. . . . For more than a century and a half the supreme power has been exercised by a nation which bases its code of justice on the equality of all men in the sight of the law. . . . Superstition reigns, and the material framework of society is such that it is ordinarily impossible for those who are lowest economically to improve their position. . . . There must be adopted a national policy of betterment."

Gradually, I am certain, the popular conception of the Aga Khan as a person who devotes himself to the Turf and to golf, almost to the exclusion of more mundane matters, will have been dissipated among those who read this character sketch. This belief is largely fostered by the popular press, to whom the Aga Khan is "news," and whose records of his activities are mainly confined to the spectacular and that which appeals pictorially.

In the Aga Khan the Empire has an ambassador who has slaved on its behalf. At Geneva he is an exceedingly well-known figure where his views on disarmament coincided very largely with those of the Disarmament Conference's ex-President, the late Mr. Arthur Henderson. "With Muslims," he told the Conference on one great occasion, "the ideal of peace is no mere economic expedient; it is an element deep-rooted in their very name. . . . We have had the terrible lessons of the Great War . . . but we have found that armaments still hold sway, and that the feeling of insecurity persists. To-day, social and economic conditions are such that unless the fabric of organized human society is to collapse it is imperative that vigorous steps be taken forthwith. . . . On the moral side we must set ourselves to remove the paralysing effects of fear, ill-will and suspicion. On the material side it is absolutely essential that the non-productive effort devoted to warlike preparations should be reduced to the minimum."

Wherever he has gone the Aga Khan has been the Ambassador of Peace, but this has never dulled his perceptibilities to the inevitability of war in certain circumstances. He hates war, but when the first shots have been fired, then the Aga Khan believes that the nation which makes the greatest effort must necessarily prove victorious. This was his doctrine during the Great War, when he not only offered his personal services, but when asked to conduct recruiting and other campaigns instead, did so with the utmost vigour. He was untiring in studying the welfare of Indian soldiers, and was a frequent visitor at their depots and regimental bases.

The facet of his character which His Highness displays to the multitude is not vastly different to that which is seen in the privacy of his home life. There were twenty-five thousand guests at his first wedding, for this marriage to a Muslim lady was a matter of high ceremonial. It was celebrated in Poona, soon after the Aga Khan returned from his first European travels, and the bride was the daughter of his uncle, the late Aga Jungishah. The world took a great interest in this union, for His Highness had already been critical of Muslim convention in so far as it affected the status of women, and Muslims especially were anxious to determine how their leader would put his principles into practice. At the time of his marriage, His Highness made it clear that he would expect his bride to take her place by his side, and to be more to him in his home life than are the sheltered, secluded wives of so many of the Faith.

This wedding was more than a great occasion;

it was an event in Shiah history. It was not just a social event to be marked by a day's festivities. It meant to millions of Muslims the first concrete step toward the furtherance of the line of direct descent from the Prophet. In matters such as this the Orient is perhaps a little more outspoken than the West where, but for a few lines in the marriage ceremony, the topic is practically taboo. In the East there is a natural delicacy, but also a natural directness, and the birth of a son is the signal for great family rejoicings, and for ardent and sincere congratulations. There the begetting of a son is the *raison d'être* of marriage, and it is as vital and as important to the poorest as to the richest of Muslims.

Many of those who attended the nuptial ceremonies of the Aga Khan had travelled many thousands of miles in order to do him honour. Others had travelled hundreds—by rail, road, bullock cart, horse, and even on camels. Many thousands from the near and distant countryside accomplished the journey across the mountains of the Western Ghats on foot. Such guests could not be regaled to a single ceremonial meal, however sumptuous, and then be requested silently to depart. Sleeping accommodation was provided for twenty-five thousand, and accommodation of a more temporary character for many thousands more. Great canvas camps sprang up over many miles of the beautiful Poona countryside, and the great assemblage was entertained, not for a single night, but for a whole fortnight.

The official and invited guests were outnumbered

by those of the poorer classes who had gathered from the villages hundreds of miles around. On an occasion such as this, largesse is plentiful, and there is no limit to the entertainment of any who care to present themselves. Special police in large numbers had to be requisitioned to regulate the great throngs which gathered, none of whom went empty away. Apart from the large sums of money distributed personally by the Aga Khan in Poona, His Highness directed that special grants should be made to all Ismailian communities suitably to mark the occasion of his marriage.

It was a great grief to the Aga Khan when his first wife died, for she had loyally taken the place beside him which he had indicated, and had become a pioneer in demonstrating the new status of Muslim women. Nor was the loss of his second wife—an Italian princess—felt less by all. For many years the Aga Khan remained a widower, and it was not until quite recently that he contracted a third marriage with the beautiful and accomplished Mlle. Andree Carron. In remarkable contrast, there were no thousands at this ceremony—just a handful of near relatives and intimate friends.

In his home life, and whenever he can afford the leisure—for he regards physical fitness as pre-eminent, and much time in these days is taken up with golf—the Aga Khan is a voracious reader. Here he is somewhat of a savant, and there is little of Oriental, and especially Persian, poetry which he has not perused and studied. His reading, however, has necessarily to be diverse, for his interests are many and varied. Quite apart from the religious and political problems which continually exercise his mind, he believes in keeping abreast of modern trends in the many commercial concerns from which so much of his private income is derived. Trade journals concerning newspapers, coffee-planting, tea-planting, coconut-planting, and a host of others receive his attention, for here is indicated but a tithe of his varied interests.

The Aga Khan has never forgotten a remark made to him by his English tutor at a time when he was ploughing his way through such representative examples of English literature as "The Queen's Prime Ministers" and "The Lives of Eminent Men." The tutor said, "read Gladstone," and His Highness is one of the few who have found the answer to an oft-repeated query. He found that Gladstone said that recreation was nothing but a change from one fruitful reading to another. If this is so, the Aga Khan spends much time on recreation. Sometimes the Begum Aga Khan speaks somewhat critically of the many hours spent in reading. Then the Aga Khan, with that slow smile of his, promptly quotes Gladstone.

The Aga Khan is exceedingly fond of quotations, and he has a great store of them into which he readily dips. They come from a bewildering variety of sources—from the old Persian poets, from the German, from the Greek classics, and—from Gladstone. Sometimes they come with such astonishing rapidity that they leave one rather breathless, but they constitute a very strong conversational armoury. The Aga Khan has found that an apt quotation and a smile can perform wonders in a conversational gambit that shows signs of becoming an embroglio. Also they are an adequate foil to the many who have designs on his bank balance, the majority of whom leave the Aga Khan somewhat bewildered, and still working out the implication of quotations which are entirely new to them, yet still with the impression that they have had a delightful conversation with an urbane and cultivated business man. It is only on mature cogitation, and laborious rumination, that it is discovered that the door has been firmly, but politely, indicated.

The stream of seekers of capital is steady and constant. Nothing can damp the optimism of those who build immensely profitable fabrics upon paper, but the majority approach His Highness having made one fundamental error in their calculations. They see in the Aga Khan a great figure of the Turf, and they jump to the erroneous conclusion that he is a gambler. He is not, and never has been, and is unlikely to become one. This man, frequently seen in Continental casinos, and very frequently upon the racecourse, has never turned a card for money or had a transaction with a bookmaker. He occasionally visits a casino because he is drawn there by the kaleidoscopic maelstrom which humanity there provides. He goes to the racecourse to race. In the one he has never held a bank, and prefers only to watch, and on the other he is there to see in magnificent action the horses upon which he has expended so much selective and individual care. His Highness has never allowed himself the pleasure of a bet. He is perfectly satisfied with the spectacle of perfectly trained, superb horseflesh, cheerfully and willingly responding to the behests of man.

There never has been another large owner so completely of the racecourse, and yet so completely detached. The owner of Blenheim which won the Derby for him in 1930, and of such famous thoroughbreds as Diophon, Salmon Trout, Ut Majeur and that great public favourite, Mumtaz Mahal, not to take into account those which have provided him with more recent and highly spectacular successes, would willingly pass on information to his friends, but never sought to make money in a mere betting transaction. He makes his stables pay without the assistance of the bookmaker, and this is largely because he is able to buy the best. He has a fine appreciation of the best points of a horse inherited from a long line of animal-lovers. Also, he has his own views upon training. Every animal requires individual treatment, and he insists that it is accorded. It has to be admitted that his methods, if somewhat his own when compared with the accepted English standard, have been uniformly successful.

Even here we have an example of that earnestness of purpose which is the Aga Khan's, and which has stood the Near Eastern world in such very good stead over what has probably been the most chaotic period this vexed world has ever known.

With the Aga Khan, it is impossible not to look back over the centuries. One senses the power and influence which his forbears have wielded—the meteoric rise and falls of their fortunes, the romances which have attached to their names. The assassin with his knife, the machinations of court dignitaries, and the displeasure of Kings failed to break the line of succession, though there were numerous occasions when this was perilously near accomplishment. The chances of battle, and the rigours of frequent and forced migration rendered the stock virile, and produced a background which has enabled successive Ismailian heads to cope with situations which called for the highest endeavour and steel-like resolve. The history of the line is redolent of astonishing incident, and that of our own time has been little less remarkable. It has seen many astounding changes in the world of Islam, just as there have been vast upheavals in the world without.

The present Aga Khan has weathered a tempest of long duration, and he, as head of his sect, finds himself more firmly in the saddle while others have been ejected and cast into the night.

In the cosmopolitan complex which the vicissitudes besetting his House engendered he found the strength and that breadth of outlook which enabled him to steer a course through events where the slightest mishandling would have precipitated a Near-Eastern conflagration of terrifying proportions. Too frequently the train was laid, and it required only a spark to set millions on the road to religious war, yet always was the Aga Khan there fighting for the cause of moderation and sanity. The West is largely unappreciative of the achievements of this man in the cause of peace, principally because it does not know, and the Aga Khan is no publicist.

NADIR SHAH

NADIR SHAH

HIS Majesty, King Nadir Shah of Afghanistan, ruled for a comparatively short period before he was struck down by the assassin, but he reigned sufficiently long to leave his mark, and to earn for himself an important niche among the pre-eminent Orientals of our time. He was called to rule over a bankrupt country which had been outraged and scourged by one of the most remorseless tyrants this world has ever known, to keep for Islam a people who had Red Russia on their doorstep, and to resurrect from the grim ashes of civil war a national prestige which was in danger of being lost in a reversal to the elementary and the feudal. A spare, wiry man, almost an ascetic in his veneration of the simple, he was quite unlike the accepted conception of an Afghan. He had culture, he had learning, and he had military genius. Above all, he had the will to conquer adversity, and that terrific stamina which is necessary when a national fabric has to be rebuilt upon sources so remarkably slender as to be practically non-existent. He was to know the adversity of exile—he was, indeed, born in exile—and to know hunger and ill-health. He was an exceedingly sick man when the call came to rid his country of a Satanic incubus. He fought a fierce and bitter campaign as a sick man, and he ruled as a sick man, yet he was sustained throughout by the love of Fatherland which is inherent in every Afghan. When as a child in Dehra Dun he declared that his destiny lay beyond the Khyber Pass. When lying upon a sick bed in a European sanatorium, Destiny called, and he responded, and to-day Afghanistan is once more a nation, and not a tribal conglomeration. He restored the stamp of Amir Abdur Rahman Khan, who died in 1901 and who brought about the subjugation of refractory elements and gave to Afghanistan a political entity.

From the reign of the Amir Dost Mohamed Khan in 1826, and until the arrival upon the scene of Abdur Rahman, the country had been wracked by dissension, and though Abdur Rahman was in the saddle for an appreciable period, Afghan memories are long. It required several more decades of settled rule indelibly to stamp upon the tribesmen the mould of nationalism and unity. The mould was smashed by a ruler who displayed qualities of too rapid absorption. Amanullah went to Europe, and came back fired with the urge for "progress." The pace he set was too fast, and he lost his head and his throne, and Afghanistan reverted to anarchy. Only just in time did Nadir Shah impress his personality upon the scene of utter desolation which resulted. But for his timely intervention the Afghan national ideal might have been dissipated for all time.

During the disquiet which obtained prior to the accession of the Amir Abdur Rahman many Afghan nobles had been exiled from their country, and

HIS LATE MAJESTY MOHAMED NADIR SHAH GHAZI
King of Afghanistan

among them was Sirdar Yahya Khan, the grandfather of Nadir Shah. With the son of the Amir Shair Ali Khan, whose brother-in-law he was, Nadir Shah's grandfather settled in Dehra Dun, in British India. It was in this delightfully picturesque centre —now the home of the Indian Sandhurst—that Nadir was born and had his early being. His family had money and, even though exiles, were welcome guests in the homes of the Dehra Dun military officers; yet this colony of Afghans, notwithstanding its many years of intercourse with an alien people, never lost its national perspective. The setting of Dehra Dun is sylvan; it is a small paradise of colour, delightful streams and romantic gardens; yet this small colony of exiles pined for the crags and the barren rocks of their native hills. They had but one criticism of Dehra Dun, but it was destructive. " The air of India is too soft for Afghans," they said. With that there was little more that could be said.

Nadir was eighteen years of age when the Amir Abdur Rahman died, and his successor, Amir Habibullah Khan, addressed a request to his family to return to the home of their ancestors. By that time he had run the gamut of youthful expression, and his ambitions were concrete and set. He had resolved upon a military career even when this was unlikely of attainment and, with the enthusiasm of youth, he had set out wholeheartedly to qualify himself for the rôle.

His military zeal had been fired in the first instance by one of those tiny, almost insignificant, gestures of Fate, and it was upon a chance and a vagary that

I

Nadir Shah was to build a military reputation which was to become formidable.

A route-marching British column halted at Dehra Dun, and there was the inevitable gymkhana. The Afghan colony, as was natural, took the utmost interest in the rifle-shooting competitions, and, observing this, the British Colonel, whose guest Nadir Shah and his family were, handed a rifle to Nadir's father. The latter, in turn, handed it to his sons who were grouped around him. It chanced that Nadir was nearest, and he it was who shot, and incidentally carried off the trophy, though he had never fired at a target before. Thereafter he changed. He banished from his quarters everything that pertained to civilian luxury. The soft divans disappeared, and silks and rich carpets were removed. Military maps appeared on the walls, and treatises on military law and strategy filled the youthful Nadir's bookshelves. This proved to be more than a caprice of boyhood, and the enthusiasm then fired did not wane as do so- many conceived in adolescence, and so it was that when the family returned to take its rightful place in the Kabul court, Nadir was given a commission in the army, and attached to the Royal Bodyguard with the rank of captain.

This young soldier, who was later to meet and excel the troops of Great Britain in honourable combat, had little regard for the soft luxuries of court life. Although one of the Royal household—his sister Ulya Jinab became the Queen of Afghanistan—his life was spent upon the parade ground and in military study. It is said that his Queenly sister, chancing to visit his quarters, recoiled in horror at the stark, Spartan simplicity which she discovered. As sisters will, she felt his bed, and discovered that the Queen's brother slept on two hard planks with two ordinary blankets for covering. He hammered the same iron discipline into the soldiery, and within two years of receiving his original commission was gazetted a colonel. He held his men because it was patent to them that although an officer and a prince, he practised what he so sedulously preached. If his demands of his men necessitated hardship, it naturally followed that these hardships would be shared by the commander. He asked none to do what he would not do. And, if he shared his men's hardships, he also shared their companionship. He drank tea with them as a matter of course, and was deaf to those courtiers who would remind him of his rank and suggest that there was a distinct line of demarcation between the private soldier and a princely commander of the Royal Bodyguard.

The Amir showed too much preference for the company of Nadir, and showered too many unsought honours upon him for the young colonel to be entirely popular. He had the ear of the King, and this provoked more than ordinary jealousy in many influential quarters and, years later, it was to be this ill-feeling which was to encompass his death. One of those who took a violent dislike to the young favourite was General Ghulam Haider Khan Charkhi, from whose stock sprang one Ghulam Nabi, who was to die a traitor's death for invading his country. It was the slave boy of Ghulam Nabi who was to be the instrument of the assassination of a noble ruler.

The tragedy of this jealousy, so easily invoked in a country where blood runs hot and wild, was that it was so unnecessary, for the higher Nadir rode in military attainments and military rank the more humble seemed to grow his nature. "If only you said your prayers half as many times as you salute me," he once observed to a sentry, "you would have been a saint ten years ago." The Afghans could understand a mentality which so closely approximated to their own, even though courtiers misunderstood. Nadir swept aside the ancient shibboleth that it demeans one of rank to walk when he may ride, or to work when he is able to command others. He both marched with his men, worked, and saw that they worked. On the very day when he was promoted to the rank of general—he was then twenty-seven years of age—he found fault with a trooper in the cavalry lines, and an amazed general staff stood by while their commander, in the light of a lantern held by the inefficient *sawar*, gave the man a practical lesson in grooming.

At the age of thirty (in 1913) General Nadir was called upon to demonstrate the martial gifts which so many had no hesitation in saying only existed on paper and in book learning. Habibullah Khan's throne was toppling, and the whole of the south was in revolt. The loyal garrisons had been surrounded, and a general march on Kabul was imminent. The harassed monarch called a secret durbar at which the calamitous event was discussed, and among the greybeards there was an openly expressed diffidence to entrusting the army to a youthful officer such as Nadir. Others, even more outspoken than the rest, did not hesitate to give vent to diatribes against one who had basked in the royal favour for so long. The Amir listened, but when he asked, " Then who shall lead ? " there was an embarrassed silence. The Kabuli detachments trusted their general, and none other, and the situation was a delicate one. The place-seekers at court, wishing to play for safety in the event of the rebellious tribesmen winning the day, prevailed upon the Amir to despatch only a relatively small detachment against the rebels, and with this Nadir had to be content. He placed his hardly-learned strategy to the test of battle, and in one short, sharp engagement was so manifestly the victor that the south capitulated, and a civil war was brought to nought with the loss of a surprisingly few number of lives. Nadir did not immediately return to Kabul. He remained to discover what had evoked the revolt, and when he went back to Kabul to receive a Field-Marshal's baton, he informed the Amir of circumstances of which Habibullah had no conception. For years the tribal chiefs of the south had attempted to penetrate the cordon of place-seekers with petitions to the Amir, and had been rebuffed. Believing themselves oppressed, they resorted to arms. Speedily wrongs were righted, and there was no more loyal element than that in the south, but this did not advance Nadir in the good graces of the courtiers. He was now regarded as a dangerous man and as one who refused to enter into the intrigue and counter-intrigue of the court, one who must be ousted at all costs.

His position was not rendered any the more comfortable by the unyielding confidence which the Amir continued to display in his youthful marshal, and in the preference he sometimes displayed even before his own sons. There was one notable occasion which occasioned much speculation and considerable murmuring through Afghanistan, and that the celebrations in connection with the ruler's birthday. The heir to the throne, Sirday Ināyatullah Khan, later to be king in name for a few sorry hectic hours, bowed the knee in homage, and retired. When Nadir placed his sword upon his knee, thus signifying the loyalty and allegiance of the army, Amir Habibullah Khan, normally punctilious in etiquette and form when in open durbar, broke amazingly through precedent, and murmured : " Arise, my gallant son, for thou art the pride of thy country."

When the full history of the present century in the East comes to be written, if ever it is, the spare figure of Nadir should emerge if only because of his essential simplicity and his steadfast refusal to be dazzled by the glamour of office or position. He was a patriot in the truest sense, and one who bowed, in all humiliation, to many storms. Yet Destiny was to decree that he should weather the storm, and Fate to declare that he should die at the hands of those for whom he had given a life's work. Nadir was thrown to the forefront in the convulsive storm which rocked the East with the coming of the World War—for it was indeed a world war, though there were some nations whose names were not inscribed on the roll of actual combatants.

It is said that in thought, at least, the exile lives more in his country than does he who remains in situ. So, and perhaps because his boyhood was spent in a foreign clime when all conversation turned on the Fatherland, Nadir was more austerely Afghan than many who thronged the Afghan court. Intrigue angered him, and the mere thought of the secret midnight meeting appalled him and filled him with indignation. Progressively with his military advancement lashed the tide of his unpopularity in the court circle, and when he was promoted Commander-in-Chief, there were those to whisper to the Amir the suggestion that perhaps it was not safe to entrust the one bulwark of the throne to a youthful zealot who had shown, by his acts and by his treatment of the rebellious tribesmen of the south, that his thoughts were not so much with the regime as with the people.

The Amir Habibullah Khan remained deaf to all such insinuations, and readily agreed, just prior to the outbreak of the World War, to the many reforms which Nadir was anxious to introduce in the army. For the first time Afghan officers were presented with authenticated maps of the terrain over which they might be called upon to fight, and the pay of the soldiers was brought up to an economic level.

In an atmosphere pulsating with personal and social interests, Nadir held to his ideal, and each intrigue which had his downfall as its motive, he was only to scale the heights yet further. Throughout the period of the Great War, his influence was on the side of peace. Although a professional soldier, temperamentally he instinctively turned to peace. It was not that he preferred ease to conflict, but he placed a higher value upon human life than did many of his type and his time.

At a time when distrust or suspicion of the motives of Afghanistan would have held thousands of sorely needed troops at the mouths of the frontier passes, the good sense of Nadir, more than anything else, made for that attitude of neighbourliness so strikingly demonstrated by Afghanistan during the critical days of the war, though there were many at the court to whisper into the ears of Habibullah Khan the famous words of the Amir Shair Ali Khan, who once observed: " Friendship with the Ferunghi is written on ice. It melts when the sun shines on it."

Many said that Habibullah Khan and his Commander-in-Chief were inclining too far towards the Ferunghi, and should approach, with a greater display of that spirit which was Afghan, the question of British recognition of Afghanistan's complete independence. Nadir Shah, however, realized the British Empire's pre-occupation in war, and knowing the tortuous ways of diplomacy, was prepared to display patience. At a moment when the negotiations on this subject had all but culminated in complete success, the steadily rising wall of intrigue broke from its foundations. There was a wild scurry for safety, and in that moment another Afghan monarch had been assassinated by those who feared that too much would come to light when the debris was inspected. The Amir Habibullah Khan was done to death while in camp at Lughman in February, 1919, and the scenes that followed were but a typical reversion to dark practice of centuries ago.

Sirdar Nasrullah Khan, the younger brother of the dead Amir, proclaimed himself the ruler, it being given out that the heir, Sirdar Inayatullah Khan, had waived his claims before those of his uncle.

The Amir's third son, Amanullah Khan, was then Governor of Kabul—a key position—and it had been arranged that the second son, Hidayatullah Khan, should exchange duties with him and take over the Kabul Governorship. Unaccountably, however, the car conveying the second son to Kabul broke down by the wayside, and he who was the rightful heir if the first son adhered to his reported decision to abdicate, was mysteriously marooned in a district where communications were practically non-existent.

The world knows that Amanullah leaped into the saddle from which he was eventually to fall with such dramatic suddenness. As Governor of Kabul he paraded the garrison, and with tears in his eyes referred to the untimely death of his beloved father. "Before even the murderer of my father has been found and tried," he cried, "my uncle had proclaimed himself king. Is this right? Is it true to the Afghan tradition?" and with one voice the garrison of Kabul thundered, "No."

Eight days after the assassination of his father, Amanullah had crowned himself king, and securely to cement his position, he gave orders for the immediate arrest of his uncle, his eldest brother, and the Commander-in-Chief, Nadir Shah. They were taken to Kabul and imprisoned. The uncle who would be king died while in confinement, and a colonel, said to be implicated in intrigue, was taken out and shot. A trial ensued, after which it was deemed expedient to release both Nadir Shah and Inayatullah Khan, but it meant that Afghanistan's future king was without a command, and without a hearing at court. Amanullah could afford to reshuffle his court as he pleased, because he had been present in Kabul when his father was done to death, and the State treasury was intact and in his hands. That in a country where money is not raised with the readiness discernible in states more economically advanced, meant power and security. He immediately increased the pay of his army, and although justifiably creating a din due to his father's assassination, yet he was not accepted as King, till he proclaimed the demand of unqualified Afghan independence, for which the people had fretted for more than a generation; thenceforward he became a national hero.

Having commenced as Ajax, he had to maintain the rôle, and he addressed a letter to the British Government which was tantamount to a demand for an acknowledgment of independence, and for non-interference in Afghan foreign affairs. There was delay in Simla, and no immediate answer to the letter was forthcoming. Afghanistan watched to see what this ruler of a few weeks would do. In order further to maintain the rôle which he had appropriated, he mobilized his troops. There then came a hanging back, and for a month the Afghan court was in a state of turmoil and conflict. There were those who did not hesitate to tell Amanullah that he was acting precipitately, and the new king blew hot and cold. One day it was to be war, and the next diplomacy, but Fate settled the matter for him, and hurled him into the third Afghan war. An Afghan tribal chieftain killed a number of British coolies working near the frontier, and he alleged that he had been acting under instructions. Thus was manufactured the *casus belli*.

Amanullah's eye did not light up with righteous frenzy when he harangued his people into war, for he was an orator rather than a fighter, as later events were abundantly to prove. The war party about him, however, convinced him that never at any other time would he have an opportunity so golden. Not only were the troops of India war weary and indisposed to subject themselves to the rigours of further service (there was a widespread demand for prolonged leave and disbandment as there was in England), but India itself was ablaze with revolution.

Here again we have the pious platitudes of the saintly Gandhi making for bloodshed and the horrors of conflict, for it was upon his propaganda that were built the violent outbreaks in the Punjab and elsewhere in April, 1919, which finally decided Amanullah that Hindustan was under the bane of revolution, and that the revolutionaries would espouse his cause.

Quickly the war developed on three fronts, namely the Khyber, Kandahar and Khost. Barely a month before Nadir Shah had been hailed to Kabul in disgrace and as a prisoner. In his extremity Amanullah now turned to the erstwhile commander-in-chief and begged his assistance. Nadir Shah was sufficiently a patriot, and an Afghan, not to refuse, even though the military dispositions which were made were entirely contrary to his views and his teachings. With but a small body of troops and an insufficiency of ammunition, Nadir Shah was accorded the Khost command, and it is noteworthy that this was the only one which reaped success. Fighting on the other fronts the war was not successfully waged for the Afghan cause, and it was upon the military successes of Nadir Khan, who led his forces where the military strategists said that none could go, that was founded the Afghan Treaty, negotiated at Rawalpindi, which was so highly satisfactory to Afghan aims and ideals.

Again out of adversity Nadir Shah found advancement, for though he had little liking for him, Amanullah could not do less than make him Minister for War after his victories on the Khost front. But Nadir was not meant for the exotic Court life of a ruler such as Amanullah. He was for the plain and unadorned, and his speech was stripped bare of courtly platitudes, or of appeals to emotionalism or easy-sounding falsities. He was the soldier who had to be accepted on his merits, and who was to be received on these terms and none other. He was without personal ambition outside his military career, and he was the reverse to self-assertive, but on matters military he could be dogmatic.

Amanullah, having wrested a highly satisfactory treaty from the British, and having sustained in full measure the part he had set out to play when he seized the reins of government, felt himself secure. He reduced the pay of his soldiers, and ordered the disbandment of many units. Nadir Shah protested, and did not hesitate to say that such an action was a breaking of faith with those who had served. Stung by the bluntness of words which in an atmosphere of sycophantic adulation sounded almost gauche, Amanullah bitingly observed: " Our friend still lives in the last century. Could someone not tell him that a new age has dawned, and that I am its leader? And lead, I shall!" There were not wanting those who accepted Amanullah's invitation. Nadir Shah knew then that there could be no further syncretism and he resigned his portfolio as Minister of War. To save his face outside the Court circle, Amanullah appointed Nadir as the Afghan Minister in Paris, and to Paris he proceeded, to virtual banishment.

A great moderating influence was removed from Kabul, and a mind which worked with a certain mechanical precision and which refused to be affected by Court excess or inadequacy was banished beyond the seas. That an intellectual force had departed was soon apparent, for courtiers, gleefully assuring themselves that at long last an upright, and therefore hateful, figure had been removed, urged their ruler on to escapades which might have had their inspiration in the Dark Ages.

On the surface, the country began to move forward at a rate which was hourly accelerated by an impatient monarch towards those reforms upon which he had set his heart. Below the surface it began to flounder. The Ministerial coterie appointed by Amanullah appointed, in its turn, its own hirelings in the provinces, and there was hardly a post which had not its "working arrangement," and a scheduled percentage of taxes to be forwarded *sub rosa* to the appointing Minister. An official who delayed more than a week in the dispatch of the stipulated graft was confronted on the following morning by his successor to office. Graft descended on a sliding scale down to the humblest Government clerk. The inkwells of these lesser functionaries incontinently dried, and unless they were "watered," no petitioner could so much as secure a form on which to inscribe a plaint.

Amanullah instituted a lottery system for the army, those to be called to the colours being determined by the drawing of slips of paper. Much money changed hands in order that certain names should not appear in the draws, and the army was filled with dissension.

Amanullah conceived the notion that the priestly class had held the kingdom in thraldom, and it was his wont to "invite" the mullahs to his court, where he played the part of court jester at their expense. He ridiculed their dress, their enormous turbans, and their voluminous trousers, and contrasted them with the ultra-Western habiliments of himself and his courtiers. As an exhibition of bad taste it was outstanding; as a political blunder it was astounding. He hung on to this throne for ten years, mortgaging and collecting his taxes years in advance in order that he might expedite the monument to personal edification. His European tour, from which he was to garner the ideas which were finally to bring about his decline, cost the country three years' taxes, and if Amanullah excelled, it was as a tax-gatherer.

Afghanistan could ill afford to send its monarch on a glorified tour, but the financial shocks which attended his going were as nothing to that sustained when he landed in Egypt, and Queen Souriya, at his command, stood before all beholders, attired in European garb, and with face unveiled. He returned to a sorely perplexed country, convinced that he had only to act to transfer much of the lucrative industrialism of the West to the hills of his own country.

Prior to Amanullah's European tour, Nadir Shah, appalled by Amanullah's mismanagement of Afghanistan, resigned his post in the diplomatic service, and retired to the South of France, there to nurse his failing health. When in Europe, Amanullah made an unsuccessful endeavour to win Nadir Shah to his side, but Nadir, with his customary directness, declared that he could have nothing to do with a court which was rotten with intrigue and bribery. Seething at this rebuff, Amanullah made the atmosphere so unpleasant for anyone related to Nadir, that Nadir's brothers deemed it expedient to leave the country and to join him in exile.

On his return to Kabul, Amanullah issued the edict which was to spell dishonourable flight. " The face of the Afghans " was to be changed, and to this end orders were broadcast that everyone should wear European dress and European hats, and that women should go unveiled. The news spread like an epidemic. The ruler was forcing un-Afghan ways upon the Afghans, and the priestly class saw their long-awaited chance. This king, who had pulled their beards and treated them with ribaldry and jest, should be made to smart. The people, taxed to the limit, turned with baleful eyes on the officials who waxed fat on their distress. The nobles had largely been ejected from the court circle, where they had not left it in disgust because of the discourtesies of the misnamed courtiers, and the army had found that Amanullah's promises lent themselves to the cadaverous. Not only had pay been reduced, but it was in arrears, but that did not prevent the officers demanding the commission on their pay which, since the departure of Nadir Shah, had become the privilege of the gazetted.

The banner of revolt was unfurled by the Shinwaris, and the officers sent to quell the disturbance were imprisoned by the much-tried tribesmen. Amanullah so misunderstood his country and his kingly duties that he resorted to the expedient of arming tribe against tribe, and clan against clan, but although there was some fighting, there was even more cohesion, and Amanullah grew apprehensive. He sent emissaries to the rebels to open peace negotiations, but before these officials could fulfil their mission, he had lost Jalalabad, the capital of the eastern province, and the rebel principals were on their way to Kabul with demands contained in twenty-one articles, not the least of which asked for the banishment of Queen Souriya and the abdication of Amanullah.

Amanullah sent the majority of his troops away from Kabul to deal with the rebels, but there was lurking in the hills, awaiting just such a chance, the low-born bandit, Bacha Saquo, a brigand with a lengthy cut-throat entourage with a reputation extending over many years of successful caravan rustling and lucrative pilfering. He descended on the capital, and though brought up short by fire from the walls, invested Kabul, and commenced a reign of terror such as no country had known before or since. In the Arg Palace, Amanullah gave way to panic. He endeavoured to communicate with his far-flung troops, but found that the resourceful Bacha had cut all the telephone and telegraph lines. He saw spies everywhere, especially among the mullahs, and had them executed. He made a pathetic attempt to ingratiate himself in the good graces of the Kabulis, but when he appeared before them they reviled him.

Now convinced that his people no longer wanted him, Amanullah returned to the Arg, and with candles as an illuminant, for by now Bacha had also cut off the electric current, he decided to abdicate, and hand the throne to his brother, Inayatullah. Before abdicating, Amanullah took the useful precaution of appropriating the court jewels and that which remained in the treasury, and set out for Kandahar by car, hotly pursued by Bacha. A few miles from the capital the car became bogged, and the pounding hoofs of Bacha's cavalcade came perilously close. When almost within rifle shot, the car was dug out, and Amanullah made good his escape. Returning to Kabul, Bacha soon entered the city, and within a few hours Inayatullah also had to abdicate. He made his egress by aeroplane, and made for Peshawar.

When Amanullah reached Kandahar he learned of the flight of Inayatullah, and shortly afterwards the news was confirmed by his brother in person, and the Kandaharis were regaled by the sight of two ex-monarchs. They had no cause to love either, but both were infinitely preferable to the inglorious Bacha, so Amanullah withdrew his abdication, and again proclaimed himself king. In order to soften the blow, he informed the Kandaharis that he would rescind all his reforms; then he asked for their support. There was a pregnant silence until a greybeard spokesman, with vitriolic sarcasm, suggested that this mercurial monarch should seek assistance from those courtiers whose soft words he had so sedulously cherished, and not from those he had denounced as traitors.

It was borne in upon Amanullah that he had misjudged his moment, so collecting what forces he could, and summoning others to his aid, he shook the dust of outspoken Kandahar from his feet and marched northwards toward Ghanzi, on the high road to Kabul, once more to try conclusions with the Bacha. To be king in Kabul, is one thing; to be king without, is another, as Amanullah found.

So mistrustful were the tribesmen that they insisted that cash down should be the rule before they parted with any supplies; while those on the flanks of Amanullah's march, remembering the taxes of which they had been mulcted, and the undignified charades in European clothes in which they had been forced to play a leading rôle, threw shots from their fastnesses among the mountain crags, and severely harried Amanullah's forces.

The people of Ghanzi proved to be as outspoken as those of Kandahar, and they were, if anything, a trifle more forceful. They intimated that the oncoming guest was not only uninvited, but unwelcome, by closing their gates and firing upon his advance guard from the towers. Disconsolately, Amanullah wandered about for a further fortnight, and on May 14th, 1929, his nerve gave, and he gave orders for a general retreat upon Kandahar. He fled ahead of his dispirited troops, who had all along lacked a general, and sent word to Kandahar that Queen Souriya and his relations should immediately proceed toward the British frontier, where he would join them. At 2 a.m. the following morning Amanullah's car crossed the border at Chaman. It stopped a yard or so inside British territory, and Amanullah broke down and wept.

" This is the end of my ten years' reign," he cried. " I leave my country as a rejected monarch . . . but why ? "

He could not have been listening when he appealed to the Kandaharis for assistance.

With the menacing figure of Bacha still in the background, other personalities danced for a brief period upon this bizarre stage. In the east, one Ali Ahmad Jan had proclaimed himself king, and set himself up at Jalalabad. He had taken a post-graduate course in licentiousness, and the local tribesmen were not enamoured. They advanced on Jalalabad, and sacked it, just after Ali Ahmad Jan had fled to Kandahar. This third deposed monarch was actually in that city when Amanullah and Inayatullah arrived in their initial flight from Kabul. He was still there when Amanullah made for the British frontier, his decision to abdicate now irrevocable, and again he set himself up as king. He held the self-conferred title for exactly two months, when he was captured by Bacha, and executed with the brigand's usual thoroughness and celerity.

Bacha marched into the Arg Palace in his muddy boots and frowsy sheepskin, and found the treasury empty. There was no bullion, so he struck leather rupees, and if the merchants demurred when requested to exchange their goods for this novel coin of the realm, they were bayoneted. He mobilized his fellow bandits as secret service agents, whose task it was to tour the country and render an estimate of the probable worth of individuals.

In a villa on the French Riviera sat a man of fifty or more, with ashen face. The medicine bottles around him, even more than his countenance, testified to the severity of his illness, and he it was who was called to the task not only of ridding Afghanistan from this ghastly incubus, but the far more difficult one of remodelling the social fabric. He did not seek the task; indeed, his physical exhaustion was sufficient to deter any man from self-aggrandizement, but when he was handed a newspaper which told him of the ravages of the bandit king, and of the imprisonment of his family, and all he held most dear in the dungeons of the Arg, where milk was refused for the children and even water was difficult to obtain, he considered that his life would be worthless unless he made the supreme effort. He was ill; he was to all intents and purposes penniless; the difficulties in his way seemed insuperable. Yet he was sustained by a divine faith.

He was profoundly moved by what he learned, and he trembled with emotion. What could he do for his Fatherland?

Nadir Shah had never attempted to amass money. He had contributed more than half of his army pay to the establishment of the National school, and more than half the proceeds from his estates went to its upkeep. He had barely sufficient means to convey himself and his two brothers to Afghanistan. Nevertheless, they would go, and Allah would provide.

He and his brothers sailed for their native land, and they crossed the border in the south, minus arms and minus finances, and with only the prestige that attached to their names with which to do battle with a formidable foe who had possession of Kabul and the public treasury, the people in an iron grasp, and an army, large and well disciplined, fed and sustained with the promise of more and yet more loot. Yet Nadir Shah's manifest ideals, and his perfect freedom from the paltry motive of private gain, was to prove in the end a sufficient weapon for the routing of a mad killer gone berserk, and for the great work of reconstruction which remained. Nadir and his brothers had stepped into the poorest province of the country, where the tribesmen, if they left their homes, would expect to be fed. Although it was patent to all that even the barest rations would be scarce, the tribesmen thronged around him, and prayed that this Marshal, whose military achievements they knew, and whose moral integrity was a byword through the country-side, should deliver them from the monster who ravaged and sabotaged the people and the hills of Afghanistan.

Bacha, with his secret-service brigands, was early informed of Nadir Shah's incursion, and he laughed brutally and raucously at the thought that one who was without men and financial resources could oust from the throne Habibullah Ghazi—meaning the Beloved of Allah—for this was the style and title which Bacha, the water-carrier's son, had had the temerity to assume. Nevertheless, when his laughter had subsided, he took the precaution of dispatching to the south the most trusted of his regiments and his most capable officers. He was fully determined that Nadir Shah should be overwhelmed at the very inception of his campaign. Not only did he send a great force, but he secretly dispatched trusted emissaries whose duty it was to buy the allegiance of the southern tribesmen, some of whom succumbed to the lure of money.

Surrounded by treacherous tribesmen, Nadir Shah took to little known valleys among the rugged hills, and though the military forces sent against him could not pin him down, yet the secret-service agents of Bacha did their work well. They could only advance one criticism against the Marshal, but this they hammered home with virulence and invective. They made what capital they could out of the fact that Nadir Shah had been War Minister in the Government of the hated Amanullah.

From this it was easy to suggest, and to emphasize with manufactured evidence, that Nadir Shah was there in the interests of the ex-king, and that his real purpose was to re-establish Amanullah on the throne. This was clever propaganda, and for a time it bore fruit. Wherever the Marshal showed his face he was greeted with marked hostility, and it was necessary for him to preach, and to declare to these ignorant people that his sole aim was to rescue them and the country from the remorseless grip of a tyrant.

Every day, and at every halt, it became incumbent upon him to insist that he himself belonged to no party, and that he was a soldier first and foremost. Furthermore he emphasized that if and when he succeeded in driving out Bacha, he would leave the question of who should rule to the nation itself. He promised that representatives from all parts of the country should gather in Grand Assembly to elect a king. It was no easy task to convince a people who were accustomed to the despotic, and some tribes indeed remained unconvinced until the end, preferring the ignoble rule of Bacha to the return of Amanullah.

The mere fact that Nadir refused to make a personal bid for the throne lent colour to the belief entertained by some that he was acting in consort and on behalf of the discredited Amanullah who, by running away, had committed the unforgivable Afghan sin. There was, however, no need to fear

Nadir Shah, for, though one versed in war, his temperament was that of the dove.

He was so remote from personal gain, and so altruistic that he was something apart. He was beyond the comprehension of a people who had learned to expect the worst, and to see in an amiable exterior and a disposition to consider the feelings of others a cloak for the sinister and the avaricious. That a man could be entirely honourable and veracious, and entirely without venom, was beyond their understanding, and for long such powerful tribes as the Suleiman Khel and the Dari Khel assiduously hindered his progress, and did their utmost to exterminate the small force which was slowly penetrating into Afghanistan from the south. Another tremendous obstacle to cohesion confronting one who could not back his appeals by force were the long-standing jealousies and feuds among the tribesmen, who sought the opportunities presented by unrest to settle personal differences and to engage in hostilities which took into account neither Nadir Shah nor Bacha.

More than once Nadir saw his men fade away while they engaged in battle one with the other; yet in spite of these early disappointments and hindrances he and his brothers resolved to maintain their fight and, if necessary, lay down their lives for the honour of their country. In their Faith they found the strength to cut their way through to Khost, where the achievements of Marshal Nadir Shah against the British were still a matter for jubilation and for resuscitation in song. Here he was understood and known. The tribes of Khost had seen a brilliant commander at work. He had passed and repassed through their country-side, and there had been no depredations. There had been no commandeering of cattle or supplies, and the Marshal's men had not been accorded a looting licence.

From the comparative security of Khost, Nadir Shah dispatched letters to the principal tribes, informing them that he had returned to Afghanistan with the express purpose of restoring law and order to a troubled land and of giving the brigand king his *congé*. He exhorted the tribes to lay aside their petty personal jealousies, and to combine in a great national movement for the resurrection of Afghanistan from the ruins.

That appeal was issued on the first day of Id. On the second the first batch of one thousand men marched in, to be followed on succeeding days by others. Gradually the diverse groups grew into a formidable lashkar, and then, for a moment, all appeared lost. The lashkar split. Old tribal jealousies had come uppermost, and the tribesmen were on the point of exterminating each other, instead of the Bacha and his bandits.

The Marshal went among the disputants and succeeded, in the last split second, in inducing the contesting chieftains to take a solemn oath to cooperate with each other and to bury tribal antipathies. More tribes came in, and the time came to hold a jirgah at which, after considerable discussion, the tribal elders demanded that before leaving Khost, Nadir Shah should accept their allegiance, and give an assurance that in the event of success attending their arms, he would be their king. Specially was he asked to have no connection with Amanullah Khan for "we have lost faith in him, and any connection with him is regarded as a great offence."

The Marshal remained adamant. His purpose, he assured the elders, was not to take the throne, and he advised all not to pay allegiance to one who had not been universally elected by the people, otherwise, he insisted, civil war and disunion would never end. This refusal to advance to Kabul as the Pretender to the throne caused murmurs of disappointment, but the jirgah had to be content.

Faced with almost incredible difficulties the Marshal's very mixed force—it could not be termed an army—set out for Gardez, three days' march distant. Such were the obstacles that had to be overcome that seventeen days were to pass before the walls of this strategic centre were sighted. Bacha, in Kabul, and exceedingly wrath that Nadir Shah should still be existing, concentrated all his transport, and rushed a well-accoutred force, over ten thousand strong, to stop this forward thrust at the capital. A heavy battle ensued, and at the close of the first day the Marshal's men ran short of ammunition. During the night Nadir Shah scoured the country, buying what ammunition he could, but with daybreak a rumour ran through the camp that all was lost. The lashkar broke and retreated pell-mell, and the situation was rendered the more difficult by the attentions of neighbouring tribesmen who had hitherto assumed the rôle of spectators, waiting for a decisive move before coming down on the side of the victor. These tribesmen rushed down upon the dispersing lashkar, slaying and looting, and Nadir Shah was left with but a handful of stalwarts to act as a bodyguard. He made his way from the field of battle, hotly pursued, but his topographical knowledge stood him in good stead, and he was able to reach the concealment afforded by the wild crags of the Altamoor Pass. Bacha's men surrounded the Pass, and even retreat was cut off, but Nadir refused to become disheartened. "I am determined to fight to the last," he declared. "Even if there is none to help me I, with my rifle, will continue singlehanded to fight the enemy with the idea of doing my duty and averting from my nation this catastrophe. Either I will achieve my object, or lay down my life in the attempt to secure national peace and prosperity."

These were brave words, but they have been heard so often before in the world's history, and with so little effect upon contemporary history, and the tribesmen had lost heart. Once again Nadir Shah called a jirgah, indicating that the recent reverse had not been due to lack of bravery on the part of the tribes, or to deficiencies in military skill, but to treachery. This, of course, was the case, but this appeal from a single source was drowned in the mass propaganda of the Bacha, who let it be known that he had overwhelming strength and was determined to crush any signs of revolt with more than ordinary severity. Bacha must have been indulging in fantastically imaginative flights if he had conceived anything more severe than that which Afghans had by now learned to accept as the *status quo*.

At a previous jirgah the elders had denounced Bacha as a usurper, and had declared him an outlaw, and it is not enough to say hard things unless one is prepared to hurt, and receive hurt. The elders began to consider their position, and more heed was paid to the Marshal's appeals. Gradually confidence was restored, and preparations were made for a fresh attack. Emissaries were sent farther afield, and their accounts were encouraging, though when at last a jirgah was called, the tribesmen remained undecided for several days, the majority holding that to try conclusions with the might of Bacha would be tantamount to courting irretrievable disaster. In the end Nadir Shah stood up before the waverers. He depicted the horrors of the day, and spoke of the untold miseries of the people. In impassioned tones he called for a concerted effort for national emancipation. Nadir Shah was ordinarily no orator. He preferred the simple and direct language of the soldier to the flowery flights of the courtier or the politician, yet on this occasion he was inspired. From indecision the tribesmen were lashed into decision, and from decision into wild enthusiasm. They left with the determination to raise a lashkar for the common cause.

Anticipating the gathering of the lashkar, Bacha despatched a force of fifteen thousand regular troops to dominate the country-side, while secret-service agents visited the tribes and offered large rewards for treachery toward the Marshal.

The Bacha also sent a letter to Nadir Shah in which, in return for the Marshal's allegiance, he promised to instal Nadir in any post that he desired, and to return to him all his property. Failing this, he assured Nadir that all the members of his family—sixty-nine in all—now imprisoned in the Arg, would be done to death.

Nadir Shah's response was characteristic. He addressed his reply to "Habibullah, the son of a water-carrier," in itself at once a sneering and calculated insult, and one which was necessary to pierce the skin of an ignorant barbarian such as the bandit. "My object," wrote Nadir, "is neither to have the throne nor to share it with you. I have come here simply to do away with internal unrest, and to put an end to this bloody civil war which is corroding the foundation of the nation."

Nadir went on to refer to the fact that a tribal jirgah had already named him outlaw, and had called upon him to retire from Kabul. "You have had the audacity to refuse," he proceeded, "and I once more advise you to vacate the throne."

Nadir was sorely troubled by the threats to his relatives, and he lingered long before inscribing the final paragraph to his letter. Then, with tears in his eyes, for the Bacha held blood to be the cheapest commodity upon earth, he wrote: ". . . if in the cause of the national welfare I should lose all my relatives, or even my own life, I will feel proud of such noble sacrifices. Remember, O tyrant, that these threats cannot deter me from my determination."

So easily might this have been bravado. In an

era when braggadocio is the rule rather than the exception and national leaders are more wont than not to scream defiance and imprecations at one another across the ether, words are held cheap. In the case of Nadir Shah he was to prove that words and values were co-related, for before he was to see the ramparts of Kabul he was to suffer many more reverses, and there were occasions when his own rifle was, to all intents and purposes, the solitary armament opposed to the victorious forces of the arch-sadist.

Time and time again the lashkars of Nadir and his brothers broke or wilted before the storm, and Bacha rose from strength to strength. He was aroused to a military endeavour lacking before the advent of the Marshal, and he brought under his dominance tribesmen in outlying areas who had hitherto scoffed at Kabul. Every arsenal and every military post was in his possession, yet still the will-o'-the-wisp remained to harry and torment him. Where armies of ten thousand and fifteen thousand had failed to corner him, he despatched a force over fifty thousand strong, but the Marshal drew to his banner a small but doughty following. For the first time he had a force which was immune from treachery and the wiles of propagandists, and he became the strategist of old.

He so confused the fifty thousand that its commanders were forced to detail it in segments. First one flank would be threatened, and then another, and the fifty thousand became weary with marching and counter-marching. The Marshal sent invitations to the trans-border tribes, and there was a ready response, and with the trans-border men rushed the waverers and doubters.

Nadir Shah joined battle near a pass twenty miles from Kabul. Into it he threw every man at his disposal. It raged for forty-eight hours, during which time the Marshal was everywhere, encouraging his men, hauling ammunition and serving guns. The Pass was taken, and the supporters of Bacha retired discomfited.

The panic-stricken and famished inhabitants of Kabul were too excited to sleep. A long drawn-out deliverance was at hand. Rumour said that the Bacha troops were retiring on the capital. They could see the hurried preparations being made to man the walls and the forts. It was said that the worst had happened to the Marshal's relatives in the Arg Palace.

The next day dawned with Kabul in sight, and the Marshal's men advanced. Thrice they were swept back by the hails of grape from the forts and the walls, but under cover of darkness Nadir Shah's men succeeded in gaining possession of playing fields on the edge of the city. Sirdar Shah Wali Khan, the Marshal's brother, forced an entry under a withering artillery fire, and Bacha withdrew to the Arg to make his last stand.

The Bacha's tax-gatherers and hired fled their posts, pursued by an incensed populace delirious with the joy of deliverance. Bands played, and the rejoicing was general, but in the heart of the victorious Nadir was a deep hurt and an all-abiding sorrow.

Bacha had called his bluff, if bluff it was, and Nadir wrestled with himself, for he was in the throes of a great and momentous decision.

The Bacha had sent word that with the first shot fired at the Arg so would a relative of the Marshal be put to death, and with each succeeding shot so would another die, to the number of sixty-one. Yet he who ruled the Arg ruled Afghanistan. The citadel had to be taken at all costs. Anxiously Nadir Shah's officers awaited his fateful decision.

At length he made up his mind and called for a pen. It was worthy that such a response to patriotism should be recorded in black and white, and not be left to the maladjustments of memory and the ear. He inscribed the following:

"At this crisis, when the choice lies between the safety of my family and that of the nation, I do not hesitate to sacrifice the former. I therefore command you to begin the bombardment of Arg immediately without the slightest consideration for our dear ones."

This command was handed to his brother who, with tears in his eyes, commenced the bombardment. It was maintained throughout the night, and ceased only when an abortive attack was made on the citadel. It was maintained the next day, when the magazine caught fire and the defenders lost heart. Bacha remained in the Arg, cowering until darkness fell, when he made his escape to his native hills.

The major portion of the beautiful palace was burned to ashes, yet every member of the Marshal's family was safe. Bacha's great bluff had failed, and he had hesitated to carry his threats into execution when possible retribution was so imminent. In the deep dungeons in which they had been incarcerated the Nadir family had found safety. Neither shot nor flames had reached them.

Overcome with emotion, Nadir Shah proceeded to the smouldering Salaam Khana—the hall of reception—where an enthusiastic people hailed the conqueror, and begged him to accept the throne as the fruits of victory, then and there. To the pleas that he should become king Nadir Shah, a sick man, and now feeling the inevitable reactions to an arduous campaign and to the terrific nervous strain imposed by the necessity of giving an order which, as far as he was aware, meant the death-knell of all he held beloved, begged to be allowed to retire into private life on his estates two miles from Kabul at Aliabad. The representatives of the people, however, were not to be gainsaid, and the hall resounded with the repeated cries of " Long live the King. Long live His Majesty, King Mohamed Nadir Shah ! "

There was a quality of heroism about this man which was irresistible ; it was undeniable ; and without it the people refused to face the appalling task of reconstruction which awaited. The smouldering ruins of the Arg Palace around was only a symbol of what was to be found without.

Few had really understood Nadir Shah when he declared that he was fighting solely for the nation. Now, with success in his hands and his obvious preferment for retirement, they felt that they did. Here was no Judge Jeffreys, who would demand an eye for an eye for all that had transpired during the previous nine months of odious existence. Here was no Salisbury who would glibly ordain "twenty years of resolute government," to eradicate the stains of the past. Here was a man whose passion for his country's nationhood had transfigured him from a patient, whom European doctors had ordained death should he leave his sick bed, to a mighty conqueror.

There was something in his very simplicity of purpose and utter lack of the artificial which was greater than the sickness still obvious within his spare frame. It made him at once a shattering force and a masterful leader. He had that quality of unaffected seriousness which could be relieved by a quick and ready smile which displayed, not the conqueror, but the passionate humanity and love of country beneath.

His eyes, when they lighted with his smile, gave an insight into the high-souled being within. Here was one who had passion and logic balanced to an unfailing degree; one who could take decisions, feel, and feel terribly, and yet not be racked by remorse. Unthinkingly, he played the part of king, but he was no actor. The stage was beyond his realm.

Every impulse was dictated by the fundamentals of intelligence and purpose. Here was one who was a philosopher, and yet possessed of quick sensibilities. He could appreciate beauty, yet he had little patience with beauty allied to pomp. His castles were on the earth and not in the clouds, and, amazingly and suddenly, Afghans felt that they understood.

The cynical and the satirical, who had believed that Nadir Shah had made his protestations against accepting the throne with his tongue in his cheek, saw that they had wronged a simple-minded soldier. With this high-minded spirit at the head of the State, a new era might dawn when values would be re-orientated, and a great upward thrust made through the mire of rapine and spoliation to an even-tempered and sane normality.

"Long live the king!"

Nadir spoke.

"My object was only to free you from the cruel hold of Bacha," he said, "and to put an end to the reign of terror, and this, by the grace of God and your co-operation, has been achieved. Now, I hope, you will kindly permit me to retire and take rest. It is for you to choose your king. Let your choice fall on some worthy person. As for myself, to tell you the truth, I am not in a position, nor am I willing, to take up this onerous duty."

The people's representatives crowded round.

"There is none worthier," they cried. "Long live King Nadir Shah."

Thus it was that the man who would not be king took over the reins of Afghanistan's government on October 16th, 1929. If Amanullah had been an Ajax, Bacha a robber, Nadir Shah had to be a Titan. Reluctantly he accepted the throne, and gazed sadly upon a realm devoid of law and order, on a treasury utterly empty, on a people who had been clubbed and terrified into parting with their last possessions, on to a civil service rendered rotten from top to bottom with corruption.

There would have to be a clean sweep, but even the sweep is unable to sweep without the tools of his trade, and tools cost money. Nadir Shah and his brothers were not afraid of the commonplace. They were not abashed by work. The glories of conquest had still left them as men, and they toiled night and day, with each cycle of the clock, bodily and mental exhaustion determining the time for sleep.

As he toiled he made others, relying upon the old-time maxim, "Work must bring its own reward," to hearten those who dallied or contemplated the grim prospect of reconstruction with despair. To assist the State, his first decree made over all royal private property to the public treasury, and it was with the aid of this thin financial stream that the cumbrous wheels of State were first made to revolve.

Gradually, with Nadir Shah toiling far into the night, the wheels' momentum became greater, and Afghanistan began to realize that here was a stable and rational government. The provinces, convulsed with disorder, began to quieten down, and men's thoughts began to turn not to the necessity of protecting their lives and that of their dependents, but to the long-neglected soil.

This new king, intolerant of both despotism and Communism, broke through the tyranny of plutocracy, and the taxes which were levied were so designed that their burden rested with equal weight upon all shoulders. No longer was the rich man able to buy his way out of obligations. No longer was the peasant intimidated into making up the difference. One of Nadir's first orders was to prohibit bribery. He made all employees of the government swear on the Koran that they would neither accept bribes nor presents from the people. At the same time he banned intoxicants, both for public and private use.

Nadir Shah attained his end. He lived to see his country once more upon the path of advance and moral rectitude. He should have lived longer, but Nadir Shah, one of the finest characters ever to come out of the East, is dead. He commanded to an extraordinary degree the faith and the confidence of his people, yet he was laid low by an assassin and an unbalanced youth. He died while reviewing the youth of his country, perhaps as he would have wished to die—in the service of a country to which he had given so much. Certain it is that in those few moments which divided life from death he was happy in that he was giving his all, and that his then nineteen-year-old son had been worthily trained, and had worthily responded, to maintain a noble tradition.

FEISAL

FEISAL

I

PROPHETS are as the pebbles upon the seashore in world history. Saids, mullahs, prophets, name them as you will, and they are legion. Of those who have leaped for a short space into the Islamic firmament, but few have sustained the rôle in the memory of man, and those that have found an abiding place have necessarily been outstanding, and men of unusual calibre. The Arabs, who are somewhat pedantic in such matters, and who invariably strive for colloquial effect, even when this calls for the repression of fringing detail, maintain that there have been forty thousand saints. If their computation is correct, and there is no one to say them nay, then Feisal, son of Hussein, Sherif of Mecca, was to be accounted the forty thousand and first.

Notwithstanding the generous tributes of Colonel T. E. Lawrence, the public still entertains a remarkably erroneous impression of this man, for it is biased, and has made up its mind. Feisal, in the Western conception, must remain as the living embodiment of the sheikh of the desert as envisaged by lady novelists—writers who have fed successive generations of their grimly-environed Western sisters with that romantic and colourful soporific so necessary to under-nourished imaginations and souls nurtured on the mechanical and the unfeeling.

In the eyes of the men he remains as a personage of fine vision and generous impulse, who rose against the domination of an alien race to the assistance of his nation. He was a glorious hero, who imparted dash and movement to a grisly war scene which lacked mobility, and where all were locked in a ghastly wrestle with death.

Both men and women of the West have been hypnotized by the canvas skilfully painted by wartime propagandists, and no amount of argument, and certainly no mere pen-picture, will move them. Feisal will probably remain for all time in the Western view as the romantic and dashing Pied Piper of the Near East who, on gaily-caparisoned camel or highly-curvetting Arab, tore across the desert wastes raising the tribesmen to the succour of his national cause.

There is sufficient of truth in this picture to give the canvas an air of verisimilitude, and that is sufficient for the enthusiastic, but it fails to portray the Feisal that was, or to give any real indication of the motives which were behind his spectacular and highly-successful forays.

To accept the view of Feisal which is so generally held, it is necessary to assume that the Arabs were oppressed and inarticulate, and that the mismanagement of the Turk was such that they hailed the advent of the war opportunity in their midst as a beam direct from heaven. Like so many premises, some of the assumptions are correct. The Turks not only mismanaged, but they were corrupt. Their administration was rotten, from the Porte itself down to the lowliest time-server. They were more than brutal, and certainly oppressive.

HIS LATE MAJESTY KING FEISAL OF IRAQ

But the Arab was not the dour, inarticulate, poorly being which so many would have us believe. His outlook was not confined to the desert and the oasis, and life meant more to him than pasturage for his camels, sheep and goats. There is in the world to-day a great Arabic-speaking *bloc* which extends from Egypt, Palestine, Syria, trans-Jordania, Hedjaz and Iraq, and this is something which was evolved by the World War.

The War achieved much, as it was responsible for much, but this was the outcome of no peace treaty. The intense Nationalist spirit now permeating these peoples was not a spark of the War to be fanned into wild conflagration by Feisal and his comperes.

It was there, lying dormant and awaiting expression in some of these countries, but decidedly active and vocal in others. There is to-day a very close affinity between Egypt and the rest of the Arab-speaking *bloc*. Post-war events have tended to emphasize this liaison.

But it followed that there were tremendous repercussions in the pre-war era to the struggle of the Egyptian fellaheen, in the first instance against the crippling dominance of the Porte, latterly against the high-handedness of the Porte's Viceroy, the Khedive, and more recently against the yoke implied by Western militarism, the presence of which was excused by a desire to protect the foreign millions sunk in the development of the country.

These repercussions had resulted in a strong Arab Nationalist movement; in the formation of secret societies, and a ripe appreciation of world events. If the army of the Turkish Sultan was riddled by officers who executed the Porte's commands indifferently—Mustapha Kamal was a case in point—so was it pitted by Arab officers who obeyed the orders of their Turkish superiors only because they had not the power to do otherwise, and who waited the day when they could throw off the mask of subservience and strike for freedom.

Such a one was Feisal. There was an occasion when even the redoubtable Enver Pasha stood within an inch of death because of this feeling, and when his life was saved only by Feisal, and by Feisal's highly-developed Arab sense of the fitness of things.

Those with Feisal said: "Now is the time . . . a mere knife thrust will do it." Enver was more than unpopular. He was a braggart, and one who used the cloak of office for legalized injustice. Feisal's hand was at the hidden girdle beneath his mantle, and his fingers itched to perform that lightning stroke which would remove for all time an oppressor of the Arabs, but he held his hand and turned away. "This man is our guest," he said sadly and regretfully, and Enver lived.

Feisal was no stripling torn from an Arab tent and flung into the gambit of war by those who deemed it wise that a Turkish enemy should be harried and embarrassed by a revolt from within. He did not rise to tales of derring-do as a trout does to a fly, and with wild and youthful impetuousness proceed to paint the country-side a rich shade of vermilion. His every movement was logical and calculated. Not a step was taken without thought and consideration. There was a complete absence of the gloriously impromptu; everything was governed by the cold and impassionate dictates of reason.

Feisal knew, his father, Hussein, knew, and his brothers knew far more of the international body politic than the outside world credited. They were all, without exception, close students of the Nationalist idea, and they had been presented with unrivalled opportunities to pursue their studies. They were not merely Arabs who knew nothing of the great beyond, and who accepted the jibes and the buffetings of destiny with a fatalistic phlegm.

They had seen, and their minds had been trained to function, and they looked upon world events, not so much from the perspective of the pasturage and the oasis, as from that of the cosmopolitan. For more than seventeen years Hussein had been a guest, but a virtual prisoner, in Constantinople, where he had the stern and apprehensive eye of the custodian of the Yeldiz Palace ever upon him.

One could not spend nearly two decades in such an environment without assimilating the atmosphere, for Abdul Hamid was the centre of world intrigue, and the diplomats ever clustered thickly around him. Hussein and his sons were spectators in a tragic comedy. The Powers were around the almost moribund corpse like vultures awaiting the death. While Germany undertook to dry nurse the Turkish Army, much to the chagrin and mortification of Great Britain, Great Britain, no less high-souled, accepted the more onerous task of wet-nursing the Turkish navy, to the ex-Kaiser's rage and Kiel's fury. They had the respective merits and demerits of the Powers appraised to a fraction, and they knew to an iota what value there was to be placed either on the written or spoken word.

Turkey was discounted in its entirety. They knew all about the movement of the Young Turks—far too much, for the Young Turks, after their prewar *coup de théâtre* before Constantinople and their accession to Ministerial eminence, proved to be harder taskmasters of the Arab than the old-time Porte. Nation-conscious themselves, they deplored the rise of this spirit among the Arabs, and they went to extreme lengths in order to eradicate it.

They believed that they had succeeded, whereas they had merely driven it beneath ground. That is how the grandiloquent Enver came so near to death without realizing his danger. In Enver's eyes any Arab whose obeisance was not sufficiently low and obsequious was a potential Nationalist, and was hanged forthwith. I, who have seen much of the Assyrian, the Palestinian, the trans-Jordian and the dweller among the reeds of the Tigris and the Euphrates, cannot speak too strongly either of Enver or of the Turkish governors and Turkish jacks-in-office, who regarded the unfortunates within their power as so much carrion to be devoured. Here I have in mind not so much repression as it would be interpreted in the West, or, shall I say, in Great Britain?

There, kings have overtaxed and bloody-minded tyrants such as Judge Jeffreys have stalked the land, halter in hand, yet Great Britain has never known repression such as I have seen it. Blood and greed are virtues in comparison with what can emanate from brains warped by hereditary and cultured disease, and much of that which I saw was unspeakable. It sapped not only at the *moral*, but at the bodily virility of subject peoples.

Hussein and his sons returned to Mecca when the Young Turks clipped the talons of Abdul Hamid, and the sons took with them a modern education and a wide grip on international affairs. They returned to the desert as beacons of light in a night where even the stars refused their radiance. Thus equipped, they were to lead a groping people over many diverse and difficult paths before the day dawned and the sun made of God came to give warmth and colour to the scene.

Thus it was, when Germany declared war in 1914, Hussein and his family were able to take stock of a situation pregnant with possibilities. They judged, and judged rightly, that Turkey would be drawn into the conflict, but they were unable to say upon which side. The diplomats were still bargaining. True, Germany was early in the picture, and the military mission, headed by General Liman von Sanders, was more than missionary in purpose, and had assumed virtual control of Turkish military affairs, but the Porte wavered.

It is now no secret that Turkey could have been bought by Great Britain with money, but that is by the way. Soon Turkish neutrality became a farce, and more and more did she incline towards belligerency, and it was only a matter of time before she would be lined up with Germany against the Allies. The Porte, vain and boastful, declared itself an ally of the Kaiser, and one who fought on equal terms, but Mecca, more observant, and reading more correctly from the hand of fate, asked how could this be so. Turkey, effete, rotten, broken by a long succession of wars, ill-armed and badly equipped, how could she remain as an equal in a battle among the giants of the earth? If Germany won, she would be in the invidious position of the poor relative, perhaps even a vassal; if the Allies won, a certain dismemberment of the top-heavy and lop-sided Ottoman Empire could be safely expected.

Turkey declared war, and called to the Faithful. From the minarets of St. Sophia, in Constantinople, the Caliph radiated the call to Islam. He voiced a challenge to the Christian Infidel, and breathed the magic word "Jehad." It was to be a Holy War against the forces of Christianity, which should embrace not only Turkey proper, but Assyria, Palestine, the Jordan Valley, Hedjaz, Mesopotamia, India, Persia, Afghanistan and Turkestan. The Caliph, spiritual head of the Sunis, called, and the entire East was to rise as one man to the call of Jehad. There was to be a spiritual awakening; pan-Islamism was to be triumphant.

The Caliph and Sultan was not of this world. The "Pavilion of Stars" was as a world unto itself. It was at least a kingdom in miniature, with a range of buildings the size of a town, numerous lesser palaces, gardens and parks, and around the whole, not one wall, but three. Once inside that triple-guarded fortress, whether resident or visitor, the only way to get out was to secure an Imperial decree. Here lived an army of retainers, and hundreds of cooks to serve the aged Sultan and Caliph. He had seen his Empire crumbling at its outer edges.

Lost in all but name before the War, Egypt was British for the nonce, and though professedly a non-belligerent, its "neutrality" was perched upon a crazy and precarious pyramid—an edifice in farcical imitation of those at Mena. Tunis had gone, and the French were colonizing Morocco. Austria had advanced in the Balkans, and Greece, the ancient enemy, was watching, under the steely eye of Venezilos. Russia—of course, Russia—was advancing toward Constantinople.

This much he saw in the seclusion of the Yeldiz Palace, but he, who had been a match for the most able of European diplomatists, had lost his sense of values. Secure behind his triple walls, he was secure from the current and cross-currents of intrigue and self-determination, but even the Sultan could not see through bricks and mortar. The foreign ravagers had been eating of the fringes of his vast domains, and he sought to consolidate that which remained by an absolute despotism.

The Young Turks could find what solace they could in their hollow victory. They could have their Assembly, but the real strands of government led to the Yeldiz Kiosk. In his more virile days, the Sultan had sensed the coming of Nationalism in the conglomeration of States and peoples which made up his unwieldy Empire. He knew that if this movement was not rigorously repressed, it would swell until it burst through the bonds which held together the segments of the Ottoman union.

The Sultan had a wonderful conception of Empire. It must sprawl across the map and be limitless. He had a still more grandiose picture of his status as

M

Caliph. As the Padishah, he believed that he was the living embodiment of Islam, and his Islamic conception was not religious but political. As he viewed Islam, it had necessarily to be universal. It must be all-embracing, and must eschew Nationalism. Once the National element was allowed to intrude, then Islam, as he saw it, became merely a tradition, and—I hesitate to say it—merely a religion. Dimly he perceived that all was not well with the body politic, and more and more did he draw the reins of the administration into his white-gloved hands. Before the slightest administrative move could be taken, his scrawling pen had to go into action.

His successor also had lost touch with realities, but he saw in the World War a relief from his growing sense of impotence to stop the rot in his realms. This man really believed that a triumphant Christendom was seeking to engulf the Muslim world. A call to Holy War from the minarets would circumvent this; it would cement the ever-recurring crevices in the Ottoman structure; millions would fight for the honour and glory of the Crescent.

He invited the Islamic world to the vast Golgotha —this man, afraid of his own shadow, whose sense of fear and mistrust had grown into a horrible and revolting mania; this arch-priest of the morbid.

Hussein, Sherif of Mecca, was ordered to give his seal to the Jehad, but if a man of great piety, his enforced sojourn in Constantinople had made him worldly wise, and the pros and cons of this situation had to be well considered. No matter what happened, Turkey could not emerge well from a conflict which had Great Britain on the other side—and

Great Britain, although she entered upon war with the air of one participating in a game, had a highly irritating habit of selecting the victorious faction. Hussein knew his history. Then there was Germany. Could Islam ally itself to a State so aggressively Christian—a State where the Hun was pre-eminent; where the spirit of compromise and toleration was so conspicuously absent? The Sherif thought not. On the other hand, there was *la grande nation.* France was a desperate enemy of the Moors, and there had been that revolution with its paganistic trend, and more repugnant in Muslim eyes to the acceptance of Isa as the True Prophet rather than Mohamed. These things had to be considered.

The countless thousands who came to Mecca on the pilgrimage were, in amazing proportion, people who dwelled under the security of the foreign flag. That, too, had to be borne in mind. These people might grumble and cavil, but not only could they afford to undertake the Haj, but obviously no disability attached to them for being Muslims. They had perfect freedom of speech and of religion, and there had been advances toward constitutional freedom, with promises of more. And if the British had a negligible army, they had a mighty fleet. The situation bristled with complexities, and required thought.

A more pressing problem called for solution. There was a considerable interim between August 4th, 1914, and Turkey's formal declaration of hostilities and the Caliph's call for a Jehad, and the stream of pilgrims had dried up, and with it the resources of Hedjaz. Mecca, Medina and the other holy cities were non-productive. They dispensed spiritual equanimity and a sense of achievement and grace. There they ceased. The outlook was unpleasant, and more so as Mecca, and the Hedjaz as a whole, had become accustomed to depend in large measure upon the Indian pilgrim ships for the wherewithal to eat. Could the Sherif depend upon the Porte for supplies? He had seen something of Turkish supineness, and now that the Empire was to be further racked with war—well, he thought not.

There could be no Jehad, and the Caliph's call echoed across the Bosphorus to mock him. Only echo answered. Mecca was unaccountably silent.

The secret Nationalist societies were not quiescent. They, too, sensed the coming avalanche of events, and they turned instinctively to Mecca for guidance and for assistance. Secretly, Hussein dispersed his sons to various points of the compass to feel the pulse of this infant nationhood.

Yet it was food which turned the scale. Great Britain held the seas, and that was the way sustenance must come if Mecca was to be fed. Hussein asked the Allies if he was to starve. They said not, and provisions were landed at Jedda. Then, at this very early stage, and long before the world had heard either of Feisal or Lawrence, was the die really cast.

With Hussein's refusal to countenance a Jehad, the Sultan's suspicions were aroused, and the Imperial edict went forth. As far as possible, every Arab soldier was to be concentrated without delay on distant battle fronts, and Turkish troops were to be quartered in the Hedjaz. A great reshuffle ensued, and with that efficiency which only fear and war induces, Hussein, whatever secret thoughts he then entertained regarding the success or otherwise attaching to a recourse to arms, saw those warriors upon whom he would have to call scattered to the four winds, and a Turkish division at full strength intimidating him from the near distance of Medina.

Nevertheless, the Arab revolt could not be restrained. It broke out in many places far distant from Mecca, and the Sherif, whether he considered the moment ripe or not, became embroiled. We know that the Arab cause met with early reverses, and when Lawrence found Feisal he spoke of him thus: "So I went down to Arabia to see and consider its great men. The first, the Sherif of Mecca, we knew to be aged. I found Abdulla too clever, Ali too clean, Zeid too cool. I rode up-country to Feisal, and found in him the leader with the necessary fire, and yet with reason to give effect to science. His tribesmen seemed sufficient instrument, and his hills to provide natural advantage. So I returned, pleased and confident, to Egypt, and told my chiefs how Mecca was defended not by the obstacle of Rabegh, but by the flank-threat of Feisal in Jebel Subh."

There is an Old Testament mellowness in the words of Lawrence which lend themselves to the Eastern page. Their simplicity is at once expressive and impressive. They live and portray. They open up a vista at the end of which one can see a leader clearly and without redundant shadow. Themselves, sharp and clearly defined, they throw their object into relief. They pluck Feisal from the obscurity of the desert, and place him squarely and surely upon the international canvas. He stands there, a quietly imposing figure, magnificently poised, ready for the action which Allah dictates. A leader of men!

Although not strictly a man of the Hedjaz, Feisal was an Arab and, first and foremost, he was an Arab leading Arabs for an Arab cause. The Allies were only incidental, and in that charming, quiet voice of his, Feisal made this abundantly clear on innumerable occasions. He was willing, far more willing than was the Sherif, his father, to accept assistance from the Powers and from sources outside the Hedjaz, but this assistance, though it was against a common enemy, was primarily for the Arabs against Turkey, and not for the embarrassment of the German Higher Command, who entered but faintly into the picture.

From first to last the Arab revolt, sedulously fostered and encouraged by such men as Lawrence, was a Nationalist uprising against the maladministration of the Porte. In its broad aspect it was comparable to the movement in Egypt, where the fires of Nationalism, although kept in check for the time being by a rigorously-applied martial law, were in reality obtaining a progressively firmer hold upon the political fabric.

The Arab revolt was, of course, not confined to the Hedjaz, and though this was the pivot, and though much of its inspiration was derived from the attitude of the Sherif of Mecca, and though the separate waves of revolt overlapped and intermingled, the spirit of race was clearly manifest throughout. The

Sherif demurred when it was suggested to him that Arabs other than those domiciled within his domains should be given commands of importance.

He objected, in the strongest terms, to the appointment of one who was to become Feisal's Commander-in-Chief, not because of his race, for the man was an Arab, but because he hailed from Mesopotamia. Fortunately, Feisal was above such prejudices, and he had the courage of his convictions. Always quietly and without any parade, he frequently acted on his own responsibility, and in the face of criticisms from Mecca. He had a wider and a clearer conception of his duty than had Hassein.

The Sherif, notwithstanding his long stay in Constantinople, was in some matters essentially parochial. His very piety induced a rigid line of conduct, and Mecca overshadowed his every thought and action. Moreover, he had advanced beyond the age when decisions came easily. When Turkey declared war, and the Caliph called for a Jehad, he spent much time in anxious meditation, so long, indeed, that the Nationalist forces in the Arabic-speaking countries lost patience, and raised the banner of revolt before Mecca showed the way.

He was burningly enthusiastic for the cause, but years had rendered him timorous. He desired not only to see the path clearly indicated before he would move, but the way lay clear, shorn of all obstacles and gradients, and efficiently paved and metalled.

His thirty-one-year-old Feisal was cast in different mould. His military studies in Constantinople had equipped him for the rôle which destiny had ear-marked for him. He was well acquainted with modern conditions of war, yet he had the good sense to realize from the outset that these could never be applied in their entirety to the Arab legions, who must combine soldiering with husbandry. He had the fire and dash to a degree which made him a thorn in the side of the Turkish armies.

Although the Arabs for long fought under the disability of antiquated and frequently useless equipment, they retained their mobility. They could harry a flank, enfilade a centre, and be gone. When almost surrounded, the same mobility enabled them to depart whole from the scene in the bottle-neck left by a slowly-moving Turk, pressed down into the sands by the weight of heavy and cumbrous equipment, pressed upon them by the metal-bound mentality of Germany.

The light Turkish magazine rifle, more generally distributed at a later period in the War, was an admirable weapon for lengthy marches across sand which became heavier with the passage of each succeeding file of fours. It weighs not much more than the British Lee-Enfield, and it was capable of brief bursts of demoralizing fire. Had those at the triggers of these very efficient instruments of death remembered in their excitement that these weapons were also provided with sights and range-gauges, I should not be writing this.

That, however, is by the way. On the other hand, the German machine-gun was a ponderous piece of ordnance, a terrifying cannon which required a man's utmost strength to move. Even the tripod upon which it was mounted was not an inconsequential something to be picked up nonchalantly by an infantryman who wished either to advance or retire.

Perhaps the German mentality of those days came out in this also. Once provided with such a weapon and ordered to hold or defend some salient point, the unfortunate gunners were shackled. Without wishing in any way to detract from the fighting qualities of the Turk, the fact that one had to fire to the last or lose one's armament, was undoubtedly a factor in the sturdy defensive actions so frequently put up by these troops. It also explains the frequent fading away during the hours of darkness, when these heavy machines could be handled out of view of the enemy.

Although the combination of military life with home duties had its defects—any Western military commander would have been hopelessly bewildered by the problems it invoked—it at least solved in large measure the all-important question of supplies.

Feisal was probably unique as a general, in that he killed camels rather than his men. He would make his long dashes far away from his bases, and it was the camel that paid. He had men with him, well nurtured in their home life, who were prepared and content to undertake such an expedition with a handful of dates as provender. To lumber oneself with more than the barest of necessities was to invite the derision of the remainder.

These men were hard, and lived hard. At first glance they appeared weak and weedy, but in reality they were as attendants in a Turkish bath. They had had every ounce of superfluous flesh sweated from them, and though not perhaps capable of sustained feats of endurance, they were wonderful material for the thruster who required concentrated effort packed into a relatively short period.

At such work no other race could touch them. How different were they in their light equipment—knife, rifle, bandolier and half a dozen dates—to many of their unfortunate compatriots in the ranks of the Turks.

I saw thousands of the latter, and one could not but be sorry for them. Shod with makeshift grass shoes, if they were shod at all, or with filthy bandages curled round their feet, and with but the remnants of a tattered uniform, they were the most ill-served soldiers I have ever seen. With a complete absence of sanitation, their every movement was accomplished in a dense cloud of flies. Their Turkish officers either knew nothing of hygiene, or considered its practice effeminate. Perhaps the most censorious person in the British lines was the doctor. He did not wait in his tent for disease to come to him. He went out to find it, and the individual was singularly unfortunate if he was successful.

Allenby, a superb *generalissimo*, owed more to the swagger cane than he did to his guns for his successes —the swagger cane, directed by the battalion and brigade medical officer, which prodded and dug its inquisitive way around field-cookers, through horse, mule and camel lines, and terrorized the sanitary squad into frantic action. A fly was a blot upon the regimental escutcheon. Its presence was attended by dire penalties, and the strategy which accomplished its demise was more carefully planned than that which made for victory in the biggest battle.

One of the most amazing sights of the Palestine campaign was that which accompanied an advance by the British forces. From the remarkably clear atmosphere of the hills or the desert they would march into a veritable wall of flies and disease. So numerous and so adhesive were these noxious insects that men and horses would disappear beneath a wildly humming covering of buzzing filthiness. They could not have been more completely enveloped by bee swarms. The medico's swagger cane would thrust and parry, and shortly the plague would disappear in one great incineration.

So poorly served were these soldiers of the Porte that the first consideration, on capturing them, was to inflate their stomachs. Time and time again I came across men who for days had lived on the husks which they had garnered from the fields at night.

If Feisal killed his camels in his lightning passes, the Turks tortured theirs. Feisal maintained his animals in the pink of condition. They had to be supremely fit to answer the calls he made upon them. The Turks treated the dumb even worse than the occasionally articulate. Fodder had to give way to ammunition, and I seldom saw a Turkish camel or pony which was not a hat-rack. Never was the saddlery removed, and the British troops, after their first essays at doing so, desisted. So galled and calloused were these unfortunate beasts that to remove a saddle was to take with it much that remained of the animal. More often than not the answer was a deep trench cut in the sand, with a ramp at one end down which these sadly maltreated beasts were coaxed in a last ambling shuffle. A revolver muzzle, mercifully applied to ear or forehead, did the rest, while the ubiquitous sanitary squad stood with shovels at the ready to hide the traces of Turkey's indifference to suffering and lack of organizing ability.

Feisal, and all those behind the Arab revolt, were Nationalists. They fought for an ideal, and they received their reward. It is unfortunate that the Nationalist principle, accepted across the Jordan Valley and in Iraq, should have been forgotten in Palestine. When Balfour made his famous declaration, he had in mind the rights of conquest, forgetting that if the principles of conquest were applicable to Palestine, they could also be applied to Iraq where the Arab population, suspicious of British motives, frequently proved a formidable enemy.

The Arabs of Palestine, acutely conscious of the Nationalist spirit on their borders, did their part in assisting the invader. The individual soldier could wander where he willed in perfect security, and they expected a reward other than that contained in the Balfour doctrine. But for the friendly disposition of the Arab populace, even Lord Allenby could not have done what he did. He balanced his front line on a railway four hundred miles long. Along the railway ran a pipe-line which conveyed water to his troops. To all intents and purposes both railway and pipe-line went unguarded.

A single lightning thrust, and the troops would have died of thirst, even if it had been found possible to convoy rations. Even if it was only forbearance, which it was not, the Palestinian Arab played a noble part. He can be forgiven if he shows distaste in the realization that the status of Palestine is not comparable with that of Iraq and elsewhere. I have no passionate bias against the Jew. One of the most outstanding Viceroy's India ever had was a Jew. The principle would be the same if the Balfour declaration had given the land to Hottentots or the Eskimo.

It has to be remembered also that the British, when convinced that the Arab revolt was more than a local insurrection, and was something which, if properly bolstered and accoutred, could do much to roll up the Turkish left flank and reduce Turkish and German pressure on the main Palestine front at a time when the Palestine Expeditionary Force had to be denuded of British troops to meet the onslaughts of the Germans in France, declared in all sincerity to the Arabs that the territory they wrested from the Turks they could regard as their own.

Without Allenby's broad vision, Feisal would not have succeeded. Without Feisal, Allenby's smashing of the Turkish forces might only have been a dent, for so surely did the Arabs co-operate that Liman von Sanders was completely gulled, his communications were cut behind him, and when Allenby's pulverizing blow was delivered it met the enemy just where it was weakest. His generalship had made this possible, but Feisal made it certain.

Feisal it was, frequently against the cross-grained senility of his father, who fought sometimes a silent, yet more often a voluble battle on the red carpet of his guest tent. When the Arab revolt reared its flaming head it had no sense of cohesion.

There was but one element of unity, and that the ill-expressed desires of Rabab Nationalism and a common wish to oust the Turk. Ordinarily that would have been sufficient to weld the many diverse elements which rise in revolt. There was a common aim and a common enemy, but even more common was inter-tribal jealousy and inter-clan feud.

The hills and deserts of Arabia were split into fragments, and in each tiny segment the local sheikh was paramount, and necessarily so, for the moment he was not, so was he. As far as Feisal was concerned the revolt began by containing the Turkish forces which were rushed by a suspicious and apprehensive Porte to Medina. That force was rendered immobile, was forced to extend its perimeter until the labour of holding Medina became a task not lightly to be borne, and it was rendered so impotent that, notwithstanding the urging of the Powers, Feisal laughed at this slaving sweating slaves of militarism there in situ, and replied in effect, " Let them sweat."

The Powers were anxious for paper victories. They wanted meat for their propagandists; they desired material for headlines, and Medina was a Holy city. Nicely phrased, the ejectment of the dispirited garrison from Medina could be hailed as a great victory to Allied arms, and there would be a sharp upward sweep in the graph of morale—the bugbear of those whose task it was to maintain the spirit of war at the highest peak.

The Turkish garrison could have been ejected after a stiff fight, but the Turks were Muslims, and would not foul the Holy city, and he much preferred that the Turkish higher command should retain its responsibility. If he took the city his losses would be such that his men would have faded away. Enlistment in his forces was purely voluntary, and men came to fight for just as long as the spirit moved them. If he captured the garrison he would have to feed it, and that was more than even he could contemplate. Instead he cut communications, and kept large Turkish forces at work repairing them. He allowed just so much food to enter Medina, and no more, and the garrison gradually demobilized itself by eating its transport animals.

The Powers, whose military mind was circumscribed by weight of metal and weight of men, failed for long to see in this delicate Arab irony a victory for Feisal. They could not understand his cut-and-run tactics. Their form-fed minds could not grasp the potentialities of a situation where the commander could not even furnish a parade state. Feisal seldom knew how many men were at his call at a moment's notice, and for long, sitting within his guest tent, his principal battle was not with the Turks, but against tribal enmities. He sat there, gradually piecing together the bewildering and complex jig-saw puzzle, and it was not until it was suddenly realized by a bewildered and half-unbelieving British Intelligence that he was engaging more Turks than the British forces in Palestine, was he taken with the seriousness that his movement and his qualities demanded.

Sitting prettily, according to the Turkish point of view, on the right, and to the rear of the British line in Palestine, was the port of Akaba. True, British warships had shelled the town, and reduced it to ruins, but the Turks dug fresh trenches on the outskirts, and held the port as strongly as ever. Could Feisal do something about this? He could. He took the port, and the British right wing was rendered less vulnerable.

The question of Medina loomed up again. A long-suffering Turkish command came to the conclusion that the Holy city was not worth the effort. It took so much effort to maintain the twenty-odd thousand troops there that they were becoming a drain on Turkish resources, as well as a nuisance, as they were unable to obey any of the orders relayed to them by Jemal Pasha. Orders were given for the city's evacuation, and now the British were doubly alarmed.

It was assumed that this force would march from Medina, and eventually appear on the Beersheba-Gaza front where British arms were not faring too well. Could Feisal do something about this? He could have replied that he had already done it, for it is one thing to order an army to march, and quite another to get it on the move, and the Medina Turks had long since eaten their baggage train. However he took precautions, made doubly certain that the Turks should imprison themselves, and there they remained almost to the end of the war, a continual source of worry and irritation to Liman von Sanders

In all his operations Feisal had to proceed with more than ordinary wariness. He could not afford heavy casualties, for the very spirit which made cohesion possible was against a heavy death roll

The men who rallied to his pennant would fight for the fruits of victory, and fight well, but there was no point in fighting unless they were to live to taste the sweet fruits of victory. Not for the Arab were the mass tactics of the modern text-book. He appreciated the power of modern arms, the gun of heavy calibre, the machine-gun, the aeroplane, and he took almost an infantile delight in the pyroclastic efficiency of modern high explosive, but only so far as they served the individual or the unit.

He could not envisage a vast mass movement where the action of many diverse arms was co-related. True, there were one or two remarkable occasions when the seemingly impossible actually occurred, but these were fortuitous and freaks of a freakish war. Feisal, although well versed in modern tactics, had to mould his campaign upon tribal temperament and individual aspirations, and he sought mobility as his chief weapon. By day he was like the snipe in the heavens, zig-zagging, erratic, difficult to kill. A good shot is he who bags a snipe, and with the Turks he was never in much danger.

At night he was as a wolf, silent padded on his swift-moving camels, fangs always bared, and invariably at that spot where he was least expected. His very name induced terror in a much harassed enemy; the mere deployment of his unruly soldiery within sight of post or fort the harbinger of death or ignominious surrender. He had his way because everything that he did was in inverse proportion to modern military discipline. The better disciplined the enemy, the more it relied upon form and set manœuvre.

This was a trench warfare. The first thing the soldier did after an advance was to dig a hole and sit in it. It afforded some protection, but it marked the limit of his horizon. If he would see farther, he had to call science to his aid and extend a periscope.

Feisal would have no trenches. His men would not have known what to do with them even if they could have been induced to dig them. When they wanted protection they either disappeared into the mirage, or urged their trotting camels forward into wild, headlong gallop, and anyone who has seen a brigade of tanks in full cry can gain some conception of Feisal's Arabs when fully extended to the charge, screaming, yelling, and shooting from the shoulder with uncanny precision, synchronizing their shots with the gait of their camels as the aeroplanes have learned to do through the blades of their propellors. It did not require the dust they raised to bring a dry feeling to the mouth.

This was always the final thrust to a wider tactical manœuvre based on the success which had corralled a Turkish army in Medina. Until he had gained strength it was no desire of Feisal's to meet the Turk face to face in stand-up combat. Face to face he had to come, but only sufficiently long to pummel the enemy in the commissariat, and then only sufficiently hard to wind him and to disturb his digestive organs. The more men he strung out along the railway lines and along the caravan trails, maintaining communications and repairing the damage which he wrought unceasingly, the less were there for the firing line against his British allies.

He and the British met as far as they had a common enemy. There came to be mutual regard on each side, but never for one moment did Feisal forget that he was an Arab, fighting for an Arab cause. When it was realized that he was a fighting force, and the British desired to increase his mobility, he gladly accepted what they offered and worked to plan with Lord Allenby, but the issue was never clouded. It was clear in his mind if not in that of the British, who were apt to see in his readiness to serve a suggestion of the subservient.

Feisal was subservient to one thing, and that the cause of Arab Nationalism, though there were occasions when his father failed to see this. Hassein, upon whom each passing year added progressive senility, saw his son caught in the net of British wiliness. He and his other sons, though ostensibly for the Arab revolt, talked but did little. It was Feisal who acted, and finally who reaped the kudos, and the old man grew inordinately jealous of his son.

They were difficult days for Feisal, but he had that clarity of judgment which enabled him to see that, in accepting British assistance in large measure and in working in close liaison with the British generalissimo, he was bringing within grasp that which at any time to the capture of Damascus might have been no more real than the mirage which so frequently gave him sanctuary.

It was long before the British command in Cairo would accept Feisal as a potential Turk beater. When it did, there was another hiatus before the name of Feisal percolated through to Downing Street. It did in the end, when a ghastly stalemate had closed upon the Western front, and the previously despised side-shows were called upon to fashion the key which would once more provide mobility.

Until then Feisal had been a rebel—a likeable rebel it is true, but one to be treated with that cold and distant courtesy which Whitehall specially manufactures for those who act *contra bonos mores*. Suddenly it was realized that, although weight of men, and weight of metal, and the heavy war machine which had its roots in trenches sufficed for the main tourney, if a war was to be won the old weapon of mobility and flank attack had to be resuscitated. Germany's northern flank was impregnable, but some hope offered in the East. Turkey was to be lifted at the edges and energetically rolled up until she fell upon her German ally and smothered her.

In the eyes of the Cabinet Feisal became part of the British army in Palestine. He was away across the Jordan, it is true, but he was the right flank. Could he take Maan while the British took Es Salt? Maan was too strong for him, as he could not spare men to batter themselves to death against a defensive position rendered practically impregnable against Arabs lightly armed, but he did the next best thing.

He knit the rails of the Hedjaz Railway into an intricate pattern and caused its engines to compete in altitude records, and cut it off and isolated it. So flustered were the Turks that they wasted their substance in relieving an unbeleaguered Maan instead of smiting the embarrassed British off Es Salt, and Allenby was able to regain his old lines without undue hurt.

Allenby had been rendered weak by the calls of the army in the West. The great German offensive which was to break through the Allied lines and end the war was at full tide. Palestine must fill the many breaches in the British ranks. He was divested of most of his British troops. His army had to be remodelled. A call was sent to India for troops, that is more troops, and the old balance of the infantry brigade on Eastern service was tipped alarmingly. Brigades were to consist of two or three Indian battalions and one British, and to find the nucleus for the new Indian battalions each service battalion was lopped of a company. To make up for the lost company, each company was lopped of a platoon and the holes were stuffed with recruits. Three lopped companies formed a new battalion. Here again the companies lost each a platoon, and recruits filled the missing files.

It was a clever scheme, and deserved the success which it attained, even though men grumbled when suddenly torn from the cherished regimental associations which were theirs and coldly told that they were now the glory of a new unit so ultra-modern as to be designated not by a cognomen rich in military romance and atmosphere, but with an ugly prosaic number which came oddly and unfamiliarly to the tongue. " Who are you ? " would call the regiments on the march, and the new units would remain silent for very shame, for who had heard of a three-figure number which savoured more of the convict than regimental tradition.

Allenby's army, or what remained of it, was caught up in grand transition. Like ants scurrying to their orderly and manifold duties, so did the lopped companies descend from the heights of Jerusalem to the sands of Ludd, emerge from the olive groves of Ramleh and the orange groves of Jaffa to take up station at Jericho, while slowly the troopships disembarked raw men from the hills and plains of Hindustan, who gazed with astonishment and awe at the aridness of El Kantara and wondered what lay in wait for them beyond.

The fighting reached a fierce crescendo in France, and Germany called for a similar effort on the part of her Allies. Allenby's army appeared not so much as a force but as the opening day at a West-end sale. It was in remnants, and it invited attack.

Again the old cry went forth : " Could Feisal do something ? " He could.

While this great game of musical chairs without the music proceeded, Allenby was vulnerable. Big in stature and big in soul, he stamped up and down the line in his patched field-boots, giving encouragement here, a gentle chiding there. So easily could he have provided the musical accompaniment which was lacking from this grandly-conceived charade, but he withheld his trumpetings, and merely asked that the limelight be deflected from the stage which he dominated.

Feisal should have some, and Feisal was not averse. The Turks were using the Dead Sea as a means of transport. He destroyed the transports. He became supremely active, and then ominously quiet. He showed the Turks his strength and then, fading into the mirage, called mockingly, " Find me ! " Instead of detaching troops to gorge the trenches of the Palestine front, the Turks had to reinforce here, there and everywhere on their left wing to be prepared for the hornet when he should display his sting.

Every day of respite which Feisal could give Allenby meant that the kaleidoscopic segments of the British army were clicking into their allotted sockets. Every day, every hour, meant an accretion of strength, an addition to the main structure, a progressive alignment of an inspired picture.

Until September, 1918, Feisal danced willingly to Allenby's bidding. In September the new army was to be ready. In September the last tiny fragment would snap into position, for the West was now calling again for that diversion upon the flanks which would end the war. There was to be no respite while battalion commanders looked over their men, while men looked over their battalion commanders, and brigade commanders did those things which they do to brigades. In many cases the senior battalion commander brigaded the brigade, while inside the battalions they fared as best they could.

Not only were the men strange to one another, but officers had had to be found for this hurried huddle of men. They had been rushed from England with frantic haste, without one word of Urdu, Pushtu, Gurmukhi or Gujerati between them. The Indian troops had been taught the English words of command, and everything depended upon systematic progression. The pukka Indian Army officer was rather lost in the influx, but as the men were spread out, so did these endeavour to emulate them.

Allenby knew that his men and officers were doing their best under the strangest of conditions, and he must not fail them. Neither could he fail Whitehall, which was screaming for action. The moment that last platoon was in place, then zero hour obtained, and the great advance was on.

Liman von Sanders had little cause to be anxious. At his back, and running the entire distance of his front from Haifa to Deraa, was a railway most excellently served. From Deraa, on his left, the railway junctioned with the line to Damascus and beyond, and that to Amman and Maan in the south. He was most comfortably served with communications, and he had that mobility which makes for peace within the general's mind.

The Haifa-Deraa railway at his back was sufficiently far in the distance for him to be elastic. His line could be bent and dented. He could be pushed back for miles, and he could still retain his equanimity, because the railway would allow him quickly to reinforce, and even pinch in and isolate those sufficiently intrepid to pierce his front. He had done all that a good general could do, for with the fall of Jerusalem he had retired to selected ground, and the Germans knew a salient when they saw one.

The constant marching of troops as the newly-modelled army sought its format, of course puzzled the Turks, and he desired to answer the riddle which he had set them, though not necessarily with the correct solution. Turkish aeroplanes were allowed a certain licence over his right flank. They were chased away half-heartedly, and then only when they had observed. The British machines sent against the Turkish observation balloons on this sector developed a strange inaccuracy, and parachutes were no longer at a premium. Tents despised even by an optimistic quartermaster-general were erected in their thousands. Sick animals were staked in magnificent line. Captured cannon was brigaded, and with limberage far beyond its first youth, looked imposing and martial from the air. Men marched and countermarched, and raised great columns of dust. Empty convoys burnt unlimited petrol in the same cause, while regimental bands bellowed derisively across no-man's-land the individual calls and marches of a hundred regiments.

The enemy had to be deceived into believing that a great onslaught was impending on their left, and they were; while Allenby's cavalry was quietly and unobtrusively assembling in the orange and olive groves of Ramleh and Jaffa for a vital thrust along the Mediterranean coast. The cavalry's purpose was to get to the enemy rear, while the infantry rolled back the Turkish line on to its sabres and carbines.

Much—almost too much—depended upon the cavalry for the success of the scheme, for there was that railway which would enable von Sanders quickly to re-align his front when he found that he was the victim of a grim jest.

Yes—the railway. Could Feisal do anything? He could.

It was asking a great deal, for the key to the railway was the junction of Deraa, where the railways from Haifa, Damascus and Amman joined. Feisal was far away from Deraa, and if he moved thither he would have to contend with the Turkish Fourth Army. If he could take Deraa, or render it untenable, the British would have their way. If he failed, then the issue was on the lap of the gods.

"Can you do something to this railway?" asked Allenby.

"I think so," replied the cautious Feisal.

"I can make you a gift of two thousand riding camels," responded Allenby cunningly.

"Then I am certain," said Feisal, with wonderful schemes of dashing mobility already in his mind's eye.

With two thousand additional riding camels, Feisal was more than content, for on them he could mount tried warriors. He marched a strong force in the direction of Deraa, and just below it, to the south, he blew up bridges and culverts, thus denying the Turks assistance from the south. Armoured cars dashed across to the west of Deraa to Sheikh Said, and severely damaged the line and cut all the telegraphs.

The northern line to Damascus was cut at Arar, and by withdrawing into the desert at Taiyibe, he dominated the three railways so that working parties could not repair the damage, and the Turkish Fourth Army was fully engaged in scouting for him. Not only were the railway communications cut at the three vital points which put the entire system out of gear, but the Turkish Fourth Army was contained on the very flank where it could least trouble Allenby. Moreover, these actions confirmed in the mind of the Turks the belief that the British blow would fall on their left. Feisal's spies went through the villages declaring that he was but the advance guard to a mighty force, and when Allenby struck there was no holding the Turk. His telephones were down and his railways would not work. The British right flank worked forward to seize Deraa. It found the work done by Feisal. Feisal preceded it all the way to Damascus, his troops leaving notes at conspicuous places by the wayside informing the British that the path was clear. The Turkish Fourth Army broke, and as it pursued its way northward, it took toll of the Arab villages. The Fourth Turkish Army was harried, chivvied, and charged, until but a remnant, and that the compact German stiffening, escaped into Anatolia, there to have its wounds dressed by Mustapha Kamal, who took over command from a disgusted General von Sanders, and held the line on Turkey's own frontier.

Feisal and his Arabs were called upon to play a great and glorious rôle, and they sustained it. By their efforts, Turkey was first reduced to that state where General Allenby and the British Cabinet could envisage collapse. Feisal held the fort while Allenby was reforming his army, and he played a conspicuous part in the manœuvres which were to blind the Turk as to the British general's intentions, and a glorious one in the final endeavour.

He hastened the end of the War for the Allies, and caused Turkey to sue for a separate peace. It was the beginning of the end for Germany. It opened up the vista of peace to a war-weary world, and it saw the Arabs in Damascus where Feisal's foresight had provided a civil government even before the Turks marched out.

In a very large measure the Arabs were responsible for the success of British arms in Palestine. Without Feisal's vision, without his gift of leadership, and without his power of inclining toward a set goal undeterred by family or tribal jealousies, that success would not have come so quickly and not in such full measure.

He proved himself to be no less an administrator than a fighter, for his work was by no means finished when his Arab legions marched triumphantly into Damascus. There was a large population to be disarmed, and an Arab does not lightly give up what he has gained in the battlefield.

As King Feisal of Iraq he had a difficult furrow to plough, but that furrow remained straight and clean, no matter the terrain he was called upon to traverse. Never did he look down, but always up, and here he was fortunate, because he was excused those bouts of moodiness which are common among his countrymen. He held his position high, not so much by force, but because Arabs in general recognized his integrity of purpose, and the simplicity of his ideals. Not for him was pomp and state, but rather the desk where he could further his aims and those whom destiny had decreed he should lead.

II

IT is a long step from Damascus to Baghdad, and Feisal found it such. Feisal and his officers believed that Damascus was the all of their endeavour, and he was not prepared for the lengthy negotiations between the Powers which were to determine the status of Syria. He had acted blindly, believing implicitly in the good faith of Lawrence and his promises, though he was not aware of the agreement between France and Great Britain which apportioned the Arab territories before they were won. His mind was centred upon Syria, and he and those with him gave little thought to the other facets of the Arab revolt, and for long evinced but little interest in what was happening in Mesopotamia. If, in 1919, it had been suggested that Feisal would eventually rule Iraq, the matter would have been laughed out of court. Feisal himself would have been the first to lead the revelry, for he loved a joke.

The Sykes-Picot Agreement, however, proved to be a stumbling-block to the rapid attainment of Arab ideals, and the situation as it was with the entry of Damascus underwent some fundamental changes. Lawrence's suggestion that Feisal and his two brothers should be rewarded with Arab States in Syria, Upper Mesopotamia and Lower Mesopotamia, was found to be impracticable. It fell to the ground because the autonomous Arab Government in Syria was costing the British exchequer £150,000 a month, and the old Greek conception of Mesopotamia as the plain of the Tigris and the Euphrates no longer held good economically. The modern Mesopotamia, if it was to be an entity, must include the vilayets of Basra, Baghdad and Mosul. Moreover, Iraq, as we now know it, had little in common with the rest of Arabia. Politically and racially it was poles apart.

In the Powers' partition of the spoils of war, it must be confessed that the Arabs became a back number, and in disgust Lawrence retired from the peace counsels to seek seclusion as Aircraftsman Shaw. He believed that his promises to the Arabs could now be regarded as so much piecrust. Feisal could only regard his own position with apprehension. By the Picot Agreement, France was to have Syria, Great Britain Palestine, France Mosul, and Great Britain Lower Mesopotamia.

As the position was revealed about the time of the Versailles Treaty, Great Britain was in Palestine, she was in both Lower and Upper Mesopotamia, including Mosul, and she was financing an Arab State in territory which should have been French, viz. Syria. Feisal knew that there must be a rearrangement. If the British withdrew their subsidy at the behest of the French, his government would fall. He began to cast his net in other waters.

In this haggling among friends, Britain found herself in a quandary. She had no desire to see the Arabs go to the wall, yet she could not indefinitely maintain a State which was almost of necessity anti-French. Feisal began to look toward Basra and the Mesopotamian plains. Many of his officers were Iraqians, and they furthered his aims. Thus, into this already Gilbertian situation crept another factor. Emissaries spreading the name of Feisal appeared in Baghdad, and they were financed from Syria. In its turn, Syria was financed from London!

When it was seen that the Arabs might lose Damascus under the terms of the French Syrian mandate, efforts to secure an Arab kingdom in Mesopotamia were redoubled. Yet, in his heart, Feisal was still wedded to Syria. In an endeavour to present the Allies with a *fait accompli*, so-called Syrian Congresses proclaimed Feisal King of Syria, and his brother Abdullah, King of Iraq, but this was no more than an empty gesture, because there was no real force behind it. The British had only to withdraw their financial support and the entire Arab façade would collapse.

Moreover, in respect to the selection of a constitutional head of Iraq, there were many difficulties. The British were far from certain in their own minds that Feisal would fill the picture, because he was a Sunni from Mecca, and the Iraqians are predominantly Shiah. Also, the Iraqians, if uncertain of the desires of the British, were far less certain of their own wishes. Actually, when Feisal did put in an appearance at long last, many Iraqians made it abundantly clear that they did not want him.

When he arrived at Basra from Mecca, the Basra vilayet immediately submitted a request for independence, and the people held back, any attempt at popular acclamation being sternly repressed by those who regarded with askance the prospect of a Sunni ruler. Incidentally, when a vote was taken among the tribes, Feisal secured an eight per cent. majority, but this was attained because the tribesmen approached the British for advance, and the political officers told the sheikhs to vote for Feisal.

Before Feisal's entry upon the Mesopotamian scene, many other potential leaders had been weighed in the balance and found wanting, the British desire, in the first instance, being to secure an Iraqian of power and influence for the honour. For some time they toyed with the idea of selecting Sayyid Talib Pasha, a man of extraordinary force of character living in armed state a few miles from Basra. He was little more than a powerful chief with modern ideas (his sons had all received a Western education), and his name spread terror wherever it was mentioned. Such a man, it was thought, might hold the Iraqian tribesmen in awe. Fortunately, Sayyid settled the matter by conduct so bold and audacious that it was found necessary to round him up and transport him to Ceylon.

Feisal's claims only received a hearing when other considerations had been discarded, and it was realized that his transference to Baghdad would remove a thorn in the flesh of the French and at the same time enable the British to demonstrate their gratitude to the Arabs.

It was made abundantly clear to Feisal in Cairo that his candidature for the throne of Iraq would only be upheld if he upheld British policy and negotiated a treaty. Feisal agreed, and he became King of Iraq in August, 1921—three years after his triumphal entry into Damascus.

It cannot be said that Iraq reverberated with the popular acclaim, for Feisal was only a legendary figure to the Iraqians and—he was a son of Hassein of Mecca. The official records of the time are trite. They aver that Feisal's position in the Arab world, and his valuable services to the Allies during the war, appealed alike to British and Iraqi. Quite frankly, this is an overstatement of the case, for not only were there those who were suspicious of a Sunni, but there were others, powerful in their own hills, who saw no reason why they should bow the neck to Baghdad. Feisal's entry into Baghdad coincided, more or less, with fierce outbreaks among the rugged hillmen of Kurdistan.

There was no peace in Turkey, and they were in a kind of no-man's land. They saw a wonderful vista of independence which would allow them to deal with the caravans as they willed. Instead of this, here was a man in Baghdad who threatened to police their passes, and, greatest blow of all, demanded taxes of them. This was too much for their proud spirits. In the south one of those minor Emirs, who had been weighed and found wanting, vented his spleen and his sense of disappointment in fermenting an outbreak. Feisal was well qualified to meet a situation such as this, and with the assistance of the British Air Force he soon placed his mark on the recalcitrant.

Feisal had proved himself a leader in Arabia, and

one able to weld together diverse elements even more mutually unsympathetic than those in Iraq. The man who had sat in his tent and gravely pondered over problems of the desert, now accommodated in a palace, applied the same powers to meeting the problems of Iraq. His Sunnism never obtruded, and he worked—from break of day until far into the night. He brought with him the frugality of the desert, and his simple tastes went somewhat ill with those who would surround him with a certain pomp. He won the hearts of those who were working for the Iraqian National idea, for he interpreted this as Arab Nationalism, and was enthusiastically loyal.

He won the admiration and the esteem of the nomads because, on the slightest excuse, he slipped quietly away from the encircling walls of his palace and took his papers and his secretaries into the desert. Even though the cares of office chained him more and more to the Baghdad Secretariat, the desert's call was always there. Sometimes, even when he had resigned himself to the cramped life of the town dweller, he succumbed to its lure, and Feisal was missing. The desert would be scoured, and there he would be found in his tent, sitting upon his rugs.

Under his helpful guidance Iraq was the first of the mandated territories to achieve Parliamentary status, but Feisal, with the lessons of the Syrian Arab Government well in mind, had no desire to be swamped by the Nationalist ideal. There were Iraqians who agitatedly alleged that Feisal did not press with sufficient verve the representations for independence, but Feisal was founding a kingdom rather than a Royal House, and, astute Arab that he was, he saw speedy attainment through the British connection. If independence came too quickly its actual realization would, in effect, be retarded, for Iraq was far from ready for the responsibility. Sometimes Feisal was required to place considerable pressure on the constitutional brake, and the principles underlying his actions were frequently misinterpreted and misrepresented. On the first anniversary of his accession there was a hostile demonstration outside his palace, and other outbreaks occurred in Kurdistan. Feisal remained unperturbed, even when, at a later date, all the Shiahs boycotted the elections.

Feisal saw further than did the Iraqians in respect to their relations with Great Britain. His was a country which would prosper and flourish if suitable agreements could be negotiated with a great Power, and which would languish and wilt because of financial stringency if left entirely to its own devices. His principal bargaining weapon was oil, but his every action required tact and clever diplomacy.

Fortunately, he was blessed with a charm of manner which saw him through many difficult situations. But for this charm and, of course, that real ability that was his, he might very easily have found himself in that uneasy position which was Fuad's in Egypt. Even though he was several steps behind the Nationalists, and an equal number in front of the British, within two years of his accession he had the sympathy and goodwill of the vast majority of Iraqians, and the respect and good wishes of the British.

When, under the stress of the cares of office, his charm was in danger of cracking, and his sense of good humour lapsing, the tent would rise in the desert, and the King would be in conference with himself. On innumerable cups of coffee and countless cigarettes would he sustain himself for hours, reviewing the tangled skein of diplomatic endeavour. He would return to his palace, smilingly maintain the balance between the British and the Nationalists of the extreme school, suggest to this Minister that he should take a holiday, and to another that his qualifications singled him out for some special mission. For ten years he juggled, and in 1932 Iraq secured her independence.

This was in the domestic field. Elsewhere there were events which took stock of Feisal's nerves—events which would have robbed a lesser man of his imperturbable exterior, and sent him into the desert with rifle and sword. There were the events in the Hedjaz where the great enemy of his clan, Ibn Saud, was busily engaged in routing his father from the Holy City. Later, when the domains of Ibn Saud marched with those of Iraq, and before Ibn Saud could consolidate his position and bring the roving Bedouins to heel, there were incidents which, if Feisal had not been at the helm, could easily have precipitated the whole of Arabia into another conflict into which Great Britain would inevitably have been drawn. For countless ages the Bedouins have laughed at frontiers.

They were wont to travel where they willed, and the only barrier they knew was that of superior force.

They cared nothing for mandates, and had never heard of the League of Nations. If by some mischance they had they would not have been awed by its immensity, but its ponderous gravity would have appealed to their sense of humour. The Iraqians are sheep-breeders, and the Ibn Saud's Bedouins were camel-raisers, and in season both used the same pastures, the less warlike sheep-breeders securing immunity from the camelmen by liberal payments.

When the map of Arabia was redrawn, the frontiers were for long political rather than actual, and the problem of Bedouin migration proved a thorny one. The Iraqian sheep-breeders were told that they must now pay money to tax-gatherers, and with some confusion of thought they did so, believing that they were now buying immunity of new masters. When, in the season, the roving Bedouins appeared and demanded their tribute, they were met with an insuperable inability to pay. The Bedouin tribesmen accustomed to graze in Iraq were of the Akhwan clans—fighters who believed that their destiny was to remove all Shiahs and Unbelievers.

When the accustomed indemnity was not forthcoming, they reverted to normal, and in the shepherd encampments they raided not a single individual was left alive. Police posts were rapidly organized along the frontier, and almost as rapidly wiped out by the Bedouins, who saw in them the prelude to an era of unified control which would rob them of their livelihood. The Bedouins were quite candid. They had camels, of course, but unless they were allowed to raid or secure indemnities, they would starve.

Before Ibn Saud had really mastered his territories he obtained much of his support from the Akhwan, and when they protested against the erection of police posts on territory over which they had had complete freedom of movement since the time of Adam, he had perforce to listen to them. He, too, protested against the placing of police posts on his frontier.

This was adding a certain modicum of insult to injury, and Feisal—a real Arab of the desert with the tradition of the blood feud not too deeply down beneath his veneer—could not forget that Ibn Saud had ejected his father from Mecca. The strain which these events imposed upon Feisal was immense. Every fibre in his being called out insistently for action. He was a man of a warrior race, and of a clan which had a history of long feud with the family of Ibn Saud. If he interpreted Ibn Saud's actions as a challenge—and it was extremely difficult not to do so—the sword would have to flash from its scabbard.

Incidentally a literal translation of "Feisal" is "The flashing downward of the sword." On the other hand, if he ignored the offences of Saudi Arabia, he could be accused of being a traitor to his name and his cult. He chose the more difficult course of maintaining peace, steadfastly biting on the iron that he might present his usual amiable exterior when he repaired to the durbar hall. Ibn Saud, for his part, had another of the Hussein clan on his flanks in Abdullah of Trans-Jordania, and he was convinced that much of the unrest within Saudi Arabia at that time had been due to the machinations of Abdullah.

There was little love lost on either side, and it says much for Feisal's powers of self-control and of Ibn Saud's appreciation of kingship when it is recalled that a meeting between the redoubtable pair actually took place in 1930. It was deemed advisable that the conference should take place in the cheerful and neutral environment of a British warship. The broad result of the meeting was an agreement to resort to arbitration on any outstanding frontier grievances.

One of Feisal's principal tasks—and in this we discover the reason why he should have braked hard for ten years on the wheels of the chariot of independence—was to place his country on a sound financial structure. As an Arab well acquainted with the ways of Arabs, whether Meccan or Baghdadian, he did not identify himself with those rosy pictures of Iraqian riches which were painted during and immediately after the war. He was aware that there was a sure source of income in oil, but that would not suffice to provide budgetary equilibrium. In the original conception the oil revenues were to be devoted entirely to capital expenditure, and to this end Feisal was provided with masses of figures to demonstrate the taxable wealth of the country.

He was ever dubious of the efficacy of Western methods of taxation when applied to the East, but he accepted the work of the actuaries with his accustomed good humour. The doubts he expressed were not for the ears of those who had laboured, but for those of Sir Percy Cox and other sympathizers. Actually a ten years' average shows the annual revenue to have been only £3,750,000, and much of the oil revenue has had to be utilized in balancing the budget. Feisal could visualize the difficulties ahead, where merchants are for the main part illiterate and keep no books, and retain their simple Arab garb as a cloak for their hoarded riches.

The machinery for the collection of income-tax, which is so remorselessly efficient in the West, creaks and groans in a land where men habitually plead their poverty and carry all their commercial transactions in their heads. Men whose memory is so extraordinarily retentive that they recall the details of financial deals of a decade ago, do not experience difficulty in remembering the story they told the income-tax collector on his last visit.

The cumbrous engine of officialdom has no terror for them. Even in those cases where the intended victims are literate, the pains and penalties attaching to breaches of Western company laws cannot apply. There is no means of gauging a man's income by his standard of living, and if his books disclose a profit of one pound when in reality it was half a million, the income-tax collector can suspect, but he cannot prove. The only persons who regularly pay income-tax are the salaried officials.

Feisal was never enamoured of income-tax, preferring to place his faith in the probity of carefully selected customs and excise officers. Even here he knew that he would meet difficulties, but they were such as he could meet and counter. He was at home with the smuggler and the freebooter. The long land frontier with Iran, however, makes smuggling a profitable trade, and with the advent of the motor car the revenue officer is usually on the losing side.

As a law-maker, Feisal had to tread with caution, for the centuries have developed their own desert laws as distinct to those which custom has decreed for the towns. In some instances the differences between tribal custom and town practice were, and are, acute. Feisal solved the difficulty in the main by accepting tribal custom from the unlettered tribesman. Feisal was more at home with tribal custom than he was with the rigidity of town practice, but his judges were quickly to be faced with the most difficult of judicial problems in which it was discovered that, in practice, custom could be even more rigid than codified law.

The Director-General of the Ministry of the Interior in Baghdad was shot because he had offended tribal custom by marrying. He had risen to his position by merit, but he came of a lowly family. He married a girl from southern Iraq who was a member of an aristocratic clan which decreed that she could only marry outside the clan with an equal, the tribal object being to keep the tribal possessions within the clan. It was successfully pleaded that the shooting was no crime according to Arab tribal custom.

Another problem which Feisal was called upon to face was that presented by the Assyrians—a Christian race who fought their way out of the Russian debacle in 1917 and entered Iraq. Many Assyrians were enlisted by the British, but they were regarded with disfavour by the Iraqians, who saw in them both men of an alien tongue and of an alien religion. Of the forty thousand Assyrians in Iraq, approximately ten thousand were armed, many of them with rifles presented to them by the British for their defence against the rebellious and hard-fighting Kurds.

The problem presented was not easy to solve because the Assyrians had not only been admitted to Iraq, but they had served well in the disciplined British forces. All they asked was a place in which to settle, and to a minor degree Feisal saw what has happened in Palestine—feuds between Jews and Muslim. The matter was referred to the League of Nations, and while the League talked there occurred some excesses against the Assyrians. The utmost endeavours were made to hide the true facts from the world. The shooting was carried out by the Iraq army, after the Assyrians were said to have attacked an army post.

Baghdad knew nothing of what was occurring, and for five days received no information from the officer responsible for the affair. Feisal was appalled when he heard the news, and rushed medical aid and every other kind of assistance to the Assyrians, and he was able to prevent further accidents.

He was accused of being a tool of the British—and this a year after Iraq had secured her independence by his efforts.

Still the stalwart, he attempted to reshuffle his Cabinet, but under the new constitution he could demand, but not force, a Cabinet resignation unless four Ministers consented to go. He induced three to resign, but the fourth held resolutely to the sweets of office, and Feisal felt the situation slipping beyond his control.

He was now a man consumed with sickness, both physical and mental.

In sickness one's powers of resistance are impaired, and Feisal gave way on the controversial matter of decorations. These were awarded and were personally presented by the Crown Prince, who even then, though Iraq did not know, was within the shadow of bereavement.

The Iraqian populace ran wild, and shouted loudly for the Crown Prince, while the name of Feisal went unheard.

Man's ingratitude to man, coupled with his physical disabilities, wore Feisal to a shadow. He gave out that he was returning to Europe to regain his health. Actually, he was preparing to abdicate in favour of his son, for his knowledge of the reactions, had sapped his remaining strength.

Sadly he left Baghdad and the deserts for the mountains of Switzerland.

Within a week he was dead.

The news stunned Iraq, for no one had suspected that the king was ill to death. The country was without a leader in a moment of great difficulty, and his son, though he stepped manfully in the breach, was not of an age when he could bring the requisite ripe experience to bear.

A wail of mourning went up from Iraq—a wail

which was not untinged with remorse. In his hour of death, Feisal finally triumphed. Iraqians lashed themselves, for they saw their faults. They saw their dead king from a new perspective. For the first time they realized what his spare figure had meant to them. They were desolated.

Feisal, first King of Iraq, had passed over, but in the deserts of Arabia, and in the country of his adoption, his name will live for ever.

IBN SAUD

IBN SAUD

IN the East, life leap-frogs. One cannot just say of a man, as one can of so many prominent figures of the Occident, he did this and that; he started with a bicycle and now pounds metal into motor-cars, so many to the hour; or that he ran away before the mast and ended as a belted earl.

Life there is much more complex. One is an individual, yet one is of a family; one of a clan; one of a tribe. To understand why " A " suddenly goes berserk and shoots " B," one has probably to go back two generations; to understand why " C," obviously a poor man, is one to whom respect and veneration is shown by those with many of this world's goods, one has to trace back to his grandfather or great-grandfather, who was probably the paramount sheikh of the district.

The East does not forget. To-morrow is to-morrow only when it comes, and to-day is not of much consequence. It is yesterday and the day before that which really matters, because then that happened; before then, that happened, and it gives one so much to talk about. With the past one need never be at a loss for material. There, in them, are to be found good stories and much laughter, or, if the mood so takes one, ample material for a quarrel or a fight. There is plenty for argument, much for philosophy, and even more for moralizing. The past is magnificent, for it feeds the present, and every man's mind dwells in the past out in the desert and in the barren hills of Arabia.

This clan has a feud with that, and this tribe with that. Men must know each other and each other's business. There is not that sense of privacy which obtains in the West, and the knowing of each other's business is second cousin to meddling in it. Consequently it frequently happens, when one sets out to tell the story of an individual, many other personages have necessarily to intrude if the tale is to have full measure. It is for this reason, and this reason alone, that so much Oriental history is fatiguing to Western readers, who become confused with the many figures darting on and off the printed page.

In order to tell of Feisal, Hassein, Sherif of Mecca, crept on to the canvas. This was not unnatural, as Hassein was his father. General Allenby also intruded, and here he had right, for Feisal and Allenby were partners in a wonderful cause. The ubiquitous Hassein must also appear in the story of Ibn Saud, if only because Hassein ruled Mecca before Mecca and Arabia became Saudi by force of arms. No story of the Aga Khan would be complete without some historical background, and the same can be said of most of us, the Orientals.

In the case of Ibn Saud, one must necessarily hark back a little, because when Ibn Saud took the Hedjaz, he merely reclaimed it for his clan. His forebears had been there before as rulers, and when he took Mecca he was merely completing a cycle.

H.M. SULTAN IBN SAUD
King of Saudi-Arabia

Hassein, Sherif of Mecca through the efforts of the valiant Feisal, became paramount, and King of the Hedjaz. When Sultan Vahededdin, the Caliph, fled from his Constantinople palace by a side door and boarded the British warship *Malaya*, he sent out a cry for protection and assistance to Hassein in Mecca. The cry went unheeded, and Vahededdin was first to find asylum in Malta and later in San Remo, where he shortly died. Hassein, King of the Hedjaz, now a much older man, and his soul still bleeding because his son's efforts and not his own had added to his lustre, had reason in ignoring the departing and deposed Caliph. He saw himself, firmly entrenched as he was in Mecca, as the leader of the Muslim world. He wanted to have himself proclaimed Caliph, but the Muslims of Egypt, India and elsewhere were far from willing to endorse his candidature.

Hassein was not only old and senile, but he had now grown querulous, and though having sons who could have relieved him of much responsibility, he preferred to retain every administrative string in his hands. This did not make for efficiency or goodwill, for Hassein had completely failed to grasp the change in Arabia's outlook.

As Caliph it was necessary for him to be orthodox, and a Sunni before everything else, but his misty mind wavered between Sunni and Shiah, and in such a manner that he found the respect or support of neither. He was a pathetic old man, groping in the shadows for the indefinable, and that which he sought had only the substance of a blacker shadow.

P

In this he was unconsciously preparing the way for the Wahhabis, of whom Ibn Saud is the head—puritanical, almost fanatical, Sunnis, who place the most rigid interpretation upon the teachings of the Prophet, and allow no elasticity. Abdul Azeez Ibn Saud relieved Hassein of his charge in good time, and secured the Hedjaz.

Prior to his seizing the Hijaz he had been living in comparative poverty, and he had had his fill of adventures. He was a fully-fledged warrior before he came to try conclusions with Hassein, for his life had been spent in fighting, either against the Turks or against his own near relations.

The story of Abdul Azeez Ibn Saud is one of almost continual conflict, and, like so many others, has its genesis in the bygone generations.

Abdul Azeez Ibn Saud is the fifth direct descendant of the famous Emir Mohamed Ibn Saud, the founder of the al Saud dynasty, and a most powerful supporter of the teachings of Sheikh Mohamed Ibn Abdul Wahhab. Emir Mohamed Ibn Saud can be said to be the first of the great Wahhabis, and the one who really gave form and name to the sect.

The al Saud of those days had their seat at Diriyya, and though they sat firmly in the saddle, around them was a chaotic jumble of warring emirates, and their borders saw continuous disorder and bitter fighting. The pious Sheikh Mohamed Ibn Abdul Wahhab arrived in Diriyya in 1736, preaching as he went a great religious revival which would exorcise from misrepresented Islam much that savoured of excess and licence.

He preached austerity of outlook and rugged simplicity. He imbued the Emir Mohamed Ibn Saud with his fiery ideals, and the great religious revival was launched. From that moment Ibn Saud increased his sphere of influence. Forty years later, his grandson, yet another Ibn Saud, was also to complete what his grandfather had begun by establishing himself as the ruler of a vast kingdom which spread from the borders of Syria in the north to a point near Saana in the south, and from the shore of Oman to the Red Sea.

The al Saud dynasty was now a power, and with the new order peace and tranquillity replaced the disorder of former days, justice and the principle of equality being firmly established. Islam became the law of the country and everyone bowed to the law.

The al Saud were too successful. This new kingdom stood out as a beacon amidst the floundering mismanagement of the Ottomans, and the Sultan in Constantinople took umbrage. He had reason for his regal displeasure, for his Viceroy, Mohamed Ali, in Egypt was speedily forgetting that he was a vassal of the Porte, and was becoming embarrassingly regal.

In the vast solitude of the Yeldiz Kiosk, the Sultan conceived a scheme which would dispose of both upstarts. He sent his ambassadors with his own particular brand of vitriolic scandal, and these whispered into the ears of Mohamed Ali in Egypt and Ibn Saud in Arabia. Soon there was dissension, and speedily a war, which progressed with varying fortune for five years.

Then the Egyptian Khedive had Ibn Saud prisoner, and he razed Diriyya to the ground. Even the date palms were hewn down, and the Wahhabis were scattered. This was in 1815. The Turks resumed their political sway over Arabia, and disorder and chaos returned, the Porte maintaining its hold by exercising the same tactics which had set Arabia and Egypt at war. Every family of note had a feud with its neighbour, and the Turkish governors were deemed to have been lacking in enterprise if there was not turmoil between families. The members of al Saud did not escape, and their quarrels were many and serious. In 1818, the head of the clan settled in Riyad, but in 1831 he was assassinated by one of his cousins.

The murderer did not live long, as Feisal—not our Feisal, but grandfather of he who is now Ibn Saud— avenged the death of his father in true Arab style, and declared himself Emir. This was in 1832. He had to fight hard to preserve his title, and he was still embroiled in war when Khorshid Pasha, the famous Egyptian general of the time, arrived on the scene and carried him off as prisoner to Egypt, placing one of Feisal's cousins in the Emirate.

Seven years Feisal remained as prisoner in Cairo, and then he escaped. He travelled back to Nejd, and declared war. He was eminently successful, and he succeeded in large measure in restoring the ancient glories of the al Saud. The Hedjaz, however, proved too much for him, and he was unable to add it to his domains. To this day his reign is remembered in the Arabian Peninsular for its prosperity, affluence, and general justice.

On the death of Feisal, disputes broke out between his two sons, and the Ottoman Government seized the opportunity once more to intervene, and by 1888 Nejd had once again been completely reconquered. The father of Abdul Azeez Ibn Saud found life in Riyad under the tutelage of a Turkish governor completely insupportable, and as the Sultan refused to elevate him to a governorship, he retired, with many members of his family, to Koweit. This was in 1889, and a desperate effort was made by the clan to exist on the sixty pounds a month allowed by the Turkish Government. Some months the money arrived, but more often its glitter attracted the attention of some Turkish official *en route*, and the al Saud were compelled to restrain their appetites with true Arab fortitude.

Abdul Azeez Ibn Saud was then nine years of age, and his principal memories were of privation and suffering. Misfortune hung at the heels of his father, but the fire and youthful ardour of Ibn Saud could not be repressed.

In 1895, when Ibn Saud was fifteen years of age, one, Sheikh Mobarak al Sabah, rose to eminence in Koweit, and the inevitable dispute arose between this new ruler and the Porte. War followed, and it wafted into the nostrils of young Ibn Saud. Despite his years, he proclaimed himself an ally of the Sheikh against the Porte, found men to follow him, and took Riyad. However, he and his few desperadoes could not hold it.

Two years later—in 1901—he was to make a dramatic entry into the town. He had forty men of the al Saud, and a motley gathering of Bedouins, and he pitted this negligible force against the might of the Ottoman Empire.

He decided to make his attempt upon Riyad from the south. Not unnaturally, the Porte heard of his activities, and a much-tried Sultan stopped the allowance which had been made to his clan, and also forbade any of the neighbouring tribesmen, whom through he had to pass, to furnish him with provisions. Learning of this, the Bedouins in Ibn Saud's train incontinently departed, and he was left with his forty al Saud stalwarts who were pledged to follow him to the death.

Ibn Saud's father and other notables did their utmost to dissuade Ibn Saud from his mad quest, for how, they asked, could he hope to overcome the might of the Turkish Empire? Ibn Saud held on, but the situation was desperate. He bethought himself of a desperate plan.

Fired by his resolve, twenty more men of al Saud joined his party, bringing his total forces up to sixty, and he and his men arrived at the outskirts of Riyad soon after dusk. In the groves around the town, and carefully concealed, he left thirty-three of his men under the command of his brother Mohamed.

He selected a palm tree and cut it down, leaning it against the wall of the town he hoped to conquer. Leaving twenty men to guard his way, he, with the remaining six, shinned up the palm and into Riyad.

So far, and so good, but seven men grouped

inside a town's wall do not necessarily indicate that the town has fallen. Actually, Ibn Saud's six stalwarts looked around them in the darkness and felt rather ridiculous; but they had not reckoned with Ibn Saud. They saw him make his way up the street and stop at the house next door to that occupied by the Turkish Governor, Emir Ajlan. He went to the door and knocked, and a woman's voice answered querulously, " Who's there ? "

" Servants of Emir Ajlan, the Governor, come to summon your husband," remarked Ibn Saud with due meekness.

" Begone, wretch ! " screamed the woman. " You must be robber, or you would not knock at doors at this time of night."

" My good woman," returned Ibn Saud, " I assure you that my intentions are not evil, and I am bound to advise you that unless your husband appears before the Governor without delay nothing will save him from death in the morning."

Hearing this unwelcome news, the husband himself came to the door to inquire the meaning of the din. The husband was an old servant of the Sauds, and Ibn Saud was aware of this when he knocked. As soon as he appeared at the doorway, Ibn Saud whispered in the man's ear, bidding him be quiet. Pushing him over the threshold, he followed him within. There he was recognized, the woman crying : " Our master, Abdul Azeez Ibn Saud ! "

Ibn Saud was surely master, for he gathered the women together, locked them in an adjoining room, and bade them preserve silence. Remarkably enough, they obeyed him. With the husband, he climbed the garden wall and into the governor's house, where, coming upon two sentries asleep on their bedding, he rolled them up in their rugs and, tied and helpless, locked them also in a room. This done, he summoned all who had been left outside the walls, and began to search the rooms of the governor's house, one by one.

In the course of his search he came across a bed which he was certain contained the elusive governor. He shone a lantern in the face of the sleeper, and it was the governor's wife! She recognized him, and smiled.

"What do you want?" she whispered.

"Ajlan!" he said shortly and undiplomatically.

The woman became the counsellor and the mother. "My son," she urged, "do not gamble with your life. Flee while the night is still young, or you are dead."

"I have not come for advice," returned Ibn Saud, with that grim pertinacity of the Wahhabi, "but to learn when Ajlan emerges from the inner palace."

"An hour after sunrise," Ajlan's wife replied, equally shortly, for she was a woman with a grievance against her husband, and she, too, suffered from a sense of disappointment.

Not to be taken by surprise, Ibn Saud collected the rest of the women and shut them in with Ajlan's wife, and took final counsel with his men. Except for their quiet whisperings, absolute silence reigned over Riyad on this memorable night.

At last came the impatiently awaited false dawn, and then the magnificent sun of the Arabian day.

Slowly the doors of the inner palace were forced outward, and slaves emerged, leading horses, the favourite charges of Ajlan the governor. Shortly afterwards Ajlan himself appeared, and he fondled the horses as was his wont. Secreted behind a wall were Ibn Saud and ten men. They rushed at Ajlan and his guards first: then they started firing.

The governor's slaves and guards had been taken by surprise, but now they recovered their senses and fired upon these interlopers. Excited heads appeared at the palace windows, and a heavy fusilade was let loose, which killed two of Ibn Saud's men, severely wounded four, and compelled the rest to break cover and retreat.

The Governor, meanwhile, whose wound was a flesh one, and of little consequence, was gradually overpowering the youthful Ibn Saud, but his cousin Abdullah rushed to the rescue, and with a shot fired at close quarters, laid Ajlan lifeless.

Observing this, the remainder of the Wahhabis opened a heavy fire, and believing that it was engaged by a large and superior force, the garrison capitulated on condition that lives were spared.

By noon Ibn Saud had been proclaimed ruler of Riyad, and he had accomplished his object with sixty men. Twenty of whom were never called up.

He had sufficient good sense to realize that he could not hold the town, for the Porte was beating up strong forces against him, so after imposing his will upon the inhabitants and organizing a garrison of sorts, he left Riyad with a relative in charge as Governor. Wherever he went he proclaimed himself ruler, but he never remained in one place long enough to be overtaken by the Ottoman army now pursuing him. He took al Kharj, and eventually all the south of Nejd. He set his face northward, and dominated the north of Nejd. Then, deeming himself strong enough, in 1905 he turned on the Sultan's still faintly pursuing army and effectively disposed of it.

Ibn Saud was now a force, and was too near Mecca for the peace of mind of Hassein, and, in 1907, Ibn Saud found himself attacked on three sides. His cousins in al Hariq in the south still cherished the blood feud, and marched against him. The Turks attacked him in Kassim, and Hassein, Sherif of Mecca, joined in. Ibn Saud refused to be daunted. He attacked the Turks first, and routed them. He returned their camels, on condition that they marched either toward Baghdad or Medina, and kept on marching. Having disposed of the Turks, he turned his attention to his cousins, and, having trounced them in their turn, forgave them, and his treatment was both generous and indulgent. There remained Hassein, but having heard of the defeat of the Turks and the cousins, Mecca's Sherif made off and was well within the security of the Hedjaz before he could be attacked.

Ibn Saud was pious, but he was also an opportunist. In 1913, when the Turks had sustained yet another reverse in the Balkan War, he took advantage of the chaotic conditions which obtained and annexed el Hasa and el Katif. He took the Turkish garrisons prisoner, but he refused to emulate the tactics of the Porte. There was no throat-slitting, and the garrisons were allowed to return to Turkey by sea with their guns and ammunition.

In 1921 he captured Hayil, the seat of the powerful al Rashid, and put *finis* to the rule of this famous house in Nejd. The members of the al Rashid family were conveyed to Riyad, where they remain to this day in honourable and comfortable retirement.

In 1924 Ibn Saud opened his campaign for the conquest of Hedjaz. In a year he was master of the country, and in 1927 he proclaimed himself King of the Hedjaz and of Nejd. Thus it was that modern Saudi Arabia came into being.

For a quarter of a century Abdul Azeez Ibn Saud had devoted himself to war. During the first ten years of this deadly strife, he himself lived the life of a soldier on active service—an Arab soldier on active service, that is, which is something far different to that expected of the private in a Western army.

The Western soldier has to be fed at regular intervals. Long years of regularity in the West have evolved an eating and drinking complex. In many cases the stomach acts as does a clock. It registers turbulence at certain hours, and has to be quietened with sustenance. But that is not real hunger. The Arab soldier eats his fill when he can get it, and drinks at the same time. In the prime of his manhood he eats less than that accorded a Westerner of advanced years, and his gastronomic occasions are extraordinary.

For ten years Ibn Saud dwelled in tents, moving from place to place, often as a fugitive, and frequently with a price on his head, sometimes eating, and more often going hungry. He flitted across the desert fastnesses, sometimes hunting, sometimes hunted. The soft downiness of beds knew him not. A hole scratched in the sand for his hip, and he had to be content, and was content, for in that position the sword comes readily to hand, and the soft drowsiness of sleep does not linger upon bruised and aching flesh.

The Ottoman Government was never enamoured of al Saud, whom it strove to misrepresent in the eyes of the Muslim world, accusing the clan of introducing into Muslim thought matters that were outside the Koran. It made mischief between the clan and the Egyptians, split the community into warring factions, and did everything which a wily and subtle Porte could to bring about its extinction.

The gradual rise to power of the youthful descendant of the great Wahhabi Emir caused the Porte not a little uneasiness, and in Nejd the powerful al Rashid was constantly reinforced against al Saud. The Sultan dreaded more than anything else the rise of a powerful Arab kingdom, for in this he saw the death-knell of his position as Caliph.

The conquest of el Hasa in 1913 brought Ibn Saud to the Persian Gulf, and it was here, discovering that he had many interests with the British, that he first established relations with them. Shortly after his conquest of Hedjaz, he concluded a treaty of friendship with them, whereby he strengthened and consolidated the old ties, and further enhanced their purpose by establishing the first Saudi Arabian legation in London.

The dispute between Ibn Saud and the Sherif of Mecca dated back, as I have indicated, to the time when the religious programme of Sheikh Mohamed Ibn Abdul Wahhab was launched under the auspices of the first Ibn Saud, whose influence thereby received a sudden impetus, and spread rapidly through Nejd. At that time the influence of the Meccan Sherifs dominated the Hedjaz, the Porte maintaining only nominal suzerainty. Alarmed at the rapid forward march of the Wahhabis, the Sherifs leagued themselves with other Emirs in Nejd, but this was not sufficient to hold the Wahhabis who, in 1803, were able to occupy Mecca.

During the Great War, Ibn Saud remained strictly neutral, but not so neutral that he was unable to prevent al Rashid rising to the assistance of the Turks against Hassein in Mecca. Ibn Saud was in full sympathy with the Arab revolt, and to a very large extent with Hassein himself. It is probable, if Hassein had been worthy of the position which Feisal won for him, and which he appropriated, Ibn Saud would never have marched against him. Letters exchanged between Ibn Saud and Hassein during the conduct of the Arab revolt show quite clearly that al Saud was well disposed toward Mecca and entertained the liveliest feelings of respect and loyalty toward the House of the Prophet. Hassein, however, did not live up to expectations.

He had spent seventeen years in Constantinople as the Sultan's " guest " before being appointed to the Sherifate, and the Arabs expected great things of him. He was fully cognizant of the sinister aims of Turkish policy toward the Arabs, and the Arabs looked to him to utilize his Constantinople experience, and devote himself to a policy of unification. Turkish policy was always to split the Arabs and to turn tribe against tribe. With Hassein at Mecca, every Arab looked toward an era of peace and prosperity.

Hassein, however, had hardly settled in the saddle at Mecca before he began playing the old Turkish game. On the slightest pretext, or without pretext, he made war on his neighbours. It was open for Hassein, with his great experience, and with the undoubted gifts which were his in his earlier years, to make for himself a great Arab kingdom, for the Arabs were willing and, indeed, impatient.

In the dispute which rose between Ibn Saud and Hassein—a dispute which eventually meant war—the position of Great Britain was rendered especially delicate. She did her utmost to induce either side to compose its differences, and she worked hard for an understanding. If anyone was prepared to concede it was the "fanatical" Wahhabi, and the aged Hassein it was who remained uncompromisingly hostile. Great Britain evolved many opportunities for a settlement of differences, and throughout Ibn Saud displayed a willingness both to listen and be persuaded. At the last of the conferences—that arranged at Koweit in 1923—Hassein so forgot his Arabian courtesy as to neglect to send representatives.

With the almost inevitable disappearance of Hassein, and the rise of Ibn Saud, a new impetus was given to the idea of Arab nationality. Sufficient time has now passed for it to be evident that the old enmities and animosities of the desert are disappearing, and that a new order has come.

Perhaps the first real evidence of this was vouchsafed in the meeting between King Feisal of Iraq and Ibn Saud, when they amicably settled the disputes which were outstanding between them and concluded agreements which put an end to the old causes of friction. Since that historic meeting, one has been encouraged by other events in the hope that this new policy will prevail in all the new Arab kingdoms, replacing the old feuds, animosities and dissension. Other instances of Ibn Saud's peace-loving endeavours can be cited by noting that he made friendly treaties with Transjordan, and even with Imam Yahya of Yamen—whose more than half of the territory was recently conquered by the Wahhabis, but given back—and a treaty of Islamic Brotherhood was signed; the sincerity of the spirit of which the Christian West might well copy.

Unity, co-operation and friendship is becoming increasingly the keynote of the relations between the Arabic-speaking States. Here again one is encouraged, because behind this movement there is no coercion. There is no central force dragooning the States into a common weal. The force which is there is mutual attraction, and the realization that in unity and peace amongst Arabs, of whatever nation, can best devote themselves to the uplift of Arabia and to regaining that place among the nations to which the ancient civilization and culture of the East entitles them.

Ibn Saud has a distaste for the stupidly ostentatious. His tastes are simple, and his ways are frugal. Notwithstanding his staunch Wahhabi-upbringing, and the rigid Wahhabi code which colours his every action, Ibn Saud is a man of charm and of endearing personality. To find a Western counterpart one has to look to the stern old Quakers under whose immense hats and unsmiling exterior was a force at once kindly, helpful and tolerant.

His is a personality which retains friendships. Although a Wahhabi, and one who places the strictest possible interpretation upon the Muslim code, he is sufficiently modern to allow electric lights and power into Mecca. He sees no reason why the Faithful should be denied light, or electric fans to cool their bodies after the rigours of the pilgrimage.

He is not an Eastern prince who looks upon the Infidel with distaste and suspicion. For both Sir Percy Cox and the late General Clayton, Ibn Saud cherishes the warmest affection and the most pleasant memories.

Tall and muscular, this man who now dominates Holy Mecca stands well over six feet, and has broad shoulders to carry off his height. His favourite pastimes are hunting and riding—pastimes in which he indulges whenever his State duties will permit. This Napoleon of the Desert—Feisal was never that; he was a Smuts or a Kronje—is an accomplished marksman and swordsman, yet he is no tyrant. In war there were no half-way measures, but prisoners were prisoners and human, and not cattle to be led to the charnel house. In war a thruster and essentially a cavalryman, in peace he is unassuming. His manner is mild, and his address kindly. He has a lively sense of humour, and a great love of society and of men's companionship.

This Wahhabi warrior king rises an hour before dawn and reads the Koran until the Muezzin gives the call for the dawn prayer. After praying, he returns home to recite more verses from the Koran, as well as some of the traditions of the Holy Prophet. Then, after attending to urgent matters of state, he retires to his quarters to rest for a while, rising later to bathe, dress and break his fast.

Thereafter he attends his Privy Council where important matters of state are discussed and instructions issued to the sheikhs and officials. Then he receives the sheikhs of the desert and tribal chiefs in private interview, listens to their plaints and their grievances, and discusses with them important questions of the moment.

These private interviews over, Ibn Saud repairs to his General Council, where anyone who desires word with the king has already preceded him. Then there is lunch, and a short siesta, and the observance of the noon prayer. Again the Privy Council meets, when matters discussed in the morning come again under review. This Council is terminated when the king leaves for the afternoon prayer, after the recitation of which Ibn Saud is free to receive his brothers and his other relatives, who join in a homely family circle. In the cool of the evening he drives or rides, and after dinner once again holds a General Council where it is usual for someone to read for an hour and a half from one of the many books on the traditions of the Prophet, or Islamic literature.

When in Riyad Ibn Saud was wont to conclude his day with a special visit to his father and his other relatives, and only when he had concluded these ceremonial visits did he retire to bed.

Every Friday Ibn Saud visits the graveyards of his family, and he never journeys to Medina without visiting the Holy Mausoleum over the grave of the Prophet, and those of the Prophet's Family.

In Mecca he still upholds the customary evening visit to such relatives as may be in the Holy City.

Ibn Saud has diverse views on money and its value. In peace he is extremely generous, being wont to aver that money is only a means to an end and should be utilized for the benefit of humanity. "What we sow, we shall reap," he exclaims as he gives freely, " and if we sow in the days of peace and affluence we shall reap the fruit of that good in the days of war and adversity."

In war Ibn Saud proved himself the reverse of generous and earned for himself the reputation of being more than economical. One of his maxims in war was : " If you are generous to a Bedouin during war he at once suspects you of weakness."

In the Western conception the Arab, or the desert dweller, is so concerned with war, tribal feuds and vendettas that he has little time or inclination for the softer passions. Actually, of course, the Arab has a heart as have other humans, and Arab history abounds in instances of the dominating influence of women.

Ibn Saud's wife died in 1919, and he makes no secret of the sorrow which this occasioned him, or of the fact that he still mourns her passing. He treasures small articles which he has kept as souvenirs of a beautiful love—a love that is now reflected in Ibn Saud's affection for his late wife's two sons, Mohamed and Khalid.

Ibn Saud has confessed that his wife was the most charming, the wisest and the sweetest woman in Nejd. Even now he can scarcely restrain the tears which spring to his eyes when he speaks of her qualities.

In his dress, diet, and mode of living, Ibn Saud is obviously Wahhabi. He is a plain and simple man, who can scarcely be distinguished by his attire from any of his subjects. To his people he is not Ibn Saud, the king, but plain, unadorned Abdul Azeez whom they can approach at all times to claim their rights and voice their grievances in language shorn of the ceremonial. It is to Abdul Azeez that they appeal, and not to "Sire" or "Majesty." At his table the humblest Bedouin is as welcome as the son of the great sheikh or the sheikh himself.

An incident which occurred in 1928 comes to my memory. Ibn Saud was sitting at a window, and a Bedouin came and stood before it. The king asked him to move away.

The Bedouin turned and asked: "O, Abdul Azeez, can you sit there and see me starve?"

"Come in and tell me how it is that you are starving," rejoined Ibn Saud.

The Bedouin accepted the invitation, and explained

to the king how he had arrived in Mecca at nine o'clock the night before, only to be informed when he called at the guest-house, that he was too late for dinner. He had replied that he would be content with any food that was at hand, but officialdom only repeated that the appointed hour for dinner had passed, and he was forced to go empty away.

Ibn Saud sprang to his feet as if stung by a puff adder on hearing these words, and ordered the superintendent and the assistant superintendent of the guest house immediately to be brought before him. When they arrived, he demanded to know why it was that the man before him had not been given food, and they replied, taking refuge in their regulations, that the man had presented himself too late.

Ibn Saud demanded to be told why the man had not been furnished with dates or other such food if the cooked repast had been ended, and the officials fell silent.

Quivering with rage, for these servants had " blacked " his face in outraging the laws of hospitality, Ibn Saud ordered them a beating, the first instalment of which he administered with his own cane. In addition, he suspended them from their duties for a fortnight, and only allowed them to resume their duties on their promise that in future no man should be refused food, no matter what hour of the day or night he made his request.

Ibd Saud brings the same simplicity into the political sphere, where he remains the practical man and without delusions, and one who bases his judgment on a true understanding of the realities of life.

He has suffered himself, and has lived the life of an ordinary man of the desert. There is no need, therefore, for the introspective. A wise statesman, and a capable leader, he abhors flattery and hypocrisy.

The men of al Saud were the first to rise against the ineptness and the tyrannies of the Ottoman Empire. They were the first to draw their swords for an Arabian Arabia, and if one examines the tactics of Ibd Saud in his many engagements with the Turks, one can see this policy emerge time and again. He desired the removal of the Turks from the land of the Arabs. He did not want their death. When he captured them it was his invariable custom to bundle them off back to Turkey with a polite intimation to a furious Sultan that they were no longer *persona grata*. It was upon the fabric built by the clan of al Saud that Hassein of Mecca erected his pyramid of hope when the Arab revolt proper broke out, but it required Ibn Saud himself to complete the work of a bungler. It was Ibn Saud who reached the ideal. It was Ibn Saud who first achieved an Arab State completely independent of any other State or Power. When the Saudi Legation was opened in London the Arab nation, for the first time in modern history, had achieved real diplomatic representation.

Also, it was the lone hand of Ibn Saud which played the greatest part in the building of modern Arabia outside of Iraq. He took from modern progress and modern thought as much as was compatible and consistent with his strict Islamic principles, the interests of his Faith, and those of the country which he had welded together from many diverse fragments.

This great task of blending the ancient and modern was by no means easy of accomplishment, and, indeed, it is impossible for anyone who has not a deep insight into Arab mentality and Arab conservatism, to realize the immense difficulties which Ibn Saud encountered. Always did he lay himself open to the criticism that he was departing from the ways of his fathers, and it was his upholding of the ancient tradition that constituted his principal hold upon a people always ready to be noisy and turbulent once their conservatism was menaced or attacked.

The abolition of the customary annual celebrations of Ibn Saud's anniversary of accession provides an illuminating case in point.

The religious luminaries of Nejd, and with them those of the Hedjaz, passed a resolution in which they declared these annual celebrations to be an unnecessary function, adding that true Muslims knew only two festivals in their calendar. The annual celebration of the King's accession they characterized as a European custom and not an Arabic or Muslim one. Accordingly they wrote to Ibn Saud, and on these grounds asked him to discontinue the practice.

Ibn Saud might very easily have replied that the religious luminaries were stepping beyond their province and were impinging upon his preserves as the ruler. Instead, he gave one an insight into his greatness, for he saw that the celebrations did not affect anyone but himself, and he bowed to the decision.

In reply, he gave the following quotation from the Koran:

"Oh, Lord, I have sinned against myself, and if thou forgivest me not, and hast not mercy on me, I shall surely be among the losers."

He proceeded:

"Whatever good I have done is surely due to God's guidance, and whatever bad I have done is surely my own fault and Satan's influence. I do not exculpate myself; one is being perpetually prompted to evil."

A very different stand he took when these same religious luminaries opposed the installation of wireless telegraphy and the introduction of the modern sciences into Mecca. There he met their opposition with a stern refusal, and plainly told them that there is nothing in the religion of Islam that could justify their attitude of antagonism to improvement in communications or to scientific advance.

Thirty-five years ago, Arabia was nominally divided between three ruling families—the Sherifs ruling the Hedjaz, al Rashid over most of Nejd, and the greater part of the Arabian Peninsula, and al Sabah over the remainder. There was perpetual disorder, and chaos was the one static rule. The tribesmen warred one against the other, exploiting the jealousies of the Emirs, and persuading each in turn that excesses and misdeeds had been committed in their service and to embarrass one of a rival ruling house. All commerce and all caravans were completely at the mercy of the Bedouins, who knew no law but that of rapine and plunder. The Bedouin would spare no one, not even the Arabs they plundered, the Turks or their soldiers, or even the Emirs and their men, who were often held to ransom.

Ibn Saud conquered one Emirate after another, and in the space of thirty years extended his beneficent rule over the whole of Nejd, el Hasa, al Katif, Assir and the Hedjaz. His very success provided him with problems, and it is not uninteresting to see how he faced them.

The first to engage his attention was the age-old one of the Bedouin population of the deserts. Here, a large proportion had led a predatory life, moving constantly from one place to another, their direction dictated by pasturage and the presence of water. This element had no stake in the country. It had no interest in the static. Raids, plunder and highway robbery were its beginning and end. Here was a large section of the population whose activities, far from being productive to the State, and far from making for the common weal and common prosperity, was a constant deterrent to advance, and a black smudge on the deficit side of the ledger.

From a constructive point of view an administrator had to regard it as a complete loss. Even from the military standpoint it was of little value, for the old Emirs had found it necessary to recruit their armies almost exclusively from the town dwellers. The desert Bedouin was a good fighter while the battle lasted and went well, but the battle won, the commander could only sit back impotent while the Bedouins pillaged the captured and the fallen. The Bedouin would only fight for material and immediate gain, and would fight those who stood in his way or sought to deter him, with as much fiery enthusiasm as he had fought the enemy.

This lawless people had to be reclaimed to the State and taught the corporate sense. Others, in the past, had failed most abysmally in the task. He conceived the idea of erecting villages where water existed, and in these he "planted" Bedouins, trusting to the ease with which they could secure water and the greater comfort of home life for them gradually to wear down the roving propensities. He appointed men of learning to teach the Bedouins their religion, of which they were woefully ignorant, and instruct them in their duties to God, their king, and their fellow men.

This policy has borne unexpected fruit, and it is hardly possible to recognize in the prosperous agriculturists of to-day the predatory Bedouin of yesterday.

To a degree little short of extraordinary, these pillagers and cut-throats have become imbued with the principles of self-esteem, determination and courage, and they recognize the greatness of the Arab State in which they are an enthusiastic part of the whole. Land ownership and prosperity has brought out that national complex, and they are now as fearless of death in defending their own as they were in the robbing of others in the past. A Bedouin wife or mother, when bidding good-bye to the menfolk on their departure for war, says : " May God unite us in Paradise." These warriors now chant as they attack : " The perfume of Paradise is in the air ; hasten to it, all you who long for it."

Uplifted by this spirit, they have become a force which cannot be denied. Tribes which from time immemorial had been in a condition of watchful hostility, are now united in brotherly love, so much so that they have earned the name of "Ikhwan" or "The Brethren." Now they recall their former state with shame and disgust, calling it "Aljahiliyya," or "the state of ignorance," thus comparing it with the ancient "Jahiliyya," preceding the mission of Mohamed the Prophet.

Another reform initiated by Ibn Saud was in the sphere of medicine, and to him belongs the credit of introducing modern medical treatment for the first time into Nejd. Against a terrific opposition, he imposed his will, and insisted upon vaccination as a protection against the ravages of smallpox. He insisted upon great changes in the sanitation of the towns and villages, and he instituted veterinary hospitals, hospitals for the people, dispensaries and clinics.

Neither did he neglect the intellectual welfare of his people, and to Ibn Saud is due the credit of introducing, again in the face of much opposition, modern scientific education side by side with religious education in the schools. In addition to increasing the number of the schools, and enlarging their scope and importing competent teachers from sister countries such as Egypt and Syria, it was found necessary in order to maintain a steady state of progress in this sphere, to send a number of youths to study abroad, in the hope that they might become proficient in modern science and art, and return to spread the light in their own country. There are now educational missions in Egypt, and the students are displaying an intelligent receptiveness.

Quite apart from settling the Bedouins at oases and at known wells, Ibn Saud initiated a careful survey of this country in order the more fully to tap its water supplies, his object being to bring as great an area as possible under cultivation. He realizes that the old conception of wealth has gone. No longer can a man be judged by the number of camels he owns, for slowly but surely the ship of the desert is having to give way to the motor. The motor cannot go as long as a camel without liquid, but it can traverse distances which make the camel uneconomic. Discarded tyres are now taking the place of bleached camel bones along the pilgrims' way from Jeddah to Mecca.

Investigations have also been set on foot to ascertain the exact extent of the mineral wealth of the country, and the best means of developing it. Gold has already been found, and the presence of oil is more than suspected.

Ibn Saud's stern opposition to unyielding conservatism where that conservatism stood in the way of progress, led to difficulties at first, but when the processes of modern science were to be observed in practice, much of the futility of the old was realized, and the forwardists carried the others in their enthusiastic urge. An example of this can be found in Ibn Saud's introduction of modern machinery for irrigation purposes. Almost with malice aforethought did he instal his imported machinery where the old-fashioned was doing its inefficient best, and the comparison was there for all to see and to convince. The cry for modern irrigation machinery went up all over Nejd and the Hedjaz, and its use is spreading.

Similarly in respect to transport. It required a brave man to introduce the motor-car, but Ibn Saud put them on the road to Mecca. The streams of pilgrims, more accustomed to the speed and luxury of the motor than they were to the slow-moving camel, left no doubt as to their preference. Those who could secure the cars were wafted to the Holy City in hours, and soon the camel drivers were clamouring to be introduced to the mystery of the petrol engine. Now a fleet of motors is at the service of the pilgrims who proceed to the Hedjaz from all parts of the Muslim world.

In order more rapidly to knit the various parts of the country together, Ibn Saud installed wireless stations in all outlying parts. Even Mecca itself possesses a powerful plant, though this was not accomplished without a stern struggle.

As with the first introduction of the motor-car, the people believed wireless to be the work of ungodly hands and to be closely associated with witchcraft. Faintly they could understand a voice being conveyed by wires, but wireless was beyond their comprehension. I do not altogether blame them, for with a mind profoundly unmechanical, it is beyond mine. Ibn Saud had to break down this prejudice in much the same manner that he overcame fear of of the petrol engine.

I call to mind an interesting incident which attended the first introduction of motor-cars. Ibn Saud left

Riyad with some of his retinue for a pleasure drive into the desert, where engine trouble developed, and the king was delayed. When Ibn Saud failed to return at his appointed time, the rumour went round that the infidel had sold the king a bewitched vehicle which had flown him away to the lands of the ungodly, and delivered him a prisoner into their hands. In a short space of time a large number of persons had armed themselves and left the town in the direction taken by the king, but they had not proceeded far when they saw Ibn Saud returning triumphantly in his chariot.

This incident reminds me rather forcibly of the Knights of Charlemagne who, filled with alarm when they saw Arab horsemen emerge from the interior of the magnificent clock of exquisite workmanship which Haroun al-Raschid at the zenith of Arab civilization had presented to Charlemagne, believed that they were confronted with magic. They suspected the clock of evil influences, and would have destroyed it. In the centuries which have passed the West has become the custodian of " magic," and the East that to be affrighted.

Great as these reforms have been, they are really as nothing when compared with the law, order and security which Ibn Saud has evolved throughout the length and breadth of his dominions. The wisdom of Ibn Saud lies in the fact that he was alive from the very beginning to the fundamental truth that until law and order were established no reforms were possible.

Not only did Ibn Saud transform the Bedouins into citizens, God-fearing and law-abiding, but he hastened the process by establishing a strong government capable of meting out exemplary punishment to those who dared disturb the peace. Until the Bedouin women had become house-proud and to demand comforts as their right, the stick had to be there to keep the Bedouin within his newly-acquired door. Often, of course, he hungered for his tent and for the excitements of the chase, and when hunger got the better of his judgment, the stick, in the guise of the motor-car, which proved invaluable for patrolling the desert; the aeroplane, which could pick up his movements from afar; and the wireless, which told of his peccadilloes in unheard cadences. Against such a combination, if only it could be applied with prudence and patience, the Bedouin had really no chance, and it was not long before the Bedouin women displayed a marked reluctance to allow their men to forsake the plough and the greater comforts to be found beneath a firm roof.

In this manner, a vast terrain which had previously bowed only to force and to the law of the rifle and the knife, was subjected to direct control, and peace, order and security gradually came.

Now, instead of a knife-thrust, one can expect a welcome from the desert.

Let another century roll on, and who can tell?

I believe the Arab of Arabia proper to be too virile ever to hatch those problems which confront Egypt. He is too conscious of his religion, and too remote from Western contacts to drift as the Egyptians, but their story, of course, is that of Fuad.

Let me tell of Fuad.

FUAD

FUAD

*Medio de fonte leporum
Surgit amari aliquid quod in ipsis floribus angat.*
                                            LUCRETIUS.

FROM the midst of Fuad's fountain of delight there continually arose something to vex him. Bearer of the proud title of First Modern King of Egypt, he was inordinately unhappy, a prey to dire forebodings, and the victim of repressed desires. Both soul and body were racked by a sense of the impotent, for Fuad, although a man with high ideals, could not rank as a statesman. His time was a time of Oriental intrigue and back-door resource, and his was a life of galling frustration, of searing disappointment, and of cramping circumvention.

Fuad was no man of Destiny. Indeed it would have been remarkable had he been so, for he was born to an environment where the fungus flourished. A lesser princeling in a Court allied to the Ottoman, his early background could not have been more uninspiring. The Courts of Constantinople, Cairo and Teheran were then by-words in the Chancelleries of Europe. The State of Denmark was never more rotten. Tawdry magnificence and a complete contempt of the perils of bankruptcy were the least of their sins.

That Fuad was able to emerge so far from the welter of corruption and inefficacy in which he had his early being was to his credit. Much of the success which attended his reign—and when one considers the times and his countrymen Fuad finished his course with something on the credit side—was, of course, due to the brass-bound tutelage of an overseeing Power. As much as he hated the tutelage, he had frequently to appeal to the might of the tutor in order to retain his throne, and at no time was this more so than toward the closing stages of his tempestuous life.

For him the years brought no hallowed ease. The plaudits of a grateful nation were not for his ears. His excursions abroad were not conducted through a genuflecting throng of loyal subjects anxious to do honour to the head of the royal house. Instead, he grew accustomed to the presence at his palace gates of a howling mob of dissatisfied Egyptians.

Fuad was called to a task which bristled with difficulties. It demanded exceptional ability, wide perception, infinite patience, a complete understanding of those surging currents which make for Egyptian public opinion, high qualities of statesmanship, forbearance combined with resolution, and, above all, the power of making friends with a people apt to be captious. It was a large order, and Fuad would have been one in a million could he have combined a majority of these qualities.

Moreover, it has to be remembered that he was not selected as the most promising of an army of applicants. When Turkey threw in her lot with

HIS LATE MAJESTY KING FUAD OF EGYPT

Germany, and Egypt's ruler preferred the delights of the Bosphorous to those of Cairo and it was deemed expedient that another should reign in his stead, there were but few in the line of succession. Even then, the name of Fuad did not come readily to the lips. His preferment created more than a little surprise.

He was not called to the head of Egyptian affairs because of his outstanding traits. There were those who disguised their feelings of doubt as to his fitness for the great position when the decision was made. He was called because there was none other who would face the responsibility of the times, and because the Power in possession, immersed in the maelstrom of war, could devote only passing thought to the internal affairs of Egypt. It required peace and stability on the great artery of Imperial communications, and Fuad offered the only solution. The Great War saw the death throes of more than one royal house. It was to thrust Egypt's into the pangs of travail.

Fuad can best be summed up as a very ordinary man, and with the majority of human frailties well-developed. He had all those impulses which we lesser mortals do our utmost to hide and keep in subjugation—a love of power, a not inconsiderable vanity, and a ripe and ready temper. His European training during the years of his banishment had engendered in him a virility and an urge to movement and endeavour strikingly at variance with the sober lethargy of the majority of Egyptians, and this energy he applied to good works until he became bored with the project, left it to wither, and took up another which captured his passing fancy.

His record, from the time when he returned from exile in 1892 at the invitation of Abbas II, to the time when he succeeded Hussein, was littered with the broken monuments of impulsive endeavour. Societies, organizations, leagues and committees lay moribund along the path which he had strode. Later he was to return in his tracks and give succour to many of these forlorn children, but the fact remained that until he had reached middle age he enjoyed none of the confidence which is necessary if one is successfully to rule. He had married and the marriage had been annulled ; he was a confirmed woman-hater and indeed, refused to remarry until it was necessary to provide a heir to his House, and he was an irresponsible member of a royal clan which had the misfortune to be unbeloved of the people.

Also, he was the son of Ismail who had been driven into exile because of his wild excesses and almost maniacal profligacy—a handicap indeed. Because of the sins of the father Egypt had had to recede from the proud position where, although nominally part of the Ottoman Empire, her Viceroy merely commented in derisive undertones if called to heel by the Porte.

The Powers, and particularly Great Britain, had placed on her neck the metal collar of thraldom. The collar glittered, for it was gold, but it was excessively heavy nevertheless. Still, because of the sins of the father Egypt had lost her hold upon the Sudan. For years the Mahdi had done to Cairo what Cairo had previously done to Constantinople, and with a proud and sensitive people this hurt. Following the tragedy which was Gordon's, there was a partnership, the Mahdi was routed, and the Sudan became Anglo-Egyptian.

At the door of Ismail Egyptians laid the blame for the increasing sphere of influence of the British, and with the outbreak of war, the dethronement of Abbas and the succession of Hussein as Sultan, Egyptians saw with pain and humiliation the declaration of a Protectorate.

Fuad, it can be seen, had many disabilities, and it would have required a personality excessively engaging to win through the barriers of distrust which surrounded his name, and—Fuad's personality was hardly that. He had been grafted on to Egypt. His great-grandfather had been the famous Albanian adventurer, Mohamed Ali, with all southern Europe's ill-concealed contempt for that which marched eastward of the Dardanelles. He regarded his people as recalcitrant children for whom he slaved and from whom he could never expect gratitude or thanks. Here was another disability, for his complex was too patently superior, and it irked. It certainly did not make for either understanding or goodwill.

Many of the British names which are to be found in the story of Feisal also enter into that of Fuad—Kitchener, Lloyd, Storrs, Wingate, Allenby, and the rest—but here we do not see a solid phalanx working under the stress of war to a common and unified end. Rather do we see incessant wrangling, intrigue, and twisted diplomacy, and only in some instances that community of spirit which marked all relations with

Feisal. There was something clean and fragrant in the revolt of the desert against the supineness of the inglorious Porte. It captured the imagination, for it lent colour and romance to a landscape which had for far too long been excessively drab. It encompassed the Holy cities of Mecca, Medina, Jerusalem and Damascus, and one saw a war of movement against long odds. Every day presented its story of gallantry, and every week a lesson in grim fortitude.

Egypt's war against the dominance of Great Britain lacked all these high lights. The movement was not massed movement, and was largely confined to the intelligentsia.

When Fuad stepped so suddenly into the Sultanate in 1917, he found himself faced by a powerful Nationalistic *bloc*, the intentions of which were to wring freedom from the British by any means that would serve, and so to curb the powers and the aspirations of the Sultan that when freedom came he could either remain as a pleasantly innocuous figure-head, or retire in the face of republicanism, vocally militant.

America was the ideal to which all thinking Egyptian Nationalists aspired. They did homage to its constitution, and lauded its individualistic freedom. In such a picture a monarch—Sultan, Khedive, King, no matter the nomenclature—would be redundant, and when Fuad took his place in the frame politic he might have been a usurper stealing what was not his under the dominance of British guns. After the initial pleasantries demanded by etiquette and decorum, the gloves had to be removed. Little quarter was given on either side in a battle which waged until Fuad's death.

To keep track of the Ministries of France a card-index is a prime necessity, and then before committing oneself it is advisable to telephone Paris to make positive that a new Cabinet had not emerged overnight. To follow the ramifications of Fuad's political wanderings and to keep tally of the Ministers who either dragooned, or were dragooned, requires a library. Sometimes, of course, when the gauntlet had been thrown down and the day went well for the king, he dismissed the politicians with an imperious wave of the hand, and he governed without a Ministry. Palace government it was called, and the Nationalists welcomed these unconstitutional admonitions as they would another misfortune. On these occasions Fuad would keep within his palace walls, not daring to go out.

Fuad was selected as Sultan at a moment—one of the many—when feeling against Great Britain had reached a peak. It descended into the valley for a short period following his accession while the people took stock of the new ruler, but within twelve months it had scaled further heights, and the way was then opened for Fuad's great trial of strength with the famous Zaghlul Pasha. The two men were outstanding, and though both had a ripe appreciation of the capabilities and failings of the other, they had too much in common to be other than enemies.

Zaghlul undoubtedly toyed with the prospect of becoming Egypt's first President. Fuad was determined that he should be King of modern Egypt.

Both men, King and Commoner, fought each other with every tool fashioned by intrigue, sometimes one gaining the advantage, and sometimes the other. Zaghlul made a bid for popular favour by ignoring all the rules of usual procedure, and by boldly demanding Egypt's independence.

Fuad, committed to the orthodox by reason of his rank, was held up to scorn and ridicule by the Egyptian Nationalists throughout the country, and even the army became unstable. Zaghlul was winning the joust, and it seemed that Fuad's days were numbered. He still had a card up his sleeve, however, and he played it. Conversations ensued with the Residency, and Zaghlul was quietly arrested and transported to Malta.

The riots and the bloodshed which followed were only the outpourings of deeply aggrieved Egyptians. The name of Fuad was held up to execration; the mobs howled outside his palace, the military had to be called out, and the lawyers and the students called themselves out. Fuad had won the round, but the price had to be paid.

Fuad was unpopular before the arrest of Zaghlul. He was regarded as the arch-enemy of Egyptian progress thereafter, and he had, in order to secure a little of that popular regard after which he hankered with such pathetic persistency, to negotiate with Lord Allenby, the created British High Commissioner, for the release of the Zaghlulist leader. In 1919 a somewhat chastened Zaghlul was freed.

After the Great War Egyptians could see around them the successful emergence of the spirit of self-determination. The Arab-speaking peoples had achieved their ends in almost every country except Egypt, and now there was a determined effort to rid Turkey of the incubus of the Sultan. Egyptian opinion veered round from Washington to Mustapha Kamal, and the Nationalists saw in Zaghlul, now not quite so certain of his own greatness, for arrest had bitten deeply into his soul, one who could do better in Egypt what Kemal was doing in Turkey. Zaghlul was carried along on the wave of his supporters' enthusiasm, and again he and Fuad came to grips. Zaghlul outmanœuvred both Fuad and Lord Milner, and his tactics left Mr. Lloyd George as much out of his element as a newly-landed fish.

If Zaghlul had not dissipated his energies in internecine feuds, and had not political jealousies been so rampant, it is not unlikely that he would eventually have forced a position to which the only solution would have been the abdication of Fuad. It came perilously near to this on more than one occasion, but Zaghlul's burning hatred of the then Premier, Adly Pasha, deflected much of his heavier broadsides from the Sultan, and Fuad was given a breathing space in which to recover from the heat and stress of battle. Born to the campaign of intrigue himself, he is said to have initiated some of these bouts himself between the Ministers and the Zaghlulists when hard pressed. It served his purpose. It was Zaghlul's insensate jealousy of Adly Pasha which induced him to commit a grave tactical error and to disclose his hand long before time.

In the efforts being made to constitute a delegation

to meet the British which would be representative of Egyptian opinion, Zaghlul was constrained to declare that he would only work with Adly when he consented to take orders directly from him and to acknowledge his undisputed supremacy.

Here was a man with eyes and ears on what was happening at Ankara in Turkey, and borrowing both method and speech from the rapidly rising Mustapha Kemal. At this moment the regime was in real danger, and it was only the hesitancy of Egyptians to assume responsibility which precluded a popular outbreak. There was no one there with the moral courage to give the order, notwithstanding the fact that the Egyptian garrisons in the Sudan had been demoralized, and an active mass movement could not have been gainsaid.

In this side issue between Adly Pasha and Zaghlul, Fuad stood aside, though Egypt knew that it was really a struggle between the throne and the Nationalists. Inevitably it had reactions; and Zaghlul was again arrested. He was not released until Egypt was declared a sovereign State and Fuad slipped the mantle of Sultan to assume the ermine of King.

Normally this should have been an occasion of great national rejoicing. It is true that sovereign independence still retained one or two leading strings, but here was a great constitutional advance which any ruler might have sought to turn to his own advantage.

Fuad, however, was now to feel the effects of the double-handed weapon of intrigue. During his Sultanate he had used so many factions to fight others that he had scarcely a friend left, and the populace took the sound of the guns which fired the newly-acquired kingly salute as a signal for rioting and pillage. Fuad had the good sense to ignore these manifestations of ill-will with the reflection that now he was king he would govern, and that Wafdists and Zaghlulists could now do their worst.

His Ministers began to dread the daily summons to the palace, for here was a different man who had to maintain one foot in the British Residency and the other in his palace. He had both now firmly implanted beneath the desk in his study, and if his Ministers displeased him, which was almost a daily occurrence, he did not hesitate to acquaint them with the fact.

Constitution or no constitution, unless his orders were carried out, then his Ministers had reluctantly to lay aside the fruits of office. Behind him as a sure bulwark was the martial law maintained by the British because of the recent disorders—martial law proclaimed and rigorously applied by an alien race in a State lately declared sovereign and independent.

From this angle the situation then obtaining appears somewhat Gilbertian, but actually, with the murder of Sir Lee Stack and others, its presence was well justified. He marched by gradual stages from constitutionalism to despotism, believing that this was the only force which could govern a turbulent Egypt.

Paradoxically, it was the British who had to tap his knuckles and remind him that there was a Constitution and, when tapping had no effect, Lord Allenby delivered something remarkably akin to an ultimatum. With bad grace, Fuad had temporarily to recede from the iconoclasm, and again he was flouted. Zaghlul returned with banners flying, and he headed a great popular movement for the revision of the constitution and to the relegation of Fuad to the ranks of gilded impotency. Elections were held, and the Zaghlulists romped to the head of the polls. Ignoring Fuad, Zaghlul turned to Great Britain's first Socialist Premier with confidence, expecting an immediate revision of many of the clauses attaching to independence. His reception was such that he returned to Cairo determined on a further trial of strength with Fuad.

Zaghlul, however, went too far. He so inflamed popular opinion against the throne that the secret societies reappeared. There were the strongest representations from the British, and Zaghlul had to resign. He, too, changed his ground, and this seemingly irreconcilable borrowed of the tactics of his monarch, and sought a *rapprochement* with the British, to whom he hinted that a king who would not abide by the Constitution should be replaced.

The Residency, however, failed to take the hint, and once more Egypt saw Fuad revert to palace government and steadfastly refuse to countenance an election, his contention being that his countrymen were not sufficiently advanced to shoulder Parliamentary responsibility. Thereafter, Zaghlul, as Fuad's principal opponent, retired from the scene, a sick man. As a political force he was ended, and when Fuad toured Europe, he died.

Fuad's long battle with Zaghlul was one of the most remarkable in history, for the world saw a monarch who, both as Sultan and King, did not hesitate to venture into the political arena, and, indeed, to descend to all the " all-in " methods peculiar to Egypt of the time. Zaghlul was not only a bitter political opponent, but he was a personal enemy. Indeed, the issue was often one of pure personalities, in which Zaghlul had the advantage. He could stump the country, and did not hesitate to do so. Fuad could only rave at his ministers or retire to his study in a blind rage.

The odds were greatly on Zaghlul, and if he had had better material Egypt to-day might have been a republic. More probably it would have been annexed to the British Empire, but there might have been a republic with British zones of influence along the Suez Canal and in the Sudan. Great Britain was preoccupied, first of all with winning the war and latterly with paying for victory. She could only devote small attention to Egypt, and when events forced her to do so, it was with the obvious desire to settle the problem of the moment so that she might the more quickly return to the study of her own difficulties.

Great Britain was not very sympathetic toward Egypt. She took the view that the Egyptians had been spared the horrors of war; that the British Empire had fought her battles, and that she had waxed fat in the supply of the armies which had been sent to defend her. She thought that Egypt could well afford to wait before discussing something which was academic and political, and, in any event, she was not very interested. She was war weary; she had to rebuild her economic fabric; and the less

Egypt troubled her and settled her own difficulties, the better she was pleased.

This was an obvious asset to one who aspired to emulate Mustapa Kamal. Great Britain's desire to be left in peace was a weapon which might have been wielded to effect. After the elections, when the Zaghlulists were returned with such a striking majority, Zaghlul's claim to speak for the nation was a strong one, and in certain events he could not have been ignored.

Had he been more pertinacious, and had he not been sidetracked at crucial moments by a king, it is not impossible, always supposing that the material behind him was better than it was, that he would have achieved his dreams. There was, however, a deal of talk and little of action. Zaghlul lacked the steady purpose of Kamal, and Fuad could not be compared with the sorry Sultans of Turkey. He had a certain amount in common in that he was distrustful of democracy, but he was no wild spendthrift and he had executive ability.

The Egypt which he left was a vastly superior Egypt which was his when he was made Sultan, and if he had lived it would have been better still.

In business, Fuad would have been moderately successful, because he was shrewd and was careful of detail. Perhaps he was inclined to pay too much attention to detail, but he certainly believed in seeing things done for himself.

His was a mind which could not conceive greatness, but which could assimilate. He was not above learning and following example. He knew and appreciated the value of modern irrigation. He was keen on hygiene. His own personal tastes were simple. Egyptians might hate him; they might even despise a king who could fight the politicians on their own ground, but they were forced to admit that he initiated and saw through many much-needed reforms, was a deadly enemy of the corrupt, and was a great worker.

The exterior which he presented to his people might have been bitterly provocative, but at least they had the solace of the realization that this man was zealously working for his country. He had no grandiose schemes which would result in impoverishment. His sense of his own importance lay not in the accumulation of worldly goods at the expense of the fellaheen, but in power. He went after power like a tiger to the kill, and principally because the opinion he held of Egyptian efficiency was not high.

In Zaghlul, Fuad had a Gandhi of the militant type—one who could cast his spell upon the masses. Fortunately for Fuad, his domains included the Suez Canal, and there were always British bayonets in the offing to render him assistance when the crisis became acute.

Had Fuad been a great man, he must almost of necessity have failed when called upon to wield Egypt's modern sceptre. The appalling political chaos into which he was precipitated would have nauseated a man with higher ideals. The very character of the opposition he was called upon to face would have stultified the efforts of a creative builder. He was a princeling who had long hungered for a throne.

He made no secret of the fact that in becoming king he had satisfied one of his great personal ambitions, and it was this personal sense of gratification which gave him the courage and the stamina to hold out against subversive forces in what was, perhaps, the most critical period in Egypt's long history.

More than one attempt was made on his life, but he died in his bed after an illness which was wrapped in considerable mystery. Because of the political situation—he was fast being forced into that position when a further tussle with the democratic element was imminent—he strove his utmost to keep secret his indisposition. Until almost the last he believed that he would recover, for his illness, as an illness, was not unduly serious. In the end he succumbed from a throat affliction which had troubled him since he was a comparatively young man, and—he died a king, and in the knowledge that the succession was secured.

He had created the machinery for a regency which could sustain his house until his son, then in England, would reach his majority. As far as was humanly possible, he had erected safeguards against all contingencies. The way was open for a final settlement with Great Britain. Indeed, delegates to the joint conference between his countrymen and the representatives of Great Britain had been selected.

Perhaps in these, his last moments, he was reasonably happy. He died a tired man, worn out with political intrigue in which that highly-enervating personal element had invariably been present.

He passed over in the knowledge that he had done his best, and in that there is no higher praise.

REZA SHAH

REZA SHAH

> Place not thy trust upon a world like this,
> Where nothing fixed remains. The caravan
> > Goes to another city, one to-day,
> > The next to-morrow; each observes his turn
> > And time appointed.
> > > "The Shah-Namah" of Firdausi.

THROUGHOUT the three thousand years of her varied history, Iran has displayed a strong sense of nationalism and a great power of revival. When, judged by Western standards, she was irrevocably lost, when her finances had dwindled to the point of exhaustion, and when the administration appeared sunk in a torpor which was but the prelude to a long-drawn-out and painful demise, some great figure has arisen like a *deus ex machina* to lead his country from the morass to further heights of opulence and greatness.

Time and time again through Iran's colourful history—a poetical land impregnated with song and lyric of the great and glorious past—the man has appeared. In times of national stress the Iranians have awaited his emergence with a phlegm almost fatalistic. Their epic poems assure them that Iran cannot die, and this the Iranians implicitly believe. They regard stress, turmoil and economic eruption as but the prelude to yet another era of prosperity and peace, and quietly they await the turn of the tide.

The greatest of Iran's poets was Firdausi and, like Homer, he has become a national institution. His "Shah-Namah," one of the greatest epics which the world has known, dominates national life. A thousand years ago he told the Iranians of the glorious achievements of their forefathers, and it is this spirit of Firdausi which has obtained through the years in the maintenance of the Persian language and the fostering of the national spirit. Firdausi stood for all that was true, all that was colourful, and all that was chivalrous. He raised his voice against corruption and intrigue, believing implicitly in the creed of the Zoroaster that Ormuzd must finally triumph over Ahriman—the simple conception of the ultimate victory of right over wrong.

The awakening of Iran from the deep sleep of the Middle Ages is very modern. She has a liberal-minded and not unintelligent people, but there were powerful interests which sought to keep the country semi-comatose, and to retard her progress. Until 1906, Iran was in a state of stagnation, and her condition can only find a counterpart in that of Western Europe in the Middle Ages. There were Powers on her borders which were singularly averse to any progress in this land of lyric and song, and one Power in particular, which can best be identified by my stating that it is defunct, which openly encouraged the more retrograde internal elements.

A passage from the great work of Lord Curzon will, perhaps, illustrate the point. He said :

"It may safely be averred not merely that the opening of Persia to Western influence, the extension

H.M. Reza Shah Pahlavi
King of Iran

of roads and railroads, and the breaking down of the barriers of obsolete tradition, might have been hastened by years had a certain Foreign Government chosen to lend their powerful strength to the effort; but, and this is a much graver charge, that no scheme for the strengthening of Persia and the unselfish expansion of her resources can be proposed that is not certain to meet with the most strenuous opposition that the said Government can exert. . . . When a batch of Austrian officials came out to organize a postal service in Persia in 1874, the same foreign Government threw every conceivable obstacle in their way; and when, in spite of their efforts, the present system of internal post had been established, they did all in their power to prevent Persia being admitted into the International Postal Union."

In the summer of 1906 there was a minor revolution. It was the visible beginning of a radical change and of intensive national aspiration for better government. The spirit of Firdausi was once again making itself felt, and there followed fifteen years of great conflict, sacrifice and labour for more rational conditions which were more remarkable for their sustained effort than for their achievements.

Those who fought for reform had to battle with the strong retrogressive elements; against the traditional, obsolete in a modern world; and against the influences of the foreign Power which was affrighted of the mere mention of the word "Nationalism." Nevertheless, in these fifteen years a constitution was established, more modern laws were introduced, and modern institutions were set up. That none of these things was allowed to function is, perhaps, by the way. On paper, in any event, the changes in the form of government and administration were great and fundamental.

For many years a secular law had been practically unknown. One was established. Civil courts were established, the departments of State were divided into executive and administrative, and constitutional and budgetary laws were introduced which prescribed legal restrictions upon entering into engagements with foreigners. The revenue administration, previously completely uncontrolled, was overhauled.

Unfortunately for Iran, her royal house had been attacked by the same disease which was prevalent in Constantinople and Cairo, and her national assets and her heritage had been foolishly, almost criminally, squandered by a series of weak and lustful rulers, and by the encouragement of bribery and corruption within the State.

It is unnecessary to dilate on the shortcomings of Ahmad Shah, the last of the Kadjar dynasty, who preferred the delights of Europe to those of his own capital. Every penny that could be squeezed from an already impoverished people was expended in extravagant gaiety in any capital which could provide him with the exotic. He lacked ability, avoided responsibility, and the only interest he displayed in his countrymen was in the degree to which they could satisfy his insatiable appetite for extravaganza.

Iran, in spite of her neutrality, was not spared the horrors of the Great War. She found neutrality an expensive rôle to maintain, and her task was rendered the more difficult by a series of epidemics which ravaged the country, and by an appalling famine. Her resources were exhausted, and her very independence was threatened. The Great War left Persia helpless and prostrate, and the apathy of the Shah in her affairs caused the people to despair. Iranian territory was occupied by foreign troops, the treasury was empty, and the authority of the government was practically nil. She was close to the borders of Bolshevism, and it seemed almost inevitable, unless the Great Powers intervened, that Iran would fall into the net of the Soviet Union and become as Turkestan and Bokhara.

It was at that moment that the traditional figure appeared in Reza Shah, then known as Reza Khan. That was in 1921, the turning-point in Iran's modern history, and Reza Shah was then Minister for War.

A quiet-spoken man, with an impressive figure, Reza Shah Pahlavi is descended from one of the oldest families in Iran, which has had its headquarters in the region of Safad-Kouh (Mazenderan) from very ancient times. The inhabitants of this region represent the purest stock of the Iranian race, for they have always remained compact and have consistently rejected contact with heterogeneous strains. The people of Safad-Kouh have stood out throughout the chequered history of Iran both for their patriotism and the readiness with which they were prepared to defend the national ideal. In all of Iran's many vicissitudes, the people of the region were to be found fighting with dash and heroism. Their spirit and martial prowess in the course of the centuries had become traditional.

It was in this environment that Reza Shah was born in March, 1878. His father, Abbas-Ali Khan, was an officer of high rank, being the commander of the famous Safad-Kouhi Regiment, recruited entirely from the district. This Seventh Regiment of Military Scouts of the Fourth Brigade had the same social standing as the Brigade of Guards in England, and the family's connection with it was a long and honourable one. Reza Shah's grandfather, Morad-Ali Khan, had been a captain in the same corps and had died upon the field of battle in the siege of Herat in 1856.

Reza Shah's father died when his son was yet young, and the responsibility of this future king's education fell to the lot of his paternal uncle, General Nasrollah Khan, who commanded the brigade of which the Safad-Kouhi Regiment formed a part.

In accordance with the traditions of the family, Reza Shah was educated upon military lines, and in 1900 entered the Persian Cossack Brigade. His abilities won for him speedy promotion, and eventually he became Commander of the Independent Cossack Corps. He was called upon for service in all parts of Iran, and in February, 1921, he became Commander-in-Chief. Two months later the functions of the Minister of War were added to his other duties. Shortly afterwards he became Prime Minister, and Iran was shortly to become a nation.

He was the man for whom Iran had been waiting. Calm, and with an amazing simplicity of manner, he hid beneath this exterior an iron resolution and a tremendous fund of patience and perseverance. As Prime Minister he was given an opportunity to raise his country from the ashes, and he put an energy into his work which was unflagging.

Faced with almost insuperable obstacles, he had the courage to take the long view, and he commenced at the beginning by instilling law and order. He succeeded to the head of a Government which did not govern. His first resolve was that it should. He reorganized the army. He made it uniform and he created *esprit de corps*. He equipped it and disciplined it, and the heterogeneous mobs previously commanded by foreign officers were disbanded and the army became Iranian.

With this force behind him he began to remind the rebellious tribesmen in the outlying districts that there was now a Government, and order soon became the rule. The Iranian army became a force, and the old disrespect for Iran's frontiers ceased. He placed well-disciplined and well-accoutred garrisons in the outlying districts, and lawlessness was curbed. He threw roads out to his garrisons and the fear of dismemberment vanished.

He paid special attention to the country's finances, as indeed he must, for the treasury was empty when he took charge. Those who had previously defied or bribed the tax-gatherer were required to pay their dues, and those who had been the subject of extortion were asked for no more than was legally required.

As confidence increased, money began to pour into the State coffers in an increasing stream, and by dint of almost incredible economy, such as could only be exercised in an Eastern country, the budget was balanced. A national bank was founded, and this is now a flourishing institution, and it was not long before there was an excess of revenue over expenditure. During his premiership a law was passed abolishing all titles of nobility, and Reza Shah became known by his family name of Phalavi.

Slowly but surely the temper of the country was raised from despair to hope, and from hope to an abounding confidence, in which the thought of the continued retention of a monarch such as Ahmed Shah could no longer be entertained. Ahmad Shah had sensed the direction of the wind, and had absented himself from Teheran for a long period, deeming it inexpedient to return, and in October, 1925, he was formally deposed and Reza Shah was nominated as Regent.

Within a few weeks the Constitutional Assembly met in Teheran, and by a unanimous vote, Reza Shah was selected as Shah of Persia. Five days later he ascended the throne, the occasion being solemnized with great pomp and national rejoicing. Iran's new era had begun.

> In the hour of adversity be not without hope,
> For crystal rain falls from black clouds.

In this old Iranian proverb was summed up Reza Shah's mentality in those first difficult years, for he had to proceed with the utmost circumspection.

Before he was proclaimed king he had to contend with a powerful caucas which found its strength in the unworthiness of Ahmad Shah, and in those days he also borrowed of Omar Khayyam.

Although he was the pivot around which everything moved, he did not force his personality upon others. He initiated no sudden coup, and there was an interim of some years between his taking over the reins of government and his elevation to the throne. Then he practised the true spirit of humility, such as is found in the following rubaiyat of Omar, which, incidentally, Western readers will not find in the collection of FitzGerald:

> Dar rah chunnan ro ka salamat na kunand,
> Ba khlaq chunanze qayamat na kunand,
> Dar masjid agar ravi, chunan ro ka tura,
> Dar Pesha kwaband o imamat na kunand.

This can perhaps best be translated:

Walk in such a manner that they may not salute thee.
Live in such a way that the public may not know and respect thee.
When thou goest to the mosque to pray, go in such a manner that nobody may notice thee and make thee imam.

Yet Reza Shah did not miss the materialistic conception which was Omar's. He worked:

> Oh, come with old Khayyam, and leave the Wise
> To talk; one thing is certain, that Life flies;
> One thing is certain, and the Rest is Lies;
> The flower that once has blown for ever dies.

When he became monarch by popular acclamation,

Reza Shah found the way open to greater effort, and he discarded much that was obsolete :

> A man ought to possess humanity,
> And if the wood of aloes have no fragrance
> It ought to be converted into firewood.

He took his place as king, and the people of Iran, under his leadership and guidance, worked for and attained a great many of the ideals which the Nationalists of the old school had bled and died for. Once revenue exceeded expenditure he could go ahead with greater speed, and old roads were improved and new ones built all over the country. Railways were commenced, and great progress has been made with these. Once he had the roads, Reza Shah encouraged motor transport, and though Iranians were slow to take advantage of the oil which flows so abundantly within their borders, motor-cars are now quickly taking the place of the old horse carriage and the more picturesque camel and ox-cart.

Here Reza Shah literally evolved something from nothing, for when he assumed the premiership there was but one motor-car in the entire country. Most of the money for the new roads and for the new railways, many hundreds of kilometres of which have now been completed, have been derived from internal duties on tea and coffee.

This improvement in communications has brought about a great change in Iran, where the people have suddenly evinced a striking interest in travel. It is now possible to journey from Teheran to Ispahan in a day. Before Reza Shah gave the country railways and roads the time required to cover the distance was never less than a fortnight, and it was attended by some risk and danger. There is now a much closer contact between the principal cities, and the residents of the hinterland have now much more intimate relations with the town dwellers. In the pre-Pahlavi era it was the exception rather than the rule for thousands in outlying districts to have journeyed more than a hundred miles from their own villages, and news of conditions in the outside world was mainly disseminated by returned soldiers, whose lack of veracity or high powers of imagination produced many colourful but highly inaccurate accounts.

Reza Shah's work was rendered the more difficult by the fact that his reforming zeal had to cut across a long-established feudalism. In order to make national life secure, there had to be radical reforms in the administration of justice. Before Reza Shah took command it can be said that there was no justice for the poor man, and he was completely at the mercy of the official and the tribal chieftain.

When modern law courts were introduced which dealt out justice impartially and swiftly, there were tremendous reactions from those who quickly discovered that position and power no longer protected them from the consequences of their own overt acts. In brief, an end had to be put to feudalism, and Reza Shah's stoic calm was proof against the storm which he raised. It was necessary to subdue the powerful chiefs and their tribes, for this class took unkindly to the suggestion that if they would live they must work. Their means of livelihood through the centuries had been gained at the expense of others. Caravans were raided and merchants were required to pay tribute. With the gains so easily obtained the tribesmen would revert to their hills for feasting and high revel. "This must cease," said Reza Shah, and it has ceased. Migration and depredation is no more, for the army which Reza Shah raised by compulsory military service saw that his orders were carried out. Raiding tribesmen were apportioned land and informed that they were expected to till it. Reluctantly, they took to the plough. He built schools, and made the tribesmen dispatch their children thither. Gradually, illiteracy is disappearing, and with the growth of education there is coming an increasing sense of national discipline.

Reza Shah, as I have indicated, took the long view, and as it has proved, the right view. When he first assumed power it was said of him that he was devoting every resource of the country to military endeavour, and that every service, both moral and material, had to bow before the claims of the force which he was evolving. There was considerable truth in that assertion, for Reza Shah's first consideration was national security and internal peace.

The army was in effect an armed police force, and in those early days of financial chaos it required every penny which the Treasury could produce to give it force and mobility. Unquestionably, Reza Shah staked all on his army and his police, and admittedly he neglected every other service. He took the view that with the army there to impose peace, prosperity must come in its wake. When conditions improved, and money came in more readily, the balances which accrued were not spent in further policing and militarization. The budgetary provisions for the forces remained as they were, while that for other services, and notably education, has been multiplied many times.

Under Reza Shah's indomitable drive, Iran has now an educational system of which she can well be proud. Elementary schools have appeared hand in hand with teachers' colleges; there are secondary and technical schools, and a university has been founded with faculties of law, medicine, philosophy and literature. Large batches of advanced students have been sent abroad, and not a few have found their way to England. Reza Shah's desire is that these students should take back to Iran the most modern teachings of medicine, science, engineering and economics.

The Shah has a great admiration for the product of the public school. He sees in this system of education something which moulds character and provides for moral and physical well-being. His own son has been sent to a school near Geneva, which is run on public school lines.

The remarkable economic progress which the Shah has brought about is more than sufficient to meet those charges, frequently made when he first assumed power, that he was obsessed by the military idea. There is compulsory military service, but the periods with the colours are not long, and the army is organized not for aggression but for national defence. The army, *gendarmerie* and police force, when aligned to the long land frontiers, are disproportionate to the magnitude of the task that might confront them, but they are adequate for the maintenance of internal order. Reza Shah, who was labelled by many as a militarist, is the ruler of one of the most pacific countries in the world. He has clearly defined pacts of non-aggression with many of his neighbours, and, incidentally, Iran, a member of the League of Nations since its inception, is one of the most zealous supporters of that institution.

Another work which the Shah initiated, and which is now nearing completion, is a census, the first Iran has even known. Computations of Iran's population have hitherto been made by methods exceedingly rough and ready. From the compilations already made, it seems likely that that first accurate head-counting will place the population above fifteen millions.

Reza Shah has sometimes been accused of adopting an anti-foreign attitude, and of pursuing a course of exaggerated nationalism. Englishmen will call to mind, in this connection, the dispute which still languishes as to the title to the Bahrein Islands, the long negotiations with the oil companies, and the difficulties of Great Britain's Imperial Airways in flying over Iran. Much of this is due to an incompatability of ideas, and a refusal by some to realize that Iran has now advanced from the Middle Ages to an era when she has an acute appreciation of her sovereign rights, and of the value to be placed on these.

Reza Shah desires nothing more than to be left alone and undisturbed for the peaceful realization of his ideals. He has many more reforms in prospect, and although he is willing to encourage foreign enterprises within his realm, he does insist, and rightly so, that the rights of his countrymen be respected, and that foreigners when they pass his borders shall abandon their old conception of Iran, and leave behind them all their old prejudices. Nothing irritates him more than the " something-for-nothing " complex of so many foreigners who visit his country. The word " exploitation " is anathema to him. He refuses to be exploited, but he is not averse to friendly co-operation.

Reza Shah has always maintained that Iran will work out her own salvation if her freedom of action is not impaired, and he resents the suggestion still, I am afraid, frequently advanced by those who do not know, that Iran is in no need of assimilating Western ideas.

He points with some pride to the re-establishment of order, to the free development of the arts and sciences, and to the revival of the national spirit. He believes in the regeneration of his native land, and it is his hope that before he passes on, Iran will have regained all the ground lost by the weak and incompetent rulers of the previous regime.

He is not in the least antagonistic toward Great Britain, for he realizes that Teheran and London have common interests. When referring to the difficulties which have arisen since his advent to power, he frequently makes mention of the *rapprochement* between Iran and England, which dates back to the sixteenth century when, in the reigns of Shah Abbas and Queen Elizabeth, Iran's appointment of an Englishman as her Ambassador to Europe in the person of Sir Anthony Sherley testified to her cordial friendship and confidence.

He sees no reason why, when Iran's present status and intentions are better understood, that this friendship will be revived. Before it can come, however, England and the rest of the world must discard the old spectacles and be prepared to negotiate on the principles of mutual respect and equality of rights.

For foreign interests fully to understand the changed mentality of Iran, it must be realized that Reza Shah, and with him all Iranians, refer to Ahmad Shah's desperate strivings for the money with which to maintain his extravagances as the " Black Era." Rightly or wrongly, Reza Shah takes the view that Ahmad Shah illegally pledged his country's resources, and that those who received the pledges entered into exploitation which could not be upheld on the grounds of equity and justice.

Reza Shah's first task was to restore order. His second, to repair the financial condition of his country. In these spheres we have the Shah's outstanding achievements.

Iran's basic financial principles are now sound. To-day, not only the equilibrium of the balance between revenue and expenditure has been stabilized but also, in consequence of the reparation of financial conditions, the Iranian Government, in recent years, has been able to carry out its plan of connecting the north and south of the country with railways and motor roads, of developing agriculture, of enforcing conscription, of reorganizing the army, of creating an air force and a navy, and of developing public education. Municipal councils have been established in all towns and in the provinces, the tribes have been rounded up and settled, national and agricultural banks have been established, and—all this represents but a fragment of the progress and development of modern Iran.

The reparation of her financial conditions made it possible for Iran to renounce her customs and tariff obligations, and since 1928 she has been in a position to enter into trade treaties and conventions in which equity has been the guiding principle.

One of the concessions revoked at an early date was that of the Indo-European Telegraph Office. Although Reza Shah maintained that the concession had been accorded in a manner which was questionable, he honoured his country's signature, and the telegraphs were not taken over until after lengthy negotiations and the payment of compensation satisfactory to both parties.

Reza Shah took a somewhat different view in respect to the D'Arcy oil concession of 1901 for the extraction of mineral oil from the South Iranian oilfields. This he regarded as a direct challenge to Iran's integrity and her interests, and there ensued a lengthy period of tedious negotiation. In 1932, Reza Shah, abandoning hope of an agreement by negotiation, announced the cancellation of the concession, and he then entered into a new agreement with the oil company which can be said to preserve the interest of both parties on an equitable basis. The income now derived from Iran's oil resources is credited by Reza Shah to the reserve funds, and if any part of it is included in the budget, it is as an extraordinary and exceptional measure.

Indisputable proof of the soundness of Reza Shah's regime can be found in the fact that Iran is one of the few countries which has no internal debts, and her foreign obligations are less than a million sterling. Moreover, even this relatively insignificant sum is the relic and the unredeemed balance of a loan contracted under the old regime. It is being redeemed by yearly instalments. Reza Shah, by force of his example, has reawakened in his people the sense of their ancient glories. They now believe that effort counts.

Modern Iranians now suck deeply at the wisdom of their poets, and their speech is rich in proverbial allegory, and Firdausi sustains them in the upward fight from decades of oppression and poverty. They chant :

> All independent tillers of the soil,
> The sowers and the reapers—men whom none
> Upraideth when they eat. Though clad in rags,
> The wearers are not slaves, and sounds of chiding
> Reach not their ears. They are free men and labour
> Upon the soil, safe from dispute and contest.
> What said the noble man and eloquent?
> " 'Tis idleness that maketh free men slaves."

SUN YAT SEN

SUN YAT SEN

TO the Western world, Sun Yat Sen is the man who rid China of the Manchus. Thus tidily docketed, he fades from the picture, not because his name lacks romance; not because his life was negative, and without colour; but principally because he was a will-o'-the-wisp. The practical Western mind reacts in askance to one with five names, all entirely different, and to each one of which the bearer is entitled. And when these names, queer and ill-sounding to Western ears, crop up without reason or sequence, the Westerner loses patience and dubs the owner erratic, even though he should thrice become President of China.

For our purpose, although Sun Yat Sen began life as Tai Cheong, and signed his will as Sun Wen, he shall remain as Sun Yat Sen. Regarded thus, the man is less of an enigma, and he becomes what he was—a frank revolutionist, an impracticable idealist, and one who will go down in Oriental history as the man who achieved Chaos from chaos.

In world history—for any man who upsets a long-established dynasty must have a niche in world history—he will eventually go down in company with Lenin, Krassin, Trotsky and the rest, yet he will perforce stand a little apart. The Bolsheviks at least succeeded in stamping their print upon Russia.

Once they secured power they ceased, in large measure, to be idealists. Circumstances were too strong for them, and the practical had necessarily to obtrude.

Sun Yat Sen was the world's most unsuccessful revolutionist, for his principal failure was in success. To the end he remained an idealist. Nearly always was he hunted.

His life, in point of fact, was one long series of escapes, of disguises, plottings and intrigue. Yet like so many revolutionaries before him, he was to die in bed—in the case of Sun Yat Sen, of cancer of the liver. They opened him up to operate upon him, but when the doctors saw the problem he had so naively set them, they closed up the incision. Even in death he asked too much.

This man, who has puzzled the world's biographers, was born in Kwangtung, forty miles from Canton on November 2nd, 1866. I write this somewhat dogmatically, because so many authorities will have it otherwise. When Sun Yat Sen could be prevailed upon to give his age, he invariably gave the Chinese reckoning, which is different to the Western, and Sun Yat Sen never troubled to explain.

His father was a rice farmer, who did not own the land which he tilled. He was a tenant, and for rent he passed over half the crops which he raised.

This, too, I mention dogmatically, for there are many authorities who assert that he was born in Hawaii, and was, therefore, a citizen of the United States. Moreover, these authorities will produce documentary evidence to support their contention, and the indisputable signature of Sun Yat Sen testifying to the validity of the documents.

In point of fact, in 1904, when Hawaii had been taken over by the United States, Sun Yat Sen did depose before a notary public that he was born in Hawaii, but that was for the purpose of securing the temporary protection of American citizenship. At that time he was a refugee from China, and the Dowager Empress so much desired his company that she was prepared to give £100,000 to anyone who would place Sun Yat Sen before her. As Sun Yat Sen had previously been in Hawaii his deception was not difficult to sustain.

Sun Yat Sen left China when he was thirteen years of age. His elder brother had migrated to Hawaii, and made good. He sent for Sun Yat Sen, and when the lad arrived with only the rudiments of learning imparted by a Chinese village teacher, he decided that Sun Yat Sen should attend a school, not to gain proficiency in the arts, but to absorb English, which the elder brother considered to be an important business asset.

Quite by chance he was sent to a boarding establishment conducted by an Anglican minister, and so it was that an ignorant Chinese lad of peasant stock was taught history as well as the English which was stipulated. Fortuitously, too, he was brought into contact with Christianity. He began to compare the lot of the Chinese youth in Hawaii, where education was easily obtainable and where everyone was not under the heel of the tax-gatherer, with those in China, and finding the comparisons invidious, he began to think.

His thoughts raced, and he saw the weakness of idolatry. He was baptized, and had a fierce quarrel with his brother on the respective merits of Confucius and Christ, and was turned out. With the aid of friends he secured enough money to obtain a steerage passage to China, and returned home to battle almost as hotly with his father, an earnest Confucian. For a time that filial obedience which is instilled in in all Chinese caused him to light incense sticks before the idols, but the time came when he revolted. One night he stole to the village temple and played havoc with the idols. Next day, horror-stricken villagers demanded that the youthful delinquient should be cast from the village. He left, and the gods were appeased.

By devious means he reached Canton, and there a young, English-speaking Chinese stopped a foreigner and asked for a job. The foreigner was a doctor attached to the Anglo-American Hospital, and the doctor saw in Sun Yat Sen a good ward orderly. For a year he was an hospital orderly, and his interest in medicine was aroused. It chanced that at this time there was initiated a movement for the establishment of a medical school for Chinese students. Sun Yat Sen was given his chance, and in 1892 he qualified when, incidentally, he first took the name of Sun Yat Sen.

So far we have seen little of the revolutionary, but that was soon to come. Dr. Sun Yat Sen repaired to the nearby Portuguese settlement of Macao to practise his medicine, and there he met men who had formed a society called " Young China."

This society had as its aims the extension of democratic government to the villages, so that the people might have some voice in provincial and national affairs.

In Macao the members could talk without fear of arrest. The society approached the guilds in the hope that these powerful bodies would petition the Manchu Government, and when the conservative guilds refused, the society dissolved, and immediately became "The Educational Society." With considerable courage the members of the new society appended their names to a petition which they dispatched to Peking direct. Thereafter all were suspect, and the enemies of the old Dowager Empress.

It was in this peaceful beginning that the germ of revolution was born.

Throughout his long fight for the democratic ideal, Sun Yat Sen was arrayed against an extraordinary old woman of indomitable will. She began as a concubine to the Emperor Hsien Feng, and she intrigued for power. She bore a son, and such was the force of her character that he was acclaimed heir-apparent, and when the Emperor died, as the mother of the monarch, she became the real ruler. All those with foreign leanings were ruthlessly dismissed. All the nobles who had stood in her way when she was fighting her way from concubine to empress mysteriously disappeared. Her word was law, and behind her word was a rod for the backs of all.

When her son died he left a child still to be born, and she continued her regency. She had an army of spies who told her of the least suspicious movement towards the ways of the West. She declared that China had been a mighty empire for thousands of years, and had no reason to change its methods. Because of that and other beliefs, she was deeply suspicious of Christianity, which she allied with the revolutionary and, it has to be confessed, with some reason.

Dr. Sun and the majority of the young men about him were Christians, and the view was widely held in Peking that Christianity was the preaching of rebellion.

Having failed to provoke anything more than distrust in Peking, Sun Yat Sen and his Educational Society recognized that if any change was to be made on the face of China it would have to be by revolution and not by petition. As an idealist, Dr. Sun believed that the people could be aroused from their lethargy. He believed that if they were told that the Manchus were foreigners, as indeed they were, who were responsible for all China's corruption and oppression, the people would rise. He reasoned that the Manchus were not Chinese, and that they numbered a bare five millions against China's four hundred million. All the four hundred had to do was to rise against the five.

Sun Yat Sen was never one to be dismayed by obstacles. There and then he visualized a republic, though he was never clear in his mind how his republic was to be born. Even when it was achieved it came as a surprise, and he was in Europe. The people had no common language, and they had only one common interest, and that lay in filling their bellies. One in a hundred could read and write, and there was a complete absence of national consciousness. Impracticable from the beginning, he remained impracticable to the end when he handed his country over to the ravages of the war lords and to Bolshevism.

As a preliminary to revolution, Dr. Sun tackled the problem of arms. Some of the members of his society sold their tiny plots of land, and others pawned their wives' jewels. With the proceeds, arms were bought in Hong Kong and placed in a few barrels labelled " English Cement." When being landed one of the barrels was staved, and disgorged its contents before the eyes of the Dowager Empress's spies. Sun Yat Sen succeeded in escaping in disguise to Hong Kong, but his fellow plotters were taken, and after being visited with all the horrors of the torture-chamber, were removed to the execution ground and decapitated.

In order to escape those who were hot on his trail, Sun Yat Sen proceeded to Kobe, where he cut off his queue and grew a moustache. In Japanese garments, he made a passable Japanese.

From Kobe he repaired once again to Hawaii, where he preached and cajoled, and succeeded in raising a fighting fund of some £1,200 from the Chinese residents there. Thus armed, he determined to proceed to America and throw himself upon the mercy of the good republicans there. He believed that he would be showered with money.

When in America he learned that the Chinese

Minister in Washington had received orders to kidnap him and return him intact to the Dowager Empress for her pleasure, so he immediately transferred his attentions to the English whom, he had been informed, were always sympathetic toward the oppressed. All the while he proceeded disguised, and he was still disguised when he was approached by a Chinese in London who proved to be affability itself. Almost before he realized it, he was inside an imposing house, and the house proved to be the Chinese Legation.

Here he was held prisoner for ten days, while arrangements were being made to smuggle him to a Chinese vessel in the Thames. A servant in the Legation eventually spoke of the prisoner within the walls, and the British Foreign Office was informed. The police could not enter the Legation, but they could place men around it to prevent smuggling, and eventually Dr. Sun was given his freedom when the impossibility of transhipping him to the docks was realized.

From London, Sun Yat Sen went to Singapore, and then, again disguised, returned to China where, with a large sum on his head, he travelled the country as a Japanese, a Chinese coolie, and as a pedlar.

When it was safe he spoke, and he continued to speak until it was again necessary for him to make a long journey. Once more he turned up in America, where he enrolled cadets among the considerable Chinese population and carried out drills in back gardens and in enclosed halls.

Then came the Boxer Rebellion, and the Empress

had to flee from Peking while the soldiers of the Western nations indulged in an orgy of looting. The Boxer Rebellion had its reactions in China, and Sun Yat Sen began the more openly to speak of the coming republic. He travelled throughout America, and interviewed many bankers in Europe, but all whom he approached were strangely reluctant to finance him. He raised considerable sums from his own countrymen, however, who loaned him cash in return for ten-dollar notes on the "Chang Hwa Republic." It was understood that the notes could be redeemed when the republic came into being.

Sun Yat Sen made arrangements for an armed uprising in 1900, and for this purpose he drilled six hundred revolutionaries. When all was supposed to be ready, Sun Yat Sen sailed for China, for the intention was that the brave six hundred should take the small town of Waichow, and develop the insurrection from there. Everything went wrong. The military heard of the advent of the six hundred and marched against them in force. Sun Yat Sen was delayed on his way to China, and the treasurer with the revolutionary funds disappeared. After the fiasco, Dr. Sun was lucky to escape to Japan.

A lesser man would have been daunted, but Sun Yat Sen spent the next four years travelling to Hawaii, America and London; 1904 saw him back in China prepared for another revolution. He had now secured a good supply of arms, and he had secret organizations both in the north and in the south. The ammunition and arms, again in barrels labelled "Portland Cement," were consigned from

Hong Kong, and a steamer was chartered to convey three thousand armed men from the same place. As a sort of labour corps, another steamer carried seven hundred coolies, the coolies being under the impression that they had been engaged on contract for legal and lawful labour.

Sun Yat Sen was at his head-quarters ready to give the signal when he was handed a telegram. There had been a hitch in the arrangements, and the steamer containing the armed men could not sail. Meanwhile, however, the arms and ammunition were on their way, and so were the coolies. When being landed, another barrel was staved, and the contents disclosed. When the seven hundred coolies arrived the authorities thought the worst, and the majority were marched away and beheaded, notwithstanding their protests that this was not in their contract. Sun Yat Sen had to order his lieutenants to scatter, but sixteen failed to display sufficient alacrity, and lost their heads on the morn. Dr. Sun escaped over a wall and hid in by-alleys. Having gold in his belt, he got to the river where he bribed an old woman to part with her clothes. As an odoriferous dame he escaped into the Foreign Concession at Canton. Later, he wore a false queue, and sailed for Singapore. By now he had a price of £500,000 on his head.

In Singapore he started all over again, and in the next three years raised considerable sums of money. He was still unlucky in his treasurers, however, for frequently he found himself where he had begun. In the meantime the Dowager Empress was bowing

THE LATE DR. SUN YAT-SEN
President of the Chinese Republic

somewhat before the storm, and she promised reforms in the constitution. On the face of things, Sun Yat Sen had achieved all that he had set out to do, but he did not trust the Manchus. He continued his revolutionary activity from Singapore, and there ensued a number of minor outbreaks in China, all of which were miserable failures.

By 1907, however, he again declared himself ready, and Sun Yat Sen again repaired to China. He headed a revolt of the Progressives, and several small towns were taken before the Imperial troops caught up with him. There was one short, sharp, inglorious fight, and Sun Yat Sen was running for his life. He and a companion came across two beggars. Before the lure of much gold in the ever-present body belt the beggars consented to divest themselves of their rags, and as beggars Dr. Sun and his partner in misfortune eventually reached Hong Kong in a junk.

A year later the Dowager Empress died, and with the removal of her presence China became more liquid. The revolutionaries found greater scope for their activities, and they were learning how to make explosives. Toward the end of 1911 all was nearly ready for another throw of the dice, but not quite, and it was an accident which made Sun Yat Sen China's first President. He was in London, trying to induce London bankers to part with half a million sterling, when one of his bomb-making disciples blew himself up, and his house with him. In the south this was accepted as a signal for revolt, and a republic was proclaimed in the southern provinces. Dr. Sun was in London when he received a telegram informing him that he had been elected President. At once he hastened back to China.

A few weeks later, on January 1st, 1912, he was formally elected President of the Chinese Republic by the Assembly. Five weeks later, because he was told that the Manchu dynasty would not abdicate for him, but would for another, Yuan Shih Kai, he resigned, and Yuan was elected President in his stead. Yuan proved to be a despot of the old school, and although Sun Yat Sen tried to work with him, the pair never saw eye to eye. Indeed, they had many heated quarrels, and thirteen months after being elected President, Sun was again a fugitive. He heard a knocking at his door, and a voice which he recognized as belonging to the chief of police, demanding admittance. His acquaintanceship with back doors and garden walls stood him in good stead, and he was gone when the police burst their way in to maltreat his wife, drag his sick daughter from her bed, and to prod every hiding place with their bayonets. A few weeks later he arrived in Japan, again in disguise.

From Japan Dr. Sun wrote to Yuan, telling him that he was a traitor and that he had usurped the rôle of the Manchus. Therefore, as he had displaced the Manchus, so would Sun Yat Sen soon unseat Yuan. There were others who subscribed to Sun's appreciation of Yuan's qualities, for there was soon an outbreak which was quashed with true Manchu ruthlessness. Yuan conceived the idea of becoming Emperor, and he ordered that petitions to this end should be sent to him from all parts of the country.

Early in 1916, " acceding to the will of the people, and loving his country," he declared himself Emperor, but this proved to be too much for the southern provinces to swallow. They revolted, formed a confederacy and seceded.

For most of this time Sun Yat Sen had resided in Shanghai, and he had extended the olive branch to his brother in Hawaii. This gentleman had waxed rich and had retired, and he advanced large sums to his younger brother, making no secret of the fact that in the fullness of time, and with the turn of the political wheel, he expected to be repaid. At length the brother demanded his reward—a future governorship, but he was told that he was unworthy. Another brotherly quarrel ensued, which was ended by Sun Yat Sen repaying all that had been advanced to him.

So much for this family interlude. There was, however, another. As a fugitive Sun Yat Sen had seen little of his wife, and he had in his employ a pretty and attractive Chinese secretary who had been educated in America. There was some talk of divorce. In any event, Dr. Sun married his secretary.

In 1916, Sun Yat Sen returned to China, and inevitably to the south, where he was welcome. Here he was apportioned the title of *Generalissimo*. There followed more years of plotting and intrigue, but in May, 1921, the Southern Parliament met and elected him President. Many of the war barons looked upon him with a certain diffidence, however, and it was not long before he was in trouble. Believing that it was now impossible to unite the south and the north by peaceful means, he determined to try force, but he had to contend more with the jealousies in his own south than the resistance put up by a recalcitrant north.

He did, however, succeed in inaugurating internecine warfare, against the pleadings of the Powers, who assured him that China was big enough for two confederacies, and that they were quite prepared to recognize both.

President Sun believed that he could unite China with the sword, but the sword was to prove his undoing. He ordered one of his generals against the north, and the officer protested that he was ill-accoutred. The President insisted, and the battle that ensued was a sorry farce. The general returned and accused Sun Yat Sen of denying him support. There was a quarrel which ended when the general called on the remnant of his men and chased Sun Yat Sen out of his palace. Sun was forced to take refuge on a British gunboat, and was taken to Hong Kong.

It was at this time also that Sun Yat Sen came under the influence of the Russians who flocked into China in large numbers. Before his hurried departure, and later in Shanghai and Hong Kong, he met many, and he fell completely under their spell. He believed that the Soviet would assist him to achieve national unification, and full independence, and that he had " the earnest sympathy of the Russian people " and could " count on the support of Russia."

Working on Russian suggestions, he employed mercenaries to further his aims, and by the beginning of 1923 again felt strong enough to re-enter China. He was soon President for the third time at Canton. Difficulties beset him, however, like bees round a hive. His was the unfortunate habit of manufacturing them. His wild mercenaries turned on him like voracious wolves when he tried to call them to order. He had to appease them with much gold. More and more Sun Yat Sen turned to his Russian sympathisers in his extremity. He invited Borodin to call upon him, and later he entertained Chicherin.

His greatest bugbear was money, and he sat down and evolved one of the strangest documents which has ever been devised. It was entitled " The International Development of China," and it extended to many hundreds of pages. Much of this book had been prepared in earlier years. In it he garnished China with magnificent roads, countless railway lines, glorious harbours, and huge industrial centres. The scheme required billions upon billions sterling, and this idealist really believed that the Powers would agree among themselves and advance these incredible sums. He refused to believe in post-war depression —it is doubtful if he had ever heard of it. That his crazy scheme would cost more than the collective war output of the Allies he dismissed with a shrug of his shoulders, and as something unworthy of argument.

His extraordinary naivety can be better appreciated if I use his own words :—

"The goal of material progress is not private profit, but public profit. . . . Thus all will enjoy, in the same degree, the fruits of a modern civilization. . . . In a nutshell, it is my idea to make capitalism create Socialism in China, so that these two economic forces of human evolution will work side by side in future civilization."

Toward the end, appalled by the strife which his revolutionary teachings had created in China, he again appealed to his friends, the foreigners. He actually suggested that the Treaty Powers, and especially Great Britain and the United States, should virtually take over his country. They were to occupy the principal towns, take over the government, garrison the country, and send an army of officials and administrators for a period of four years. Then they were to retire. It was like a crazy mandate accorded the entire League of Nations. It goes without saying that it was doomed to failure.

More and more he was pressed for money. His highly paid mercenaries demanded their dues, and when these were not forthcoming, they took to pillage. The merchants became alarmed, and they procured arms from abroad, and commenced to drill men who could secure them safety. Sun Yat Sen saw in this a counter-revolution in embryo, and he confiscated the arms. The merchants retaliated by barricading the streets leading to the merchants' quarters, and what trade there was languished. Strikes, boycotts, riots and pillage darkened Sun Yat Sen's closing days. In despair he turned more and more to the Bolsheviks. In March, 1925, in a country torn to fragments, and with each section at enmity with the other, he was taken ill for the last time.

Before he passed over, he made a will, and left last instructions to his followers.

These last left to their care his "International Development of China."

In this he saw his epitaph, and the monument to forty years' unceasing service on behalf of his countrymen.

Sun Yat Sen had only one failing, and that was trust. He trusted everybody, and because of that trust sometimes he failed to see human frailty in others. He believed that the Chinese officialdom was as sincere and honest as himself. He could not see corruption and chicanery even when it was ingrained. Because of this trust the mirror through which he gazed at life was distorted. It was Hawaian. He often judged the people by the standard of those refined Chinese who still retained the spark of their original civilization.

He was impatient of inefficiency, his pace was too rapid for the rank and file of his 400,000,000 fellow-countrymen; but his sheer force of purpose carried him far. And there is no denying the fact that he is probably the first Chinese who gave China what that country never had—a true conception of independent nationhood. If his life's work produced chaotic conditions, it was all in the scheme of things; it produced at worst a glorious chaos out of which has sprung a New China, in which her sons should have a just pride.

BOOKS OF VARIED INTEREST

FUAD, KING OF EGYPT

By THE SIRDAR IKBAL ALI SHAH. *Illustrated.* 15s. *net*

Fuad, the great-grandson of the famous Albanian adventurer, Mohamed Ali, presented one of the constitutional romances of modern times.
This biography presents a brilliant picture of the man and the monarch.

THE AUTOBIOGRAPHY OF THOMAS WRIGHT OF OLNEY

Illustrated. 15s. *net*

In this, Thomas Wright's last monograph, the indefatigable biographer has turned the full force of his searching pen upon himself and has produced a striking portrait of himself and his times.

THE ODYSSEY OF A DIGGER

By CAPTAIN F. D. BURDETT. *Edited by* C. R. LONG.
Illustrated. 15s. *net*

These are the full-blooded reminiscences of an Englishman whose life has been devoted to adventure, and narrated with the unfailing humour that has been his saviour in so many tight corners. Those who read his earlier books will need no further introduction to Captain Burdett's latest " Odyssey."

STALKING IN THE HIMALAYAS AND NORTHERN INDIA

By LT.-COL. C. H. STOCKLEY, D.S.O. *Illustrated.* 15s. *net*

This book has been written for the man of moderate means, and with the intention of showing that the camera and the rifle are not incompatible companions on a hunting trip.
Stalking with Colonel Stockley is a most thrilling experience and one that will not readily be forgotten.

BODA, THE BUFFALO

By LT.-COL. CECIL LANG ("SKENE DHU"). *Illustrated.* 6s. *net*

Lieutenant-Colonel Cecil Lang, better known to many as "Skene Dhu, is the author of *Boda, the Buffalo* and other tales, a book of Indian animal stories. It is one of the most fascinating collections of animal yarns ever produced between the covers of a single volume.

BOOKS OF INTEREST

TUNNELLERS *Illustrated.* 15s. net.
By CAPTAIN W. GRANT GRIEVE and BERNARD NEWMAN. A remarkable book which reveals for the first time the secrets of one of the most intriguing sides of the War's story. Hastily recruited in 1915, the Tunnellers found themselves up against the determined opposition of enemy and Nature. The book is a record of the formation, growth, and victory of the Tunnelling Companies. A graphic account of the thrills and dangers surrounding the men who fought the Germans underground.

ADVENTURE IN ALGERIA *Illustrated.* 10s. 6d. net.
By BRIAN STUART, F.R.G.S. The author in the course of his travels takes us to Sidi bel Abbes and Ain Sefra, the garrison towns of the French Foreign Legion. There as a trooper he spent years of hardship and danger, of comradeship and content. When he took leave of the Legion, he began his remarkable lone trek into the desert. This is one of the most exciting and interesting of travellers' tales.

THE SEVEN PILLARS OF FIRE 8s. 6d. net.
A Symposium by DR. MAUDE ROYDEN, 'DR. L. P. JACKS, PROFESSOR A. E. RICHARDSON, THE MARQUIS OF TAVISTOCK, C. R. W. NEVINSON, CAPTAIN BERNARD ACWORTH, and SIR E. DENISON ROSS. Seven of the foremost thinkers of the day discuss in this book the question of what is wrong with the world, and especially of what is wrong with Great Britain. Starting with the idea that the world is wandering in a wilderness of doubt and confusion, each writer charts the landmarks and suggests a way out of the tangle.

SCOUTING ROUND THE WORLD
Illustrated. 2s. 6d. net.
By LORD BADEN POWELL OF GILWELL. The author relates his adventures on a voyage to Gibraltar, Ceylon, Malaya and Australia, New Zealand, Canada and Newfoundland. The Chief Scout tells his vast army just the things they want to know and brightens his pages with thumbnail sketches.

WAYFARING AROUND SCOTLAND
Illustrated. 2s. 6d. net.
By B. H. HUMBLE. Tells of the growth of the Scottish Youth Hostels Association and shows how the loveliest parts of Scotland have been opened up to the wayfarer. Each chapter concludes with notes regarding appropriate maps and the available accommodation whether at youth hostels, hotels or cottages.

BOOKS OF INTEREST

THE MAN OF ANATHOTH   7s. 6d. net.
By W. RILEY. It has been Mr. Riley's object to bring into coherent, narrative form the confused and badly-edited Scriptural accounts of one of the greatest and most interesting Biblical characters, Jeremiah, whose whole life was one long tragedy, full of exciting incidents. The story is fascinating from beginning to end.

CZECHOSLOVAKIA
The Land and Its People.   *Illustrated.*   2s. 6d. net.
By CLIVE HOLLAND, M.B.E. An up-to-date and detailed picture of the fascinating little Republic which was created out of the wreckage of Eastern Central Europe after the War.

BELGIUM
The Land and Its People.   *Illustrated.*   2s. 6d. net.
By CLIVE HOLLAND, M.B.E. A handbook to Belgium, a country that possesses within a comparatively small area a wealth of historic and beautiful towns and cities and a chain of seaside resorts which offer unrivalled facilities for bathing and sport.

YOU AND YOUR STAR   15s. net.
By CHEIRO (COUNT LOUIS HAMON). A simplified system by which any person can find from his birthday the important years of his life, the illnesses or accidents likely to occur, the most favourable persons for marriage, unions, partnerships, etc., and his lucky days as shown by Cheiro's system of numerology.

NAPHURIA : The History of the true Akhnaton.
Illustrated.   3s. 6d. net.
By E. S. G. BRISTOWE. An entirely new light is here thrown on the story of the young king of Egypt, usually known as Akhnaton. A fresh combination of evidence shows how—far from being a half-insane poetic dreamer who by neglecting his kingly duties brought disaster upon his empire—Akhnaton was the innocent victim of circumstances beyond human understanding or control.

ECHOES OF OLD WARS.   *Illustrated.*   10s. 6d. net.
Compiled by COLONEL C. FIELD. A book of intense historical interest consisting of personal accounts and unofficial letters of bygone battles both by land and sea. *Scotsman.*—" These letters are of high interest."

BOOKS FOR SPORTSMEN

GAMONIA : THE ART OF PRESERVING GAME
Ordinary Edition, 63s. net. Large Paper, 105s. net.
By LAWRENCE RAWSTORNE. New Edition with an Introduction by ERIC PARKER. Gamonia, a rare book, was privately printed for the author in 1837 and is now recognised as the earliest book dealing in detail with the planting of game coverts and the preservation of pheasants. The present volume is a reprint in facsimile.

BIG GAME HUNTING IN THE HIMALAYAS AND TIBET. *Medium 8vo. Illustrated.* 10s. 6d. net.
By MAJOR GERALD BURRARD, D.S.O. For the first time the actual geographical distributions of Himalayan and Tibetan game animals are explained scientifically and accurately with the aid of numerous maps. There can be no doubt that the possibilities of many new hunting grounds are thus thrown open to sportsmen.
Daily Chronicle.—" A classic of Indian big game."

INSTRUCTIONS TO YOUNG SPORTSMEN IN ALL THAT RELATES TO GUNS AND SHOOTING 15s. net.
By LIEUT.-COLONEL P. HAWKER. Edited with Notes and Introduction by ERIC PARKER, together with reproduction in colours of the original plates and a number of added illustrations. This book proves that a century ago Hawker knew all there was to be known about shooting.
The Field.—" The book is crammed with good advice."

THE MODERN SHOTGUN
In Three Volumes. Illustrated. 15s. net. each Vol.
By MAJOR GERALD BURRARD, D.S.O. An authoritative book on British shotguns. *The Modern Shotgun* covers the whole subject exhaustively. Divided into three parts—The Gun, The Cartridge, and The Gun and the Cartridge—the shooting man will find information that has never been published before.

THE IDENTIFICATION OF FIREARMS AND FORENSIC BALLISTICS *Illustrated.* 12s. 6d. net.
By MAJOR GERALD BURRARD, D.S.O., R.F.A. (Retd.), author of *The Modern Shotgun*. A scientific knowledge of both firearms and ballistics is essential to any investigation concerning shooting. This book by Major Burrard is the first textbook on the subject to be published in this country, and will be invaluable to all Police Officers and members of the Legal Profession whether they are prosecuting or defending.

IN THE GUNROOM. 2s. 6d. net.
By MAJOR GERALD BURRARD, D.S.O. One hundred questions answered by one of the greatest living experts concerning shotguns.

BOOKS OF INTEREST

THE BLOCKING OF ZEEBRUGGE
Illustrated. **7s. 6d. net.**
By REAR-ADMIRAL A. F. CARPENTER, V.C., R.N. The authentic story of a remarkable achievement, compiled from the Secret Admiralty Records. With an introduction and forewords by Earl Beatty, Marshal Foch, Rear-Admiral Sims, U.S.N., and nearly fifty unique plans, photographs, and drawings by permission of the Admiralty.
Evening Standard.—"The most thrilling of all the books born of the war."

EMDEN
Illustrated. **3s. 6d. net.**
By PRINCE FRANZ JOSEPH OF HOHENZOLLERN. The story of the famous raiding cruiser *Emden*, whose activities at the commencement of the war, here related by one of the ship's officers, set the world wondering. This book constitutes one of the most enthralling and remarkable war records ever penned.
Daily Telegraph.—"A book which has real value." "An historical document."

"Q" BOAT ADVENTURES
The Exploits of the famous "Mystery Ships"
2s. 6d. net.
By LT.-COM. HAROLD AUTEN, V.C. The story of the "Q" Boats forms one of the most romantic chapters in British Naval History. These apparently harmless vessels invited attack from the sinister "U" boat. Then suddenly gun-flaps would drop, invisible guns' crews spring to life, and the enemy would find the tables turned upon him.

PEDALLING POLAND
Illustrated. **10s. 6d. net.**
By BERNARD NEWMAN. A joyous travel book in the vein of *The Blue Danube*. Mounted on his trusty bicycle, "George," Mr. Newman explored the much-debated country of Poland, sometimes to plan, sometimes at random.

IN THE TRAIL OF THE THREE MUSKETEERS
Illustrated. **6s. net.**
By BERNARD NEWMAN. A joyous travel book from a new angle. Readers who can thrill to history, or who love the picturesque, and particularly the millions of friends of the Musketeers, will find in this unusual and fascinating book the lightest yet most thrilling of travellers' tales.

THE BLUE DANUBE: From Black Forest to Black Sea
Illustrated. **6s. net.**
By BERNARD NEWMAN. Author of "*In the Trail of the Three Musketeers.*" An entertaining account of an unusual journey. Starting from the source of the Danube in the Black Forest, Mr. Newman followed the course of Europe's most fascinating river 2,000 miles across seven countries to its mouth in the Black Sea.

KIPLING'S SUSSEX REVISITED *Illustrated.* 3s. 6d. net.
By R. THURSTON HOPKINS. "The object of this book," says the author, "is to examine the landscape of Rudyard Kipling's Sussex stories and poems, with a view to discovering the real places which served as models for his descriptions and backgrounds."

LET'S SEE THE LOWLANDS
Illustrated. 3s. 6d. net.
By A. A. THOMSON. This is not a guide-book; it records the carefree wanderings—"*stravagin*" is the Scots word—of two young men in the Lowlands—the country of gleaming lochs and blue hills, of old songs and stirring ballads, of peel tower and Border spear, of Scott and Burns.

LET'S SEE THE HIGHLANDS
Illustrated. 3s. 6d. net.
By A. A. THOMSON, author of "*Let's See the Lowlands.*" After the romantic Lowlands, Mr. Thomson takes us to the thrice-romantic Highlands, country of grim mountains and wild moors, of fairy lochs and enchanted woodlands, of "green days in forests and blue days at sea."

THE BREEZY COAST *Illustrated.* 3s. 6d. net.
By A. A. THOMSON. The East Coast of Scotland, swept by fresh, clean winds from the sea, has a character and an atmosphere all its own, and these Mr. Thomson has cleverly captured, together with a wealth of romantic story and much keen observation of local life and character.

TO INTRODUCE THE HEBRIDES
Illustrated. 3s. 6d. net.
By IAIN F. ANDERSON. With an introduction by the REV. KENNETH MACLEOD, D.D. For an arm-chair tour or a deck companion, this is an eminently suitable book. A Scotsman who had not visited the Isles said on reading the book: "It made me determined to see the Hebrides for myself next summer," while a reader who knows the Isles intimately said: "I re-visited the Isles when I read this book."

THE SUNSET SHORE *Illustrated.* 3s. 6d. net.
By IAIN F. ANDERSON. From the Mull of Galloway in the South to the bare, rugged Cape Wrath in the North, the whole extent of the wonderful West Coast of Scotland is described in "*The Sunset Shore.*"

SCOTTISH QUEST *Illustrated.* 3s. 6d. net.
By IAIN F. ANDERSON, F.R.S.G.S. The author tells of a journey in search of the secret of Scotland's charm. Through the Borders into Clydesdale, the Trossachs, Glen Lyon, Rannoch Moor, the Great Glen to Inverness. Southward by Foyers, Speyside, Donside, Aberdeen, Deeside, Perth to Edinburgh.

HERBERT JENKINS LTD., 3 YORK STREET, S.W.1